Introducing Analytic Theology

To my wife, Helen, and our children, James, Alice and Emma – with love.

Introducing Analytic Theology

Phil Weston

scm press

© Phil Weston 2025

Published in 2025 by SCM Press
Editorial office
3rd Floor, Invicta House,
110 Golden Lane,
London EC1Y 0TG, UK
www.scmpress.co.uk

SCM Press is an imprint of Hymns Ancient & Modern Ltd
(a registered charity)

Hymns Ancient & Modern® is a registered trademark of
Hymns Ancient & Modern Ltd
13A Hellesdon Park Road, Norwich,
Norfolk NR6 5DR, UK

All rights reserved. No part of this publication may be reproduced,
stored in a retrieval system, or transmitted,
in any form or by any means, electronic, mechanical,
photocopying or otherwise, without the prior permission of
the publisher, SCM Press.
Phil Weston has asserted his right under the Copyright, Designs and
Patents Act 1988 to be identified as the Author of this Work

Scripture quotations, unless otherwise marked, are from New Revised Standard
Version Bible: Anglicized Edition, copyright © 1989, 1995 National Council
of the Churches of Christ in the United States of America. Used by permission.
All rights reserved worldwide.

British Library Cataloguing in Publication data
A catalogue record for this book is available
from the British Library

ISBN: 978-0-33-406366-7

EU GPSR Authorised Representative
LOGOS EUROPE, 9 rue Nicolas Poussin, 17000, LA ROCHELLE, France
E-mail: Contact@logoseurope.eu

Typeset by Regent Typesetting

Contents

Preface   vii

Part One: Defining and Defending Analytic Theology

1 What is Analytic Theology?   3
2 Answering Objections to Analytic Theology   17

Part Two: Analytic Theology and Christian Doctrine

3 Trinity: The Triune God   37
4 Incarnation: The Person of Christ   59
5 Atonement: The Work of Christ   79

Part Three: Analytic Theology and the Life of the Church

6 Ecclesiology, Liturgy and the Sacraments   109
7 Spirituality and Prayer   141

8 Conclusion – The Apologetic Value of Analytic Theology   158

Bibliography   166

Preface

Analytic theology is a new and growing branch of theology that utilizes the tools and methods of contemporary analytic philosophy. This approach means that Christian analytic theologians pursue conceptual clarity, argumentative transparency and logical rigour in their exposition and examination of the Church's historic doctrines and practices. Over the past decade analytic theologians have established a thriving research community that has given birth to academic journals, books, conferences and research centres around the world, including the *Logos Institute for Analytical and Exegetical Theology* at the University of St Andrews in the UK.

This book seeks to offer a concise introduction and orientation to this new approach to theology for undergraduates, ordinands and the interested lay reader. It therefore begins by offering a basic description and defence of the discipline, before offering a survey of analytic theologians' accounts of distinctive Christian doctrines including the Trinity, the Incarnation and the Atonement.

But this work also aims to articulate the positive contribution of analytic theology to the life of the Church. More precisely, I seek to demonstrate that work by analytic theologians on subjects such as liturgy, prayer and the sacraments has opened new and promising approaches to these important topics. The contribution of analytic theologians in these fields has the potential to enhance the Church's self-understanding and enrich its spiritual life. It is my contention that the Church's mission to the world is also well served by analytic theology, to the extent to which it succeeds in publicly demonstrating the logical coherence and intrinsic plausibility of core Christian beliefs. The fruits of analytic theology are therefore not merely of interest to those within the Church, but a welcome addition to the toolkit of contemporary Christian apologetics.

I would like to extend my thanks to Emmanuel Theological College for granting me three months' study leave during the summer of 2024 to complete this book. I am also grateful to the congregation of St John the Evangelist Church, Ashton Hayes, who graciously surrendered their vicar to his word processor over this same period. My thanks too to David Shervington and his colleagues at SCM Press for their patience, support and guidance during the preparation of this work. Responsibility for any residual errors remains, of course, entirely my own.

Phil Weston

PART ONE

Defining and Defending Analytic Theology

1

What is Analytic Theology?

Even among theologians, the discipline of analytic theology is often an unknown quantity, a new branch of the 'queen of the sciences' that is viewed with a mixture of ignorance, incomprehension and even suspicion. The term 'analytic theology' is indeed new, having entered the theological vocabulary in 2009, when Oxford University Press published a volume entitled *Analytic Theology: New Essays in the Philosophy of Theology*. This work, edited by Oliver Crisp and Michael Rea, sought to 'begin a much-needed interdisciplinary conversation about the value of analytic philosophical approaches to theological topics' (2009, p. 2) and included contributions by William Abraham, Nicholas Wolterstorff, Thomas McCall, Eleonore Stump and Sarah Coakley, among others.

Since 2009 analytic theology has grown, having 'established itself as a flourishing research programme that includes academic journals, monograph series, a dedicated annual conference, research centres on several continents, and a growing and diverse body of work produced by scholars drawn from philosophy, theology, and biblical studies' (Crisp et al., 2019, p. 1). Analytic theology has already become an 'intellectual culture that has its own literature, jargon, social networks, and affiliated substantive commitments' (2019, p. 3). The rapid expansion of this new discipline is in part due to significant grant funding provided by the Templeton Foundation, reflecting its commitment to theological research that engages with contemporary science and philosophy.

In recent years, books by McCall (2015), Crisp, Arcadi and Wessling (2019), Wood (2021) and Arcadi and Turner (2021) have sought to introduce this new discipline to peers working in other areas of theology, philosophy and religious studies. These publications have defined and defended the methodology employed by analytic theologians, as well as offering an overview of analytic theologians' recent outputs and research agendas. McCall (2015) aside, however, none of these otherwise valuable works offer a brief, accessible introduction to analytic theology for the interested lay reader. It is this need that this present work seeks to address. As a result, this book is far from being the last word on the subject, but hopefully provides a helpful 'route map' for further explorations in the field of analytic theology.

Defining the discipline

So, what exactly *is* analytic theology? No universally accepted definition exists, but at its heart, *analytic theology is the application of the aims and methods of analytic philosophy to theological questions*. In his editorial introduction to the book that first coined the term, Rea offers his own influential definition of analytic theology:

> As I see it, analytic theology is just the activity of approaching theological topics with the ambitions of an analytic philosopher and in a style that conforms to the prescriptions that are distinctive of analytical philosophical discourse. It will involve, more or less, pursuing these topics in a way that engages the literature that is constitutive of the analytic tradition, employing some of the technical jargon from that tradition, and so on. But, in the end, it is the style and the ambitions that are most central. (Rea, 2009a, p. 7)

Since its publication of *Analytic Theology* in 2009, Oxford University Press has produced a further series of *Studies in Analytic Theology*, categorized according to the following definition:

> Analytic theology utilizes the tools and methods of contemporary analytic philosophy for the purposes of constructive Christian theology, paying attention to the Christian tradition and development of doctrine. (Wood, 2021, p. 50)

It's worth noting that this definition of the discipline is explicitly Christian in orientation, reflecting the fact that the majority of work by analytic theologians has addressed distinctively Christian doctrines, such as the Trinity, Christology and the Atonement. In this present work I shall similarly confine my attention to *Christian* analytic theology, but it should be noted that its methodology does not exclude other varieties of analytic theology, and indeed works of Jewish and Islamic analytic theology are already beginning to emerge (e.g. Lebens, 2020). It should also be recognized that, although existing works of analytic theology are predominantly Christian, they have been produced by scholars from across all of the main Christian denominations:

Thus you can find Christian analytic theologians who are Roman Catholic, Orthodox, Lutheran, Anglican, Reformed, evangelical, and charismatic. But you can also find Christian analytic theologians who are conservative, traditionalist, progressive, theologically liberal, or revisionist. It is also true that analytic theology crosses theological divisions that are material and not merely formal in nature. So, there are Christian analytic theologians who are Thomist, Arminian, Molinist, Calvinist, Augustinian and so on. (Crisp, 2023, p. 302)

As this evidence suggests, analytic theology is very much a theological *method*, rather than a specific theological system or precise set of doctrinal commitments.

Analytic theology and related disciplines

At the outset it is worth distinguishing analytic theology from closely related subjects such as 'analytic philosophy of religion', 'analytic philosophical theology' and 'systematic theology'. While there are no hard and fast criteria for distinguishing between these disciplines, some basic differences in their scope and method can be identified.

Analytic philosophy of religion is concerned with the application of analytic philosophical methods to generic questions in theology, such as the existence of God, the nature of miracles, the problem of evil and the possibility of life after death. Such questions are 'generic' in that they are pertinent to many different religious traditions, and in the past 50 years have been explored by such famous names as Alvin Plantinga, Antony Flew and John Hick. *Analytic philosophical theology*, in contrast, applies analytic philosophical methods to doctrines and beliefs that are held by particular religious traditions. So Christian analytic philosophical theology, for example, has addressed itself to questions surrounding the Trinity, the Incarnation, the Atonement and the Resurrection. As MacDonald (2009) has noted, philosophical theologians sometimes concern themselves with the justification of such doctrines – offering reasons to believe them to be true – while others devote their time to assessing the coherence of particular doctrines and their compatibility with other central theological convictions. Some of the earliest, most groundbreaking work in analytic philosophical theology was associated with philosophers such as Marilyn McCord Adams, Thomas Morris, Eleonore Stump and Richard Swinburne.[1]

Analytic theology is often considered to be synonymous with analytic philosophical theology, especially among professional philosophers.

On this understanding, analytic theology is simply a new, more concise way of referring to the tradition-specific theological work that has been undertaken by analytic philosophers since the early 1980s. And indeed in this present book I will be engaging with the work of Christian philosophical theologians such as William Lane Craig, Brian Leftow and Richard Swinburne who adopt an analytic approach.

However, other commentators (e.g. Crisp, 2023) do draw a subtle distinction between analytic philosophical theology and analytic theology. From this perspective it is noted that whereas analytic philosophical theology is undertaken exclusively by philosophers, those working in analytic theology are increasingly drawn from a wider range of academic backgrounds, including historical theology, systematic theology and biblical studies. In addition, as we shall explore further below, those identifying as 'analytic theologians' are more likely to personally inhabit a particular religious tradition (usually Christian) than those who simply identify as 'philosophical theologians'. As a consequence, they will tend to give greater epistemic weight to non-philosophical sources (such as Scripture and the Church's creeds) in their work. On this view, analytic theologians would recognize that their discipline 'does indeed involve an approach to the theological task that utilises the aims and methods of analytic philosophy ... But they would want to make this more specific by stating that this is analytic theology in the Christian tradition, practised in a confessional manner' (Crisp, 2023, p. 305). In other words, traditional sources of religious authority set parameters for many analytic theologians that are absent from some works of analytic philosophical theology. On this understanding of analytic theology, it is 'systematic theology attuned to the deployment of the skills, resources and virtues of analytic philosophy' (Abraham, 2009, p. 59). Analytic theology is thus a branch of systematic theology which makes use of analytic philosophy to offer an orderly, thematic account of the Christian faith, much as previous generations made use of 'Aristotelian philosophy, Neoplatonic thought, and German idealism ... to similar theological ends' (Crisp, 2023, p. 304). Throughout church history, one philosophical school after another has served as a 'handmaiden' to theology:

> Within the Christian tradition, one can point to the second-century church father, Clement of Alexandria, as the scholar who first characterised the relationship between philosophy and theology as one of a handmaiden – philosophy as the aid and assistant of the theological task. This aiding and assisting work of philosophy pervades the Christian theological project throughout the centuries, even as the

particular philosophical school serving as handmaiden may change. Analytic theology is no different in this overall methodological approach to philosophy. Its difference lies simply in that the philosophical dialogue partner is analytic philosophy – a dialogue partner often found absent from the major theological conversations of the twentieth century. (Arcadi, 2021a, pp. 1–2)

William Abraham memorably described analytic theology as 'an accident waiting to happen', since 'Christian theologians have deployed the resources of many modes of philosophical thinking from the beginning, [so] the turn to analytic philosophy as a source for systematic theology should neither surprise us nor initially trouble us' (2012, p. 6). Abraham went on to argue that this turn was especially attractive to scholars such as himself, who perceived 'conceptual problems and intellectual sloppiness' in much contemporary theology that needed addressing (p. 7). A similar conviction has been expressed by Russell Reno (2006), who wrote that 'in contemporary Western culture the English-speaking, analytic tradition in philosophy holds out the most promise as a suitable partner for theology in the crucial jobs of strengthening the doctrinal backbone of theology and restoring a culture of truth.'

Some see a particularly strong methodological resemblance between contemporary analytic theology and medieval scholastic theology, especially the work of Thomas Aquinas. Oliver Crisp, for instance, writes, 'Like scholasticism, analytic theology focuses on careful distinctions, argument, objections and counter examples, and metaphysical world-building' (2023, p. 307). William Wood agrees, noting that it 'is not an accident, and not without reason, that contemporary analytic theologians look to Aquinas as a forerunner' (Wood, 2021, p. 180). After all, his theology similarly featured 'deductive, linear arguments aimed at propositional assent', albeit drawing on Aristotelian, rather than analytic, philosophy (p. 177).

The style and ambitions of analytic philosophy

Despite their differences, all the definitions of analytic theology described above acknowledge a methodological commitment to analytic philosophy. This naturally requires us to define analytic philosophy itself, and to consider exactly what is meant by the *style* and *ambitions* of analytic philosophy that Rea (2009a) refers to in his influential definition of analytic theology. Broadly speaking, analytic philosophy is an approach to philosophy characterized by a commitment to such virtues as conceptual precision, logical rigour and transparency of argument. But Rea offers a more detailed account of the 'style' followed by analytic philosophers, which he says abides by five 'prescriptions':

P1. Write as if philosophical positions and conclusions can be adequately formulated in sentences that can be formalised and logically manipulated.
P2. Prioritise precision, clarity, and logical coherence.
P3. Avoid substantive (non-decorative) use of metaphor and other tropes whose semantic content outstrips their propositional content.
P4. Work as much as possible with well-understood primitive concepts, and concepts that can be analyzed in terms of those.
P5. Treat conceptual analysis (insofar as it is possible) as a source of evidence. (Rea, 2009a, p. 5)

A little exposition of each prescription is needed here. As Crisp et al. (2019) explain, P1 'captures the fact that the default setting for analytic philosophers is to write in such a way that the logical relationships between their key claims can be discerned effortlessly and their arguments can, with relative ease, be translated into syllogisms' (p. 6).[2] P2, meanwhile, is based on the observation that analytic philosophers make use 'of thought experiments, carefully crafted definitions, syllogisms, and the like' in an effort to communicate as precisely as possible (p. 8). Clarity, in this context, recognizes analytic philosophers' aspiration to maximize the transparency of their arguments. It means that 'analytic philosophers place a high premium on spelling out hidden assumptions, on scrupulously trying to lay bare whatever evidence one has (or lacks) for the claims one is making' (Rea, 2009a, p. 5). P2 does not mean that every work of analytic philosophy be easily understandable by a non-specialist, far from it, but it should be comprehensible 'to the appropriate audience and to the greatest possible degree' (McCall, 2015, p. 19).

Turning to P3, this prescription does not prohibit all use of metaphor, but does mean that analytic philosophers 'are not at liberty to trade loosely in metaphor without ever being able to specify just what is meant by those metaphors. They are not, then, free to make claims the meaning of which cannot be specified or spelled out' (McCall, 2015, p. 20). Analytic philosophers will therefore be particularly reticent about using imprecise metaphors 'that are central to the argument or proposal in question' (Crisp et al., 2019, p. 8). Prescription P4 recognizes that analytic philosophers 'aim, when feasible, to articulate and defend the ideas central to a given writing in terms of concepts that are difficult or impossible to break down into more easily understood bits of information' (p. 6). Lastly, P5 does not say that conceptual analysis is the only source of evidence utilized by analytic philosophers, nor does it claim that conceptual analysis is necessarily the best source of evidence. But this prescription does recognize that if conceptual analysis demonstrates that a philosophical argument is contradictory (that is, internally inconsistent), 'then that analysis gives us all the evidence we need' to reject it (McCall, 2015, p. 21). On the other hand, 'showing that a specific conception is internally consistent may provide some reason to hold that it is, or might be, true' (Crisp et al., 2019, p. 7).

If adherence to these five prescriptions constitutes the *style* of analytic philosophy, what then are its *ambitions*? For Rea, these include identifying 'the scope and limits of our powers to obtain knowledge of the world, and ... to provide such true explanatory theories as we can in areas of inquiry (metaphysics, morals, and the like) that fall outside the scope of the natural sciences' (2009a, p. 4). Given this ambition, it is no surprise that theological topics drew the attention of analytic philosophers. The initial application of analytic philosophical methods to religious questions began in the middle of the twentieth century. Anglo-American philosophers such as Basil Mitchell (in the UK) and Alvin Plantinga (in the US) began to apply the style and ambitions of analytic philosophy to foundational questions in religion. These questions included the logical coherence of theism, the existence of God, and the problem of evil. Nicholas Wolterstorff was another of the early exponents of analytic philosophy of religion and analytic philosophical theology and has offered an account of why interest in religious questions emerged among Anglo-American analytic philosophers. He summarizes his thesis as follows:

> What happened within analytic philosophy to account for the flourishing of analytic philosophical theology over the past third of a century? Thus far I have called attention to two developments: the emergence of widespread skepticism concerning all attempts to specify general conditions for the thinkable and the assertable; and the collapse of consensus concerning epistemological theory, in particular, consensus concerning any theory which implies that theistic beliefs are rational only if they are rationally grounded in certitudes. Also required was the existence of a substantial number of philosophers who thought it important to capitalise on the opportunity offered by this lifting of constraints – to capitalise on it by actually developing philosophical theology. In short, the sociological fact that a good many American philosophers are theists, Christian and Jewish especially, has a been a

decisive factor in the flourishing of philosophical theology. (Wolterstorff, 2009, p. 162)

For Wolterstorff the downfall of logical positivism (including the belief that meaningful assertions about God could only be made if they are empirically verifiable) and the general collapse of any consensus on 'the limits of the thinkable and the assertable' created intellectual space for the emergence of analytic philosophy of religion and, subsequently, analytic philosophical theology. Christians and other theists working in analytic philosophy were only too willing to take advantage of this opportunity.

The assumptions and aspirations of analytic theologians

As we have seen, analytic theology involves the application of the tools and methods of analytic philosophy to theological questions. In addition, 'analytic theological literature in the Christian tradition typically has evinced some key substantive components' (Arcadi, 2021a, p. 3). In other words, practitioners of analytic theology usually undertake their task with certain foundational theological assumptions. Thus, analytic theologians 'tend to include a commitment to (a) some form of theological realism, (b) the truth-apt and truth-aimed nature of theological enquiry, and (c) the importance of providing theological arguments for substantive doctrinal positions' (p. 3). In simple terms, this means that most analytic theologians are committed to belief in the objective reality of God; 'he is not a figment of our imaginations' (Crisp et al., 2019, p. 16). They are also committed to the belief that theological statements are 'truth-apt' in the sense that they can be true or false, and 'truth-aimed' in the sense that the theological task seeks to acquire genuine knowledge about God. The third commitment, meanwhile, implies that 'analytic theologians are interested in doing theology. They do not merely talk about doing theology' (p. 18). Whatever doctrine is under consideration, it is analytic theologians' ambition to get 'closer to the truth of the matter' by providing 'a better (that is, truth-tracking) account of a particular doctrine or doctrines' (p. 18).

Furthermore, most analytic theologians write from a confessional standpoint, self-consciously working from within a particular Christian theological tradition. Indeed, we have already noted the tendency of analytic theologians to recognize Scripture and the creeds as authoritative sources that set the agenda for doctrinal investigation and establish basic parameters for theological reflection. As William Abraham has written, analytic theologians typically stand 'inside the circle of Christian faith' and seek to 'articulate the deep contours of the vision of God that is to be found in the Church' (2012, p. 16).

Given the foundational assumptions described above, what are the intellectual aims and aspirations of those engaged in analytic theology? What do analytic theologians generally hope to achieve by their endeavours? Wood (2021) identifies two different, though not mutually exclusive, goals that have been pursued by analytic theologians. The first can be described as an agenda of 'faith seeking understanding', while the second is one of 'constructive theology'. Wood defines the first of these aspirations as follows:

> The phrase 'faith seeking understanding' comes from Anselm's *Proslogion*, and points back to Augustine's famous maxim *crede ut intelligas*, 'believe so that you may understand.' So construed, Christian theology begins with an epistemic posture of assent to scripture and tradition, or, more generally, to whatever theological resource one regards as authoritative. On this account, theology does not seek to prove that faith claims are true; it assumes their truth and then tries to understand them more deeply and elucidate their consequences. (Wood, 2021, p. 53)

He cites Timothy Pawl's *In Defence of Conciliar Christology* (2016) as an example of analytic theology in the mode of 'faith seeking understanding'. Crucially, Pawl's starting point is the assumption that the Church's historic understanding of the person of Christ (as enshrined in the Chalcedonian Definition of AD 451) is true. His stance is one of faithful acceptance of the authority of the ecumenical councils of the early Church. As Wood notes, 'At no point does he take himself to be offering arguments that conciliar Christology is true or even possibly true.' Instead, Pawl's goal is 'to answer what he regards as the most serious objections to that truth' (2021, p. 55).

In their own account of *The Nature and Promise of Analytic Theology*, Oliver Crisp, James Arcadi and Jordan Wessling describe much analytic theology as a form of '"declarative theology", a manner of theologising which was the subject of much analysis by Christian theologians of the fourteenth century' (2019, p. 20). Citing Durandus of St-Pourçain, they define declarative theology as the task by '"which the faith and those things handed down in Sacred Scripture are defended and clarified by using principles that we know better." Those things we "know better" might be *a priori* principles, empirical observations or notions derived from simple metaphysical or logical principles' (p. 21). Akin to

Wood's account of 'faith seeking understanding', Crisp et al. stress that declarative theology 'is not intended to produce assent to the truth of an article of faith, since faith is a gift of God' (2019, p. 22). In practice, this means that a declarative approach to theology works *towards* articles of the faith ('first-principle propositions'), as the conclusion of arguments. Ultimately, the purpose of declarative theology is to help believers have a deeper understanding of the articles of their faith and be better equipped to respond to objections to their beliefs. Their argument 'is that analytic theology not only ought to preserve these declarative theological values, but that analytic theologians have already been achieving the ends of this methodological antecedent' (2019, pp. 24–5).

Whether one calls it 'declarative theology' or an exercise in 'faith seeking understanding', this first aspiration of analytic theologians is defensive or apologetic in posture. It seeks to reinforce the pre-existing faith of believers and respond to the questions posed by unbelievers. The second aspiration of analytic theology, in contrast, is more creative and original in nature, and can be called *constructive* theology. The task of constructive theology, according to Wood, is to offer an 'account of the meaning or truth of some doctrine or claim of the Christian tradition. Alternatively, on a slightly broader definition, a constructive Christian theologian tries to show how the meaning and truth of some Christian doctrine or claim entails that another Christian interpretation of reality is correct' (2021, p. 62). In practice this methodology differs from a declarative approach to theology in that it argues deductively from an article of the faith, 'wherein the conclusion is an extension of the content of theology' (Crisp et al., 2019, p. 21).

One example of constructive theology cited by Wood is William Hasker's *Metaphysics and the Tri-Personal God* (2013). While seeking to be 'faithful to the Christian tradition, and consistent with its historic trinitarian creeds', Wood points out that Hasker's account of the doctrine of the Trinity

> draws heavily on contemporary analytic metaphysics, and [is] therefore not one that could have emerged in the fourth century. In other words, Hasker wants to develop a coherent, orthodox Christian account of the doctrine of the Trinity, but he does not argue that any patristic figure ever affirmed the account he develops. The difference between these two goals is the difference between constructive theology and historical theology. (2021, pp. 62–3)

Moreover, in Wood's view, 'most analytic theology is constructive theology. Understanding the difference between constructive and historical theology is, therefore, crucial for understanding what analytic theologians are trying to accomplish' (2021, p. 69).

As we shall see in subsequent chapters, model-building is a common feature of many works of analytic theology, and 'one important way in which analytic theologians have approached the constructive task of theology' (Crisp, 2021, p. 9). In the case of Hasker, for instance, he seeks 'to construct a model of the Trinity that is consistent with the historic trinitarian creeds, and also consistent with everything we know from contemporary thought' (Wood, 2021, p. 67). Analytic theologians seek to build and utilize models in a manner similar to that of the natural sciences:

> The goal of such models is to organise and simplify complex data regarding some subject (which is difficult or impossible to comprehend fully) for the purpose of gaining intellectual traction on that subject and making conceptual progress on a range of affiliated issues. Models of this kind typically (though not always) aim for the truth of the matter, or some approximation thereof. Often, the project of model-building is accompanied by a statement by the relevant analytic theologian of the ways in which a model is intended to represent its target and what is believed to constitute good evidence for supposing that there is an adequate match between the salient features of the model and its target. (Crisp et al., 2019, p. 17)

As well as the Trinity, other 'targets' of such models by analytic theologians have included the Incarnation, the Atonement, Providence and various divine attributes. This model-building exercise has not been without its critics, however, as we shall see in the next chapter. For now, however, it suffices to note its importance to many works of constructive analytic theology.

Analytic theology's research programme – past and present

Drawing together all that has been said so far, analytic theology can be defined as an approach to theology that utilizes the tools and methods of analytic philosophy to undertake *both* defensive *and* constructive, declarative *and* deductive, theological work. Analytic theologians operate with some basic shared assumptions about the truth-apt and truth-aimed nature of their task, and are invariably theological realists who affirm the mind-independent, objective reality of God. Christian analytic theology typically also operates within foundational doctrinal parameters set by Scripture and the Church's historic creeds.

One way of categorizing analytic theology is as a *research programme*, which can be defined as 'a set of inquiry-shaping strategies and methodological dispositions' that academics bring to their respective disciplines (Crisp et al., 2019, p. 55). In the case of analytic theology:

> Analytic theology is a kind of research programme in that theologians who adopt or acquire this approach tend to treat certain things as sources of evidence (e.g. conceptual analysis, as well as theological authorities like Scripture, and aspects of the Christian tradition), certain things as primitive or basic (e.g. primitive concepts), and certain things as important intellectual virtues in approaching a particular topic (prioritizing precision, clarity, logical coherence; attempting to write in such a way that one's arguments can be formalized and logically manipulated to provide as much clarity about the logical form of an argument as is feasible; and so on). Moreover, these strategies and methodological dispositions are used by the analytic theologian for the sake of identifying the scope and limits of the human ability to obtain knowledge of God and God's ways as well as for providing true explanatory theories of the central doctrines of the faith (pp. 55–6).

From the early 1980s onwards the research output of Christian analytic philosophers has focused on central doctrines of the faith, notably the Trinity, the Incarnation and the Atonement. This relatively narrow focus of enquiry is reflected in compendia of Christian philosophical theology produced prior to 2010. For example, the two-volume *Oxford Readings in Philosophical Theology* published in 2009 had six parts covering Trinity, Incarnation, Atonement, Providence, Scripture and Resurrection, while a similarly narrow list of topics is covered in T&T Clark's *A Reader in Contemporary Philosophical Theology* published in the same year.

Since 2009, however, and the identification of analytic theology as a distinct discipline, there has been a marked increase in the breadth of topics analysed. Recent compendia of analytic theology have included chapters on subjects as diverse as anthropology, ethics, the Eucharist, prayer and spirituality (e.g. Arcadi and Turner, 2021). Of particular note is the ecclesiastical and liturgical 'turn' seen among analytic theologians over the past decade (Crisp et al., 2019, p. 64). The attention of analytic theologians has been increasingly drawn to Christian praxis, especially worship, as a worthwhile subject of study. For example, Nicholas Wolterstorff (2018) and Terence Cuneo (2016) have recently examined the nature and function of liturgy, while Joshua Cockayne has produced a work entitled *Explorations in Analytic Ecclesiology* (2022).

Marilyn McCord Adams, James Arcadi and Alexander Pruss have all published analytic treatments of the Eucharist over the past decade, while authors such as Scott Davison and David Efird have looked at aspects of prayer and spirituality from an analytic theological perspective. Taken together, these works have challenged any prior sense that analytic theology is 'the preserve of an intellectual elite for whom the actual matters of ecclesiastical life are rather remote' (Crisp et al., 2019, p. 64).

Another way in which the scope of analytic theology has diversified over recent years is the emergence of contextual analytic theologies. *Voices from the Edge: Centring Marginalized Perspectives in Analytic Theology* (2020) was a groundbreaking work that for the first time explicitly sought to examine from an analytic theological perspective how experiences of race, gender, disability and sexuality shape perceptions of God and his activity in the world. This book 'focused on three central areas of analytic theology: methodological principles, the intersection of social identities with religious epistemology, and the connections among eschatology, ante-mortem suffering, and ante-mortem social perceptions of bodies' (Panchuk and Rea, 2020, p. 2).

Where do we go from here?

Having introduced analytic theology in this chapter, where do we go from here? The aims and methods of analytic theology have proved controversial in some quarters, and so the next chapter seeks to summarize these concerns and consider some of the arguments that analytic theologians have offered in reply. These include concerns about the alleged epistemic overconfidence of analytic theology and its apparent reticence about embracing mystery, allegations that analytic theology is ahistorical in its approach, and questions about the use that analytic theologians make of Scripture and church tradition.

In the second part of this book I shall seek to summarize the work of analytic theologians in more established areas of enquiry, with chapters on the Trinity, the Incarnation and the Atonement. These chapters seek to demonstrate the analytic theological method 'in action', and offer a concise account of the recent contributions by analytic theologians to discussion of these central Christian doctrines.

The third and final parts of this work seek to explain how analytic theology is beginning to serve the ministry and mission of the Church. I begin by summarizing the fruit of recent analytic theologians' work on Christian ecclesiology, liturgy and spirituality, suggesting that it has the capacity to enrich the Church's devotional life and self-understanding. I then conclude by arguing that the emerging fruits of analytic theology can serve as a new and valuable resource for Christian apologetics.

Notes

1 See, for example, Swinburne's *The Christian God* (1994) and Morris' *The Logic of God Incarnate* (1986), for early analytic philosophical accounts of the Trinity and the Incarnation.
2 A *syllogism* is a type of deductive reasoning where a conclusion is drawn from two prior premises (e.g. 'All men are mortal. Socrates is a man. Therefore, Socrates is mortal').

Recommended further reading

Crisp, O. D. and Rea, M. (eds), 2009, *Analytic Theology: New Essays in the Philosophy of Theology*, Oxford: Oxford University Press.
Arcadi, J. M. and Turner, J. T., 2021, *The T&T Clark Handbook of Analytic Theology*, London: Bloomsbury.

2

Answering Objections to Analytic Theology

In the book which launched (or at least labelled) the discipline, Oliver Crisp anticipated that objections to analytic theology 'might be raised about this proposal for theological method' (2009, p. 50) and this prediction has proved accurate. Analytic theology is not without its critics, and so this chapter seeks to summarize these concerns, which I have categorized according to the conventional sources of theology, namely Scripture, tradition, reason and experience. For instance, some critics have alleged that practitioners of analytic theology attach insufficient importance to the traditional norms of theology, including Scripture and the creeds, while others have argued that analytic theologians pay too little attention to the historical development of doctrine. Others allege that analytic theology suffers from an overconfidence in the capacity of human reasoning to comprehend the divine which leads, at best, to a reluctance to embrace mystery or, at worst, an idolatrous conception of God. While there is some initial plausibility to each of these concerns (and individual cases of bad practice can, of course, always be cited), we shall see that advocates of analytic theology have argued that these are not inherent or unavoidable features of the discipline as a whole.

Analytic theology and the norms of theology

A recurring line of concern regarding analytic theology is that it fails to acknowledge the authority of the established norms of Christian theology, notably Scripture and the Church's historic teaching. Such concerns are raised even among theologians who are otherwise supportive of the aims and aspirations of analytic theology. For example, John Frame writes:

> Analytic theology has come to dominate discussions of philosophical issues among Christians in recent years. Its aspiration to produce works of high quality thought and cogency has been acknowledged and appreciated, as has its use of more recent logical and analytic

tools. In my judgment, however, analytic theology, like previous forms of interaction between philosophy and theology, has been weak in its failure to apply theological norms to the work of philosophy itself. Many writings in the analytic theology movement, even writings by people who are unquestionably committed to Christ, sound like attempts to be religiously neutral, as if the Bible and the confessions had nothing authoritative to say to the issues at hand. (Frame, accessed 21.08.2023)

Crisp, Arcadi and Wessling have articulated a similar concern:

To carry on the theological tradition of the Church and participate in its formation, the theologian must be schooled in the art and science of biblical interpretation as well as be sure footed in the history and development of doctrine. However, this training is almost entirely absent from the intellectual culture of analytic philosophy. This gives rise to the worry that the privileging of that intellectual culture will inevitably lead to impoverished theological results. (Crisp et al., 2019, p. 12)

So to what extent do analytic theologians recognize Scripture and ecclesiastical tradition as norms and sources for their work, alongside analytic philosophical reasoning? Are concerns that works of analytic theology lack adequate biblical foundation or display insufficient knowledge of Christian tradition justified?

Analytic theology and Scripture

At the outset it must be acknowledged that any theological discipline that claims to be 'Christian' needs to engage with biblical scholarship and be attentive to the teaching of Scripture. Some would go further, of course, and argue that any Christian theology worthy of the name must regard Scripture as its supreme authority, the *norma normans* (the 'norming norm'), with which all its conclusions must concur. From this perspective there is sometimes a 'worry that analytic theologians bypass and effectively ignore God's own revelation as it occurs ultimately in the incarnation of the Holy Son and reliably in the Bible as Holy Scripture' (McCall, 2015, p. 38). Were this concern to be substantiated, it would mean that analytic theology ought to be categorized as a form of *natural* theology, rather than as a branch of *Christian* theology. However, such a definition would not adequately distinguish analytic theology from the philosophy of religion, nor is it a characterization of analytic theology held by its most prominent exponents. On the contrary, they maintain that analytic theology *does* recognize the authority of Scripture and interprets it responsibly using appropriate hermeneutical methods. Indeed, an increasing number of analytic theologians come from backgrounds in biblical studies.

In his article 'Analytic Theology and Analytic Philosophy of Religion: What's the Difference?' (2016), Max Baker-Hytch argues that an important distinction between analytic theology and analytic philosophy of religion is their differing attitude towards the authority of Scripture. Whereas practitioners of both disciplines may look to Scripture as a source of topics for study or for an account of what Christians believe, *only* analytic theologians will use scriptural teaching as a foundational premise in a philosophical argument. To use an element of biblical teaching as a foundational premise, as only analytic theologians do, reflects a belief that Scripture is a divinely inspired text 'whose trustworthiness need not and indeed should not be established by some allegedly more basic epistemic source' (Baker-Hytch, 2016, p. 357).

Furthermore, as William Wood has pointed out, recognition of the authority of Scripture does not in any way prevent analytic theologians from utilizing philosophical reasoning to better understand what God has revealed. He writes:

> Suppose we ... hold that theology must begin from a perspective of faithful assent to revelation. The history of the Church, especially in its first few centuries, is testament to the point that fundamental questions about how to understand revelation will always arise. So even if we think that theology requires an attitude of faithful assent to revealed truths, we can still legitimately wonder exactly what truths have been revealed, what they mean, and how they can be true, or at least consistent with everything else we take to be true. We can also wonder about further truths that are entailed by those that have been revealed. Analytic tools and methods are well suited to addressing such problems. (Wood, 2021, p. 99)

Crisp et al. (2019) adopt a similar position when they describe much analytic theology as a contemporary manifestation of 'declarative theology'. As we saw in the previous chapter, declarative theology seeks to defend and clarify the teaching of Scripture using empirical observations or the principles of logic. When operating in this declarative mode, analytic theology is applying the analytic philosophical method in submission to Scripture, rather than engaging in an attempt to steal its throne. One might say its use of analytic philosophy is *ministerial* rather than *magisterial*, and it is being utilized as a 'handmaid' to Scripture just as other philosophical approaches have been so used in the past.

It is worth noting at this stage that some analytic theologians have also sought to 'serve' the Scriptures by offering philosophical defence of their divine inspiration and authority. In so doing they have fulfilled William Abraham's prediction that the task of the analytic theologian 'will involve the shoring up of a vision of scripture as canon in the sense of a criterion of truth and falsehood. The crucial issues will be the meaning and epistemic status of scripture, inspiration, revelation ... [and] the inerrancy of scripture' (2013, p. 11). Indeed, one of the key figures in the emergence of analytic theology, Nicholas Wolterstorff, is the author of arguably the seminal work of analytic philosophy on the nature of Scripture. Drawing on insights from Speech-Act theory, Wolterstorff's *Divine Discourse* (1995) defends the view that

> God is the principal author of canonical Holy Scripture ... [because] God appropriates the various locutionary and illocutionary acts of the subordinate human authors as his own. The canon of Holy Scripture in its entirety, then, is the medium of the *viva vox Dei*; when one reads the humanly authored texts that compose canonical Holy Scripture, one is confronted with God's intended medium by which he testifies, promises, commands, comforts, exhorts, restores, warns, and personally discloses himself to humanity. (Inman, 2022, p. 121)

The volume that coined the term 'analytic theology' (that is, Crisp and Rea, 2009) also included two essays defending a high view of Scripture. In the first of these essays Thomas McCall defends what he calls the 'classical' view that Scripture *is* the written Word of God from 'progressive' views that the Bible merely 'contains or reflects the Word of God' and from the Barthian view that Scripture only *becomes* the Word of God at certain moments of divine sovereign self-disclosure (2009, p. 172). Responding specifically to Barth's concern that the classical view 'portrays the Word of God as a thing that can be either picked up or put down, something that can be either taken or left, accepted or rejected, handled or mishandled, revered or cherished or desecrated or destroyed', McCall writes that:

> What Barth fears to say about the written Word is exactly what the Christian believer must say about the *living* Word. Central to the orthodox Christian belief in Jesus is the conviction that, in the Incarnation, the living Word gave himself over to humanity. The living

Word put himself at our disposal. The action of the living Word is surely *God's* action, as such it is right to affirm with Barth that it is a sovereign action. But – on Barth's own doctrine of the Incarnation – the Word became flesh and allowed himself to be either taken or left, accepted or rejected, handled or mishandled. If we can (and should) affirm this of the 'revealed' living and incarnate Word, why would we insist on refraining from affirming it also of the written Word? It seems to me that, on Barth's own theological principles, we not only can affirm that scripture *is* the written Word of God but also *should* do so. (McCall, 2009, pp. 181–2)

The second essay in analytic theology's foundational volume was by Thomas Crisp (2009). Entitled 'On believing that the Scriptures are Divinely Inspired', in it Crisp investigated the epistemology of belief in the inspiration of Scripture. While being open to the possibility of historical evidence in its favour, plus the inward witness of the Holy Spirit to its inspired nature, Crisp concluded that the authoritative teaching of the Church provides the strongest justification for any individual Christian to believe in biblical inspiration. Over more recent years, analytic theologians such as Wahlberg (2014), Rea (2016) and Green (2021) have also offered their own defences of the authority and inspiration of the Scriptures.

Nevertheless, it is naïve to believe that all engaged in analytic theology have given the same epistemic weight to the Bible, or that all analytic theologians have interpreted Scripture in a way that recognizes its diversity of literary forms and genres. As the discipline develops, therefore, its practitioners would do well to heed the advice of McCall (2015), who urges those without a background in biblical studies to become sufficiently well versed in the subject to ensure that their work avoids egregious exegetical or hermeneutical errors:

First, analytic theologians should know Scripture itself well enough that they are able to relate their work to what the Bible may have to say about the topic or issue under discussion, and to know if the clear implications of scriptural affirmations impinge on it directly or indirectly. Recall Karl Barth's admonition: 'Exegesis, exegesis, exegesis.' Second, they should know enough about the scholarly study of the Bible that they are able to engage with it and benefit from it. Third, they should know enough about such scholarly work in biblical studies to offer their own questions and criticisms when these are appropriate. Throughout their work, analytic theologians … must work with the actual text of Scripture. (McCall, 2015, p. 175)

Analytic theology and church tradition

Alongside Scripture, doctrinal statements of the Church, notably the ecumenical creeds and denominational confessions, have traditionally served as a norm and guide for Christian theologians, setting the parameters of Christian (and denominational) belief. These doctrinal traditions of the Church represent *norma normata* (a 'normed norm') under the supreme norm of Scripture. But do analytic theologians recognize them as axioms and abide by them in their work? William Abraham, for instance, felt the need to remind analytic theologians that their work must

> begin by standing inside the circle of Christian faith and seeking to articulate the deep contours of the vision of God that is to be found in the Church. We speak here unapologetically of the Christian God, the God of creation and redemption, whose saving acts are laid out in the Nicene Creed and in the manifold practices of the Church. (Abraham, 2009, p. 60)

In general, it would seem that Abraham's call has been heeded. As Wood (2021) has noted, and as we saw in the previous chapter, analytic theologians operating in the declarative 'faith seeking understanding' mode and those operating in a more constructive manner do indeed recognize the historic creeds and confessions as normative for their work. Wood describes, for example, the assumptions made by Timothy Pawl in his work on Christology:

> First, he assumes that the proceedings and documents of the first seven ecumenical councils have a determinate and identifiable propositional content. Second he assumes that the councils are all mutually consistent. Third, he assumes that conciliar Christology is true. It therefore follows, obviously, that Pawl also assumes the truth of the traditional Chalcedonian account of the incarnation. Again, Pawl *assumes*, but does not argue for this claim. At no point does he take himself to be offering arguments that conciliar Christology is true or even possibly true. Rather, he assumes its truth and seeks to answer what he regards as the most serious objections to that truth. (Wood, 2021, p. 55)

Similarly, even William Hasker's avowedly constructive work on the Trinity assumes the Nicene definition of the doctrine to be foundational and true:

> His is not in any sense 'a Cartesian project, in which the objective is to demolish our existing edifice of belief, scour the building site down

to the bedrock, and build all over again with imperishable materials.'
Like Pawl, Hasker assumes without argument certain aspects of the
normative Christian tradition, accepts that they are reliable guides to
the truth and seeks to explicate their claims with the best intellectual
tools in his possession. (Wood, 2021, p. 64)

Baker-Hytch (2016) has helpfully teased out two different ways in which analytic theologians appeal to ecclesial tradition as a premise in their arguments. For some, creedal and confessional statements are a *'foundational premise*, on behalf of which no further argumentation is offered'. For others, these ecclesial pronouncements function as an *'intermediate premise*, which is a premise on behalf of which further argumentation is offered' (p. 351). This further argumentation will itself rest, ultimately, on foundational premises taken from Scripture or other ecclesial traditions.

However, even if analytic theologians do pay due heed to the creeds and other historic texts, do they nevertheless utilize them in an ahistorical manner? Do they mistakenly treat them as easily understood, timeless propositions? A number of commentators have expressed this concern that analytic theologians are guilty of wilful ignorance of the historical development of ecclesiastical statements – they are contingent, contextual documents. Analytic theologians are, it is alleged, far too 'quick to isolate a particular text and try to break it down to find the real "core" of the doctrine, or they may find the historical context of little relevance to the sober truth' (McCall, 2015, p. 84; cf. Branson, 2014). Crisp summarizes this 'worry' as 'something like this: (Christian) analytic theologians are not really interested in the history of theological positions but only in mining the literary remains of particular historical figures for arguments and concepts' (2023, p. 308). Such an attitude, if held, is said to create a real risk that historic texts will be misinterpreted and misunderstood by analytic theologians today. William Wood describes this 'Objection from History' (as he calls it) when he writes:

> Premodern ways of reading and thinking are very different from analytic ways of reading and thinking, and premodern argument typically looks very different from analytic argument. All too often analytic theology pays little attention to such complexities. So the objection is that analytic theology does not take history or historical contingency seriously enough. Sometimes, this objection takes an even more direct form: analytic theologians are simply ignorant of the history of doctrine, and of historical sources more generally. (Wood, 2021, pp. 14–15)

At the outset it is worth noting that this worry about historical illiteracy is not confined to analytic theology. It could equally be addressed to systematic theology, or indeed any theological discipline that utilizes historical texts in its work. As McCall observes, 'this is a general concern that should serve as an important reminder that all theologians who engage with the Christian intellectual tradition should do so with appropriate historical sensitivity' (2015, pp. 28–9). Second, in response to this concern it is also possible to cite examples of analytic theologians who have extensive knowledge of historical theology and are regarded as leading voices within that discipline too. Names who could be mentioned in this context include Jeffrey Brower, Richard Cross, Marilyn McCord Adams and Eleonore Stump. Together, they have displayed significant insights into patristic and medieval theology that are widely respected by other historical theologians. There therefore seems to be no necessary connection between proficiency in analytic theology and historical ignorance. Certainly, some individual analytic theologians may be guilty of historical illiteracy, but this need not (and should not) be the case. As Wood writes:

> I agree that some analytic theologians and philosophers of religion do not take historical sources seriously enough. I also agree that analytic theologians sometimes misunderstand premodern ways of reading and thinking. But in such cases the fault lies with the individual thinkers who make these mistakes, not with the analytic method itself ... it is certainly possible for analytic thinkers to treat historical sources with contextual nuance and sensitivity. The fault lies with those who do not, not with the analytic method itself. (Wood, 2021, p. 15)

A further, more substantive response can also be made to this concern about historical literacy. As we saw above, much work in analytic theology is constructive in ambition – it seeks to go beyond mere exegesis of the creeds and other historic texts to offer new, contemporary accounts of Christian belief and practice. Analysis of historic texts, notably the creeds, helps analytic theologians identify the parameters for such constructive work, and provides many of the conceptual, linguistic and other 'raw materials' they will need – but the texts are not studied as ends in and of themselves. By adopting this approach, analytic theologians are engaged in what John Webster called 'retrieval theology', namely 'the reclamation of tracts of the Christian past as a resource for present constructive work' (2007, p. 590). Once again, William Hasker's constructive work on the Trinity provides a helpful illustration. Not only does Hasker seek to remain within the parameters of orthodoxy set by the historic creeds, but his work is also an exercise in retrieval theology since he 'looks to the theology of the major fourth-century theologians (including both the Cappadocians and Augustine), and he relies on important work done by patrologists who specialise in the study of the trinitarian theology of the fourth and fifth centuries. He then critically receives, defends and develops important elements of that theology in defense of a moderate "social trinitarianism"' (McCall, 2015, p. 87).

As this example illustrates, historical sources are sometimes used by analytic theologians in a manner very different from how a historical theologian might expect them to be approached. Whereas the latter will seek to accurately exposit and explain a text in its original context, an analytic theologian operating in 'retrieval mode' will approach the same text with a more critical posture and a more constructive ambition. As Wood notes, constructive analytic theologians

> try to offer their own accounts of the meaning and truth of some doctrine or claim of the Christian tradition, rather than merely interpreting existing historical accounts. The ultimate aim is always to make true statements about God, or whatever aspect of reality is under discussion. Crucially, this means that analytic thinkers sometimes engage with historical sources in an ahistorical way – for example, by using modern modal metaphysics to try to understand the Christological claims of the Council of Chalcedon. This would be an illegitimate move if the goal were to understand Chalcedon on its own terms, or to give an account of what the fifth-century church thought about Christ. But if the goal is to develop a true or possibly true Christology, then it is perfectly legitimate to draw on contemporary philosophical tools that the fifth-century church fathers lacked. (p. 18)

In short, constructive analytic theologians often approach historical texts with their own distinctive aim and ambition. The method of textual engagement necessitated by their constructive goals should not be mistaken for wilful ignorance of their original historical context.

Analytic theology and the application of human reason

In addition to questions around analytic theologians' use of Scripture and tradition, another cluster of concerns surrounds their application of human reason. Specifically, it is alleged that the aims and methods of analytic theology exhibit excessive confidence in the ability of human reasoning to acquire sure knowledge about God. Analytic theologians fail, it is alleged, to recognize the fallible and fallen nature of human reasoning and our inability to fully comprehend a transcendent God. This failure to adequately recognize the Creator–creature distinction, it is alleged, leads analytic theologians to formulate a god of their own making rather than humbly acknowledge the mysterious nature of the true and living God. Analytic theologians have thus been accused of exhibiting such vices as 'intellectual hubris', 'idolatry', 'ontotheology' and unwarranted 'univocity' within their work (Wood, 2021, p. 18).

Taking these accusations in turn, is it fair, first, to accuse analytic theologians of intellectual hubris? In other words, do they systematically express an overconfidence in their ability to comprehend our transcendent Creator? Does their approach to theology place too much trust in human cognitive abilities and moral intuitions, overlooking the teaching of Scripture and the consensus of Christian tradition that we are fallible, fallen creatures? As Wood has written:

> The most salient version of the charge goes something like this: if the goal of analytic theology is to use the tools of human reason to come to know God better, then surely that kind of inquiry presupposes that God can be known, which in turn presupposes that our concepts can 'grasp' God, which means that God is an object in the world, fundamentally like us, just bigger and more powerful. (Wood, 2021, p. 19)

In response to this concern, Wood himself notes 'at the outset' that 'every major analytic theologian affirms a strong distinction between God, who creates out of nothing, and creatures who are entirely dependent on God at every moment of their existence' (p. 19). As created human beings, analytic theologians recognize that their (and everybody else's) cognitive powers are finite and fallible. Moreover, as individuals standing self-consciously within the Christian tradition, analytic theologians 'endorse the … noetic effects of sin and the cognitive consequences of the Fall', even if they do disagree among themselves on whether the Fall was 'a discrete historical event' (p. 91). Christian analytic theologians freely acknowledge that our fallen nature impairs human reasoning whenever our thinking succumbs to sinful biases or selfish desires. Analytic theology, like 'all forms of theology', is 'at risk of anthropomorphism, idolatry, self-serving biases, and similar errors, because all theology occurs in the wake of the Fall' (2021, p. 102).

For example, Brian Leftow is one analytic theologian who openly acknowledges his human cognitive limits when he writes:

I give many perfect-being arguments in what follows. As I give them I have a nagging fear that I am just making stuff up. This is not due to uncertainty about God's being perfect. Rather, our ideas of what it is to be perfect are inconsistent and flawed, and there is no guarantee that they match up with what God's perfection really is. (2012a, pp. 11–12)

Alert to their cognitive limits, how do analytic theologians seek to minimize errors in their work? As we saw above, one defining feature of the analytic 'style' is the 'high premium' attached to clarity and transparency of argument (Rea, 2009a, p. 5). Analytic theologians seek to lay bare the assumptions, evidence-bases and inferences that constitute their work. This stylistic commitment ensures that their work is easily subject to detailed peer review and correction. Controversial assumptions, logical missteps and questionable intuitions can then be exposed and challenged by others working in the field. As Thomas McCall rightly notes, analytic theology at its best is 'done within a community of scholars where there is appropriate division of labour, cross-fertilization, mutually beneficial correction and feedback' (2015, p. 175). Wood agrees, writing that 'part of what it means to offer a good analytic argument is to make it maximally easy for intellectual opponents to criticize or refute. This is actually a way of choosing to make oneself intellectually vulnerable, and a check against intellectual pride' (2021, p. 187).

Christian analytic theologians also subject their fallible human reasoning and imperfect intuitions to what Thomas Morris (1991) has called 'revelational control'. As we saw above, Scripture is a vital norm for analytic theologians, something that distinguishes them from analytic philosophers of religion. Rather than exhibiting intellectual hubris, the best analytic theologians pursue their work with 'a humble openness to correction in light of revelation' (McCall, 2015, p. 54). For an analytic theologian, human reasoning should not be seen as autonomous or unaided, but as guided and corrected by divine revelation. As already noted, analytic theology is not an 'a priori project, and ... leading analytic philosophers understand their work as "faith seeking understanding"' (Wood, 2021, p. 103).

Nevertheless, it is true that analytic theologians do often go 'beyond' revelation, in the sense that they seek to understand how revealed truths 'can be true, or at least consistent with everything else we take to be true' (Wood, 2021, p. 99). As we have seen, conceptual model-building is a common feature of this work. This in turn has led some to argue that analytic theologians are averse to mystery in theology and seek coherence and clarity on matters that are intrinsically beyond human comprehension (such as the mystery of the Holy Trinity). If Thomas Weinandy is correct, for example, then analytic theologians have profoundly misunderstood the task of theology. He writes, 'Because God, who can never be fully comprehended, lies at the heart of all theological enquiry, theology by its nature is not a problem-solving enterprise, but rather a mystery-discerning enterprise' (Weinandy, 2000, p. 32). From the perspective of Weinandy and others, 'The charge would be that analytic theology, with its explicit emphasis on argumentative rigor, the clean definitions of core concepts, and replete attempts to construct models of central doctrines of the faith, is not vitally concerned with the discernment of mystery' (Crisp et al., 2019, p. 47). This charge does not stand up to scrutiny, however. As Crisp, Arcadi and Wessling write:

> No analytic theologian of which we are aware foolishly thinks that she can dispel all mysteries of the faith, or even that this would be a worthwhile goal. How could the analytic theologian think otherwise? It takes little more than casual reflection upon the enduring questions of philosophy or a superficial understanding of quantum mechanics to realise how beautifully complex and intellectually inexhaustible mere creaturely existence is. If mysteries regarding mere creatures of which analytics are aware are expected to endure, surely it would be foolhardy to expect otherwise in the case of God. (pp. 47–8)

Rather, the ambition of analytic theologians is to better locate and pinpoint the irreducible mysteries of the Christian faith, rather than to eliminate them or deny their existence altogether. As McCall writes:

> The goal of analytic theology is not (or at least need not be) the removal of all mystery in theology. To the contrary, analytic philosophers of religion have long been keenly aware of the place of mystery in theology, and it may be that at certain points an important role of the theologian is to clarify just where the mystery really lies. (McCall, 2015, p. 19)

For example, Stephen T. Davis concludes his account of the Trinity with an admission that the triune nature of God is a mystery that can never be fully explained. 'But,' he adds, 'it is important for Christians to note the *essential location* of the mystery of the Trinity. It has to do with perichoresis: How are the three persons related to each other in such a way as to retain their threeness while being one God?' (2006, p. 74, emphasis added). As Wood has noted, the work of Davis and other analytic theologians

> ... actually removes a significant barrier to discerning the real mystery of the Trinity. We are better able to appreciate the mystery of the Trinity in all its depth when we appreciate that the doctrine of the Trinity is not a flat-footed falsehood like '1+1+1 = 1'. (2021, p. 20)[1]

However, even if analytic theologians do not seek to erase all mystery from theology, are they nonetheless guilty of the sin of idolatry? With their models of the Trinity (and of other aspects of the divine nature) do they not construct a god in their own image, an idol who can be analysed, dissected and manipulated at their whim? A god far removed from the living God described in Scripture and Christian tradition? As Crisp writes:

> Here the concern is something like this: analytic theologians work with a concept of God that is a kind of facsimile of the God of Christian theology and Scripture. It is a God made understandable and cut down to size in order to be a suitable subject for analysis. But such a God cannot be the ineffable, inconceivable, and incomprehensible deity of traditional Christianity. It is a kind of golem or idol created by analytic theologians for their own purposes. (Crisp, 2023, pp. 309–10)

Yet in the view of Crisp and other advocates of model-building in analytic theology, this concern is based on a misplaced understanding of the purpose and usage of such models. They are not used as objects of idolatrous worship or devotion; rather they are

> ... nearly always used in the analytic theological literature for some narrow purpose, such as understanding how it is not a contradiction to suppose that the simple God can be both three and one. Indeed, such models may be refined and replaced precisely when it is detected that they do not, even in part, aptly refer to the God theologians want to know. (Crisp et al., 2019, p. 18)

Models are, by their very nature, simplifications of theological reality, always open to revision – and explicitly acknowledged as such by those who construct them. Even the best models in analytic theology are recognized to be only 'constructive approximations' of theological truth (Crisp, 2021, p. 14).

Before moving on, it is worth addressing the accusations of 'ontotheology' and 'univocity' aimed at analytic theology. The exact meaning of ontotheology is contested, but a helpful definition of both terms is offered by William Wood. Ontotheology 'is the error of treating God as a being among beings; univocity affirms that Creator and creatures all fall under the same single concept of being. Both seemingly lead to the same theological fault: the sin of idolatry' (Wood, 2021, p. 130). In their accounts of God, analytic theologians are accused of blurring the Creator–creature distinction by applying terms such as 'being' univocally to God and creatures, rather than either using such terms analogically (for example, God's being is only similar to our being) or referring to God using entirely different expressions (for example, he is 'beyond being' or 'the ground of being'). Stephen Holmes, for example, has expressed concern that

> analytic discussions of the Trinity seem generally to proceed with a remarkable confidence about the success of language in referring to the divine. The theological question of analogy is, as far as I can observe, never raised, and the assumed answer would always seem to be that language refers univocally to the divine and the created. (2012, p. 32)

Various responses to this concern have been offered on behalf of analytic theology. First, it is by no means the case that all analytic theologians refer to God and his creatures univocally. As Wood observes, 'nothing about the analytic method requires it, and there are important analytic thinkers who defend analogical predication' (2021, p. 132). William Hasker, for example, is one analytic theologian who has asserted that '*analogical* language is very much to be expected in our assertions concerning the divine' (2013, p. 197). Moreover, some other analytic theologians have begun to advocate the use of apophatic language in reference to God. Jonathan Jacobs, for instance, is among those who have 'argued that an adequate account of the divine nature must take seriously the historic Christian apophatic claims that God is ineffable, inconceivable, and incomprehensible' (Crisp et al., 2019, p. 64).[2] Though he himself does not favour this apophatic approach, Michael Rea has also acknowledged that 'it is not impossible to do analytic theology in a way that respects the scruples of apophatic theologians' (2009a, pp. 19–20).

Second, even among those analytic theologians who do utilize a univocal account of predication there is a near universal recognition of the Creator–creature distinction. It is 'very unlikely that any analytic theologian holds the self-evidently absurd view that God is "a thing in the world" in the sense of "an object in the created universe"' (Wood, 2021, p. 138). Rather, in accordance with historic Christian orthodoxy, they conceive of God as occupying a different ontological plane to ourselves, as the transcendent Creator who formed the universe *ex nihilo*. As Thomas V. Morris has put it:

> Absolutely everything distinct from God depends on God for its existence. This is a foundational claim for any thoroughly theistic ontology. [God] is not just one more item in the inventory of reality. He is the hub of the wheel, the center and focus, the ultimate support, of all. (1991, p. 155)

Moreover, the use of univocity by some analytic theologians does not necessarily imply that they are guilty of ontotheology and of a blurring of the Creator–creature distinction. As Wood explains:

> Univocity can be understood in two ways. It can be understood as a semantic thesis, about the meaning of words, or as an ontological thesis, about sharing the same really-existing extra-mental properties. I call the latter 'ontological sameness.' When it comes to God and creatures, only the latter thesis is worrying, and only the latter is a form of ontotheology. Even though many analytic theologians do affirm semantic univocity, and do say that God is 'a being,' it does not follow that they endorse ontological sameness between God and creatures, violate the creator/creature distinction, or fall into ontotheology or idolatry. (Wood, 2021, p. 132)

In other words, all Christian analytic theologians freely affirm that the uncreated divine nature differs in essence from creaturely natures – thereby denying ontological sameness and avoiding the ontotheological error. This holds even for those who also affirm that some words do have the same linguistic meaning when applied to God and the things which he has made (that is, semantic sameness). For example, they may believe it is possible to say that both God and a creature 'exists', is an 'individual' or is a 'person' or is a 'being' without denying the Creator–creature distinction and committing the ontotheological error. Crucially, their commitment to semantic univocity in such cases does not entail that they believe God and creatures 'exist in the same way, or on the same plane, or anything like that' (Wood, 2021, p. 155). In short, the advocacy by some analytic theologians of univocal meanings of certain words in theology should not be used to convict them of ontotheological denial of the Creator–creature distinction. Indeed, a case has been made that univocity (in a semantic sense) is accurate and true (see Williams, 2005).

Analytic theology and experience

Having considered concerns relating to three foundational sources of theology, namely Scripture, tradition and reason, we conclude this chapter by addressing some questions raised about analytic theology's relationship with Christian practical experience. As with those above, concerns in this area are expressed in different forms. This 'Objection from Practice' (as he calls it) is summarized by William Wood as follows:

> Many theologians would say that all genuine theology is in the first instance practical: aimed not at achieving better explanatory theories about God, but at fostering greater love for God and neighbor. Genuine theology, in short, is a spiritual praxis, one deeply woven together with a Christian life of prayer, virtue, and participation in the sacraments. Analytic theology seemingly exhibits none of this. The worry, then, is that analytic theology is spiritually sterile and therefore not really a form of genuine theology at all. (Wood, 2021, p. 20)

This type of objection to the discipline was anticipated by Michael Rea in *Analytic Theology* (2009a). Rea accepts that analytic theology is not a spiritual practice, while denying that this is a serious objection because *all* theology (analytic or otherwise) can be classified as a secondary, theoretical exercise compared to the primacy of reading Scripture for personal spiritual growth and moral formation. He writes that

> despite the superficial attractiveness of the idea that philosophers and theologians ought to be aiming in the direction of wisdom and moral improvement, Christian philosophers as such, and theologians as well, might in fact have some reason for resisting this idea. If philosophy as a discipline (or theology) were to aim its efforts at the production of a self-contained body of wisdom, or at a general theory of right living it would (I think) be aiming at the production of a rival to scripture. (2009a, pp. 18–19)

But other analytic theologians are more optimistic about the capacity of their subject to 'foster wisdom, moral improvement and love for God' (Wood, 2021, p. 21). Analytic theology can be a spiritually nourishing and virtue-building activity, argues Wood, 'insofar as it requires us to engage in a disciplined and patient search for truth, and to subdue the prideful ego so that we will recognise the truth when we see it' (2021, p. 175). Indeed,

> some might go still further and embrace the ancient and medieval

claim that the desire for truth is the desire for God, because God is truth itself. To seek the truth in any form is implicitly to seek God, surely the very essence of any Christian spiritual practice. (p. 184)

More specifically, he argues that the analytic theological method is 'conducive to the life of virtue' since it cultivates, among other things: attention to detail; wonder and awe at God; empathy with intellectual interlocutors; humble openness to correction; perseverance; and patience. He sums up his argument by saying,

> when undertaken in the right spirit, analytic theology can become a spiritual practice: a way of seeking God, of training the mind and the will to be open to grace. Moreover, the specific techniques of analytic enquiry both presuppose and cultivate the virtue of humility. (p. 190)

A different type of concern is whether analytic theologians make use of experience as a *source* for their work, as well as Scripture, church tradition and reason. One recent example will hopefully demonstrate that analytic theologians are quite capable of reflecting on experience to inform their work. Derek King in *The Church and the Problem of Divine Hiddenness* (2023) makes the case that the unseen God reveals himself to humanity within the life and worship of the Church. What is significant is that King explicitly bases his argument on his own personal observation as well as drawing on Scripture, the writings of Gregory of Nyssa and philosophical analysis. King writes that his 'initial ruminations' on the ability of the Church to refute the problem of divine hiddenness

> grew out of observation. In Christian community it is common for nonbelievers to come to faith not as a result of apologetics or theophany, but immersion into the community of believers. Faith or belief in God often turns out to be what C. S. Lewis called the 'good infection,' spreading from one believer to another. (King, 2023, p. 3)

Analytic theologians, at their best, are not oblivious to the lived experience of the Christian community as one potential source for their work.

A final, related, line of concern is that analytic theologians allegedly have little interest in serving the practical ministry and mission of the Church. Analytic theology has been accused by some of 'hyperintellectualism that doesn't sufficiently connect with the Church's commitment to spiritual formation and worship' (Timpe, 2022, p. 98). With its focus on the finer points of doctrine, analytic theology has allegedly had little to offer to the ordinary Christian 'in the pew' – or indeed to the minister in the pulpit or to the priest presiding at the Eucharist. Writing a decade ago, Thomas McCall observed that 'a great deal of analytic philosophy of religion and Christian analytic theology has been focused on a fairly narrow, and sometimes rather predictable' range of doctrinal topics, 'but these are not the only worthy topics. Nor is it obvious that they are the most worthy topics' (2015, pp. 150-1). He suggests that analytic theologians ought to give more attention to issues in ecclesiology, liturgy, sacramental theology, missional theology, political theology and ethics.

Unlike most of the alleged weaknesses of analytic theology described in this chapter, this would seem to be a legitimate criticism, at least during the earliest years of the discipline. However, over the past decade analytic theologians have begun producing work in many of these areas – a development that has been described as an ecclesiastical or liturgical 'turn' in the discipline. In other words, analytic theologians have 'begun to generate a sophisticated literature on issues to do with the nature of the Church, worship and liturgical action, sacramental theology, religious affections and the indwelling of the Holy Spirit' (Crisp, 2023, p. 313). These developments will be described more fully in the third part of this book, and are associated with analytic theologians such as James Arcadi, Joshua Cockayne, Terence Cuneo, Scott Davison, Alexander Pruss, Nicholas Wolterstorff and a number of others.

There remain, however, new and uncharted avenues of mission and ministry for analytic theology to explore, and these too shall be identified in the final part of this present work. Before then, however, the next part of this book surveys analytic theologians' most significant contributions to some of the most important and distinctive Christian doctrines, notably the Trinity, the Incarnation and the Atonement.

Notes

1 For a recent compendium of analytic theologians' responses to the issue of mystery, see Rutledge, J. C. (ed.), 2024, *Paradox and Contradiction in Theology*, Abingdon: Routledge.

2 See Jacobs, J. D., 2015, 'The Ineffable, Inconceivable, and Incomprehensible God: Fundamentality and Apophatic Theology' in J. Kvanvig, *Oxford Studies in Philosophy of Religion: Volume 6*, Oxford: Oxford University Press, ch. 7.

Recommended further reading

Crisp, O. D., Arcadi, J. M. and Wessling, J., 2019, *The Nature and Promise of Analytic Theology*, Leiden: Brill.

Wood, W., 2021, *Analytic Theology and the Academic Study of Religion*, Oxford Studies in Analytic Theology, Oxford: Oxford University Press.

PART TWO

Analytic Theology and Christian Doctrine

3

Trinity: The Triune God

The Trinity is a central Christian doctrine, a dogma of the faith defined in the ecumenical creeds of the early Church and reaffirmed in the confessional statements of all the Church's major denominations (that is, Roman Catholic, Orthodox and most Protestant churches). For example, the Nicene-Constantinopolitan Creed of AD 381 affirms that:

> We believe in one God, the Father, almighty, maker of heaven and earth, of all things visible and invisible; And in one Lord Jesus Christ, the only-begotten Son of God, begotten from the Father before all ages, light from light, true God from true God, begotten not made, of one substance [*homoousion*] with the Father ... And in the Holy Spirit, the Lord and life-giver, Who proceeds from the Father, Who with the Father and the Son is together worshipped and together glorified, Who spoke through the prophets. (Quoted in Rea, 2009b, p. 404)

Similarly, the Athanasian Creed, authoritative within the Western Church since the sixth century, states:

> Now this is the catholic faith, that we worship one God in Trinity, and the Trinity in unity, without either confusing the persons or dividing the substance ... Thus the Father is God, the Son God and the Holy Spirit God; and yet there are not three Gods, but there is one God. (Quoted in Rea, 2009b, pp. 404–5)

But while faith in Father, Son and Holy Spirit is a shared belief across Christendom, the Trinity is a doctrine that sharply distinguishes Christianity from all other faiths, including its monotheistic cousins in Judaism and Islam. The Trinity is also deeply mysterious, an article of the faith that is far more easily confessed than comprehended.

Relevant? Revealed? Rational?

Beyond historical investigation of the development of trinitarian orthodoxy in the first four centuries of the Church, academic study of the Trinity addresses three other broad areas of enquiry – its *relevance*, *revealed nature* and *rationality*. Taking these in order, scholarly work on the relevance of the Trinity seeks to discern what practical applications can be safely derived from belief in a triune God. What implications, for example, does the Trinity have for anthropology, ethics, ecclesiology, socio-political structures, etc.? To date, at least, this has not been a major focus of attention for analytic theologians. Analysis of the revealed nature of the Trinity, meanwhile, is concerned with the biblical foundations (or otherwise) of the doctrine.[1] Here analytic theologians, including Rea (2009b) and McCall (2021), have condensed the doctrine of the Trinity down to three central affirmations which they find in Scripture. These are: (T1) There is exactly one God; (T2) Father, Son and Holy Spirit are not identical; and (T3) Father, Son and Holy Spirit are consubstantial. As Rea writes, (T1) to (T3) are supported

> ... by central claims in the Christian Scriptures. For example, both the Old and New Testaments make it clear that there is only one being who deserves worship and who deserves such titles as 'God Almighty' or the 'one true God' ... Hence (T1). Moreover, though Jesus says things such as 'I and the Father are one' it is clear that, from the point of view of the New Testament, Jesus (the Son) and the Father are distinct. Jesus prays to the Father, claims to submit to the Father's will; is blessed by the Father and so on. Likewise, the Holy Spirit is distinct from the Father and the Son: the Spirit is sent by the Son and is said to intercede for us with the Father. Hence (T2). And yet the New Testament advocates worshipping Jesus (the Son) and the Holy Spirit ... In short, there is pressure to say that the Son and Spirit are divine – and not in some derivative or degenerate sense, but *truly* divine, like the Father. The only clear way to say this without contradicting (T1), however, is to say that the Son and the Spirit are consubstantial with the Father: the divinity of the Father, which *is* the 'substance' of the Father is no different from the divinity of the Son. Hence (T3). (Rea, 2009b, p. 406)

However, as might be expected, the focus of most work by analytic theologians has been on the *rationality* of the Trinity. Can the doctrine be shown to be coherent? In the relevant literature this question of rationality is often known as the 'logical problem' of the Trinity or as the 'threeness-oneness problem'. Stated more formally, the problem that analytic theologians seek to resolve can be expressed as follows:

(LPT1) There is exactly one God, the Father Almighty;
(LPT2) The Father is God (from (LPT1));
(LPT3) The Son is consubstantial with but not identical to the Father (and Spirit);
(LPT4) If there are x and y such that x is a God, x is not identical to y, and y is consubstantial with x, then it is not the case that there is exactly one God (premise);
(LPT5) Therefore, it is not the case that there is exactly one God (from (LPT2), (LPT3), and (LPT4)).
But, of course, (LPT5) contradicts (LPT1). (McCall, 2021, p. 182)

Since LPT1, LPT2 and LPT3 are clearly affirmed in the historic creeds, the challenge that analytic theologians face is 'unpacking the notion of consubstantiality in a way that enables us to reject (LPT4) without incoherence or heterodoxy' (Rea, 2009b, p. 407). In their efforts to avoid heterodoxy analytic theologians have sought to steer clear of subordinationism, modalism and tritheism. Subordinationism denies that the Son and Spirit are consubstantial with the Father (i.e. they are not fully and equally divine). Modalism, meanwhile, denies the eternal distinctiveness of the three persons (that is, they are merely temporary manifestations or modes of appearance of God). Tritheism, lastly, defines Father, Son and Spirit as three independent, autonomous gods (that is, a form of polytheism).

In attempting to resolve the logical problem of the Trinity, analytic theologians are 'keenly aware that the doctrine likely exceeds the limits of human comprehension. What they are doing is, minimally, more akin to "playing defense" against the common charges that the doctrine is inherently contradictory and thus necessarily false' (McCall, 2021, p. 191). Towards this goal, analytic theologians have offered different *models* of the Trinity, which seek to offer 'a simplified description of more complex data that is an approximation of the truth of the matter, rather like the model of an atom in a physics textbook' (Crisp et al., 2019, p. 57).

It is possible to categorize analytic theologians' models of the Trinity into three broad types: those that are *social trinitarian*; those that are *anti-social trinitarian* (sometimes known as 'Latin' models); and, third, *constitutional* accounts of the doctrine. Various examples of these three approaches will be described in detail below, but their salient features have been summarized as follows:

The Latin account of the Trinity emphasises the oneness of the divine essence and distinguishes the divine persons by means of their relations of origin. These person-distinguishing relations are the paternity of the Father, the filiation of the Son and the spiration of the Holy Spirit. By contrast, social accounts of the Trinity emphasise the distinctions in the divine persons, and have 'thicker' descriptions of the divine persons as a consequence. On social accounts of the Trinity the divine persons are said to be distinct centres of will and action within the Godhead, on analogy with human persons. [The] constitution account … depends upon the controversial Aristotelian thesis that one can have numerical sameness without identity. The Trinity, then, is a kind of hylomorphic compound (that is, a compound of form and matter). The analog to 'matter' in the Trinity is the divine essence, whilst the divine persons of the Trinity play the role of 'forms'. (Crisp, Arcadi and Wessling, 2019, pp. 58–9)

Before elaborating on each of these alternative positions, it is worth noting that various contentious historical claims are made by advocates of these different approaches. For example, many proponents of Latin models of the Trinity argue that their view is consistent with the historical emphasis of the Western Church in general, and the thought of Augustine in particular. Social trinitarian theorists, meanwhile, argue that their perspective is consistent with the traditional emphasis of the Eastern Church and finds specific endorsement in the writings of the fourth-century Cappadocian Fathers (that is, Basil of Caesarea, Gregory of Nyssa and Gregory of Nazianzus). Evaluation of such historical claims is beyond the scope of this present work; suffice to say that they are not uncontested.[2]

Social models of the Trinity

As McCall notes, the term '"Social Trinitarianism" has acquired a broad semantic range in contemporary theology' and been utilized for a wide range of purposes (2021, p. 182). In some contexts, the term has been used to describe certain theologians' efforts to demonstrate the practical relevance of the Trinity to social, political or ethical questions. For others, as noted above, the term is used (rightly or wrongly) as shorthand for the trinitarian theology of the Eastern Church, especially of the fourth-century Cappadocian Fathers. But within analytic theology, at least, the term has come to be applied to accounts of the Trinity that share certain metaphysical claims.

What all social trinitarian models have in common is the assertion that Father, Son and Holy Spirit are genuinely and 'robustly' distinct, not mere modes or aspects of one divine subject. This primary thesis is also often articulated as the claim that each of the three persons are persons in the full, modern sense of the word, that is, three subjects or conscious minds that are 'distinct centres of knowledge, will, love and action' (Plantinga, 1989, p. 22).[3] A second metaphysical claim, held by many (but *not* all) social trinitarians, is the belief 'that the Father, the Son and the Holy Spirit are "of one essence" but are not numerically the same substance. The divine persons are, then, consubstantial or homo-ousios only in the sense that they share a divine generic or kind-essence' (McCall, 2021, p. 184). On this view, each of the persons is a 'trope' of divinity, a particular instantiation of a generic divine nature – much as three human individuals are tropes of a common human nature.

More formally stated, *all* social trinitarian models affirm:

(1) The thesis that the divine persons are genuinely and robustly distinct (as persons who know and love one another while acting in perfect co-operation in relation to all that is not God).

While 'strong' social trinitarians *also* affirm:

(2) The thesis that the divine essence is rightly understood as a generic or kind-essence. (McCall, 2021, p. 185)

Among systematic theologians, social trinitarianism has had many influential advocates over the past century, including Jürgen Moltmann and John Zizioulas. Within contemporary philosophical theology, this conception of the Trinity was first articulated by Cornelius Plantinga Jr (1989) and Richard Swinburne (1994). Plantinga, for example, described the Trinity as

> ... a divine, transcendent society or community of three fully personal and fully divine entities: the Father, the Son, and Holy Spirit. These three are wonderfully united by their common divinity, that is, by the possession of each of the whole generic divine essence ... [and] the divine persons are also unified by their joint redemptive purpose, revelation, and work. (1989, pp. 27–8)

Swinburne, meanwhile, has defended his social trinitarian view on the following grounds:

> If the Christian religion has helped us, Christians and non-Christians, to see anything about what is worthwhile, it has helped us to see that

love is a supreme good. Love involves sharing, giving to the other what of one's own is good for him and receiving from the other what of his is good for one; and love involves co-operating with another to benefit third parties ... So the love of a first divine individual G_1 would be manifested first in bringing about another divine individual G_2 with whom to share his life, and ... in bringing about another divine individual G_3 with whom G_1 and G_2 co-operatively could share their lives. (1994, pp. 177–8)

Following a similar line of reasoning, Stephen T. Davis has offered a more formal proof for a robust social trinitarian understanding of the divine persons, grounded upon the biblical axiom that 'God is love' (1 John 4.8). For Davis, as for other social trinitarians, the Father, Son and Holy Spirit are each 'a conscious, purposive agent', capable of actions, thoughts and feelings – including love (2006, p. 69). Each person of the Godhead is consequently a genuine 'other' from the perspective of the remaining two. With these foundations in place, Davis' deductive proof proceeds as follows:

(1) Necessarily, God is perfect, and perfect in love (1 John 4.8).
(2) Necessarily, if God does not experience love of another, God is imperfect.
(3) Therefore, necessarily, God experiences love of another.
(4) Necessarily, it is possible that only God exists (that is, that God does not create).
(5) Necessarily, if ST is false, there is no 'other' in the Godhead.
(6) Necessarily, if God alone exists, and if ST is false, then God does not experience love of another, and thus is not perfect.
(7) Therefore, necessarily, ST is true. (Davis, 2006, p. 65)

One hurdle facing all forms of social trinitarianism is to refute potential accusations of tritheism. How can affirmation of the robust personhood of Father, Son and Spirit still be compatible with monotheism? This problem is particularly acute for 'strong' social trinitarians (as defined above) who interpret the one divine nature in a generic sense. As McCall and Rea define the problem, 'The divine persons must each be in full possession of the divine nature and in some particular relation R to one another' for any given social trinitarian model 'to count as monotheism' (2009, p. 3). As Rea (2009b) explains, different social trinitarian models offer varied accounts of what the monotheism-securing relation 'R' is. For some, 'R' is satisfied because the three persons 'are parts of a whole that is itself divine' (e.g. Moreland and Craig, 2003), while others take 'R' to mean that the persons are 'necessarily mutually interdependent, so that none can exist without the others.' Richard Swinburne (1994) is one who takes this approach. A third option is to define 'R' as the 'perfect love and harmony of will with one another, unlike the members of pagan pantheons' (Rea, 2009b, p. 414). These alternatives for 'R' are not mutually exclusive, and 'most social trinitarians in fact opt for a combination of these' (Rea, 2009, p. 414).

The concept of *perichoresis* (first applied to the Trinity by John of Damacus in the eighth century) is particularly important in this debate, and usually taken to refer to the mutual indwelling, co-inherence or interpenetration of the divine persons with one another. In the view of social trinitarians such as Davis, affirming a perichoretic union of boundaryless relations between Father, Son and Spirit justifies them being called 'one God' – even if he is 'unable to provide a rigorous or precise explication of the concept … since perichoretically related things are not part of our ordinary experience' (2006, p. 72).

Davis' own account of the Trinity (which he calls 'Perichoretic Monotheism') is one example of strong social trinitarianism since it includes, among others, the following two claims. First, 'God is like a community. The three Persons are three distinct centres of consciousness, will and action.' And second, 'There are three instances or cases of divinity. Each of the three persons equally possess the divine essence' (Davis, 2006, pp. 69–70). Davis recognizes that, on its own, such an account of the Trinity might sound like tritheism but, as we have just seen, affirms that the persons are in a state of perichoresis which guarantees their 'metaphysical unity' (Davis and Yang, 2017, p. 223n). He offers a graphical analogy for perichoresis as follows:

> Imagine three circles, which we will call Circles 1, 2 and 3. In State A, the circles border on each other, that is, the circumference of each circle touches the circumferences of the two others. In State B, the circles overlap each other, but not entirely; there is an area that is enclosed by all three circles; there are three areas enclosed by two and only two circles; and there are areas enclosed by one circle only. In State C, the circles have wholly merged; they circumscribe the same area.

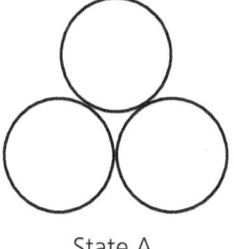
State A

State B

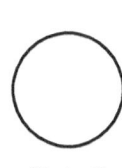
State C

Now imagine something that is impossible with geometrical objects like circles and physical objects like human persons. Imagine that the three circles are simultaneously in State A and State C. Then you could legitimately say, of any property p possessed by all three, that Circle 1 is p, that Circle 2 is p, and that Circle 3 is p. You could even speak of one circle that exists in State C – call it Circle 123 – and say that it is p. But you cannot say that there are four things that are p; that would simply be false. When we imagine that the circles are simultaneously in State A and State C, there are either three circles or one circle (or the circles are three-in-one) ... but don't try to say there are four. Perichoresis blocks this improper inference ... since Circle 123 just *is* (in my illustration) Circles 1, 2, and 3 in perichoresis. Similarly, the Godhead just *is* the Father, the Son and the Holy Spirit in perichoresis ... simultaneously one and three. (2006, pp. 72–4)

Another strong social trinitarian model is that of Richard Swinburne, a model he first articulated in 1994 and defended again in 2018. His solution to the logical problem of the Trinity is to interpret the Greek word θεός (*theos*) in the Nicene-Constantinopolitan creed (and its Latin equivalent, *deus*) in both a generic sense (that is, meaning 'divine') and a specific sense (that is, meaning 'God'), according to the context in which it appears within the creed:

It is normally acknowledged that there is an apparent contradiction here. The Creed claims that there is one God, and also three apparently different beings who are each God. But in the ancient world where it was open to serious question how many 'gods' there are and how powerful they are, θεός and *deus* can both be understood either as the name of a unique individual, or as a predicate ('divine') which can be predicated of more than one individual. While no doubt the Fathers of the Council did not have a clear view of what was the sense in which there is just one 'God' and the sense in which each of the three beings is 'God', the distinction between the two senses of the crucial words makes available one obvious way of resolving the apparent contradiction. This is by thinking of these words as having the former sense when the Creed says that there is 'one God', and as having the latter sense when it claims that each of the beings is 'God'. (Swinburne, 2018, p. 420)

In Swinburne's view, therefore, there is one 'God' comprising three 'divine' individuals, who are 'distinct centres of knowledge, love, will and action' each possessing the divine properties of omnipotence, omniscience, perfect freedom and perfect goodness (2018, p. 426). Swinburne's defence against the charge of tritheism is that these three divine persons are mutually dependent upon one another. The Father is always the cause of his begotten Son, while the Father and Son together are the cause of the Spirit who proceeds from them. The Son and the Spirit are themselves 'permissive' causes of the Father, in the sense that 'throughout any period which has a beginning he is permitted to exist' by them (Swinburne, 1994, p. 185). In Swinburne's account, these ongoing causal relations between the three persons serve *both* to distinguish each person from one another (since their causal relations differ) *and* to secure their unity (since none of them can exist independently). As Swinburne himself puts it, 'Given that they are individuated by their relations to each other, it follows that each person could not exist without the others' (2018, p. 429).[4]

Swinburne's view has also been called an example of 'Functional Monotheism' since, as well as citing the mutual dependence of the divine persons as justification for viewing them as one God, he also 'appeals to the harmonious, interrelated functioning of the divine persons. Because all of them are omnipotent and perfectly good, they cooperate in all their volitions and actions. It is logically impossible that any one person should exist or act independent of the other two' (Moreland and Craig, 2003, p. 587).

If Swinburne and Davis' two models represent examples of 'strong' social trinitarianism within the analytic tradition, the approaches of Craig (2009) and of Hasker (2013) are both of a 'weaker' form. Weaker in the sense that, although they affirm a robust modern definition of the three divine persons, they deny that they possess a generic divine nature. Rather, the persons are parts of a single divine nature, a 'soul' that simultaneously contains them all. So, for Craig, while the divine persons are 'three centers of consciousness, intentionality, and volition', they are parts of one God, understood as a 'soul' – an immaterial mental substance 'endowed with three complete sets of rational cognitive faculties, each sufficient for personhood' (2009, p. 99). This view therefore resists the charge of tritheism by asserting that the three persons are parts of a numerically single divine substance. It is important to note, however, that Craig's part-whole trinitarian model would seem to imply two types of divinity, a '*full* divine nature that is possessed by God and implies tri-unity; and a *derivative* divine nature, possessed by each person' in virtue of being part of God (Rea, 2009b, p. 415, emphasis original).

To illustrate his position, Craig suggests that the triune God is composed of the divine persons in a way analogous to the way in which

Cerberus, the three-headed watchdog of Hades in Greek mythology, is composed of three canine centres of consciousness while being only one dog:

> We may suppose that Cerberus has three brains and therefore three distinct states of consciousness of whatever it is like to be a dog. Therefore, Cerberus, while a sentient being, does not have a unified consciousness. He has three consciousnesses. We could even assign proper names to each of them: Rover, Bowser and Spike. Despite the diversity of his mental states, Cerberus is clearly one dog. He is a single biological organism having a canine nature. Rover, Bowser and Spike may be said to be canine, too, though they are not three dogs, but parts of the one dog Cerberus. If Hercules were attempting to enter Hades and Spike snarled at him or bit his leg, he might well report, 'Cerberus snarled at me' or 'Cerberus attacked me'. We can enhance the Cerberus story by investing him with rationality and self-consciousness. In that case Rover, Bowser, and Spike are plausibly personal agents and Cerberus a tri-personal being. (Moreland and Craig, 2003, p. 593)

Turning to Hasker (2013), he shares Craig's belief that the divine persons are distinct centres of consciousness and similarly denies that they 'merely ... share a common generic essence'. Rather, 'the three persons share a single concrete nature, a single instance or trope of deity' (2013, p. 226). Hasker therefore affirms what he calls the 'Trinitarian Possibility Postulate' (TPP), which he defines as follows:

> (TPP) It is possible for a single concrete divine nature – a single trope of deity – to support simultaneously three distinct lives, the lives belonging to the Father, to the Son, and to the Holy Spirit. (2013, p. 228)

In support of this postulate, Hasker offers evidence from 'the "split-brain" and "multiple personality" phenomena documented in psychology' (2013, p. 231). He begins by citing commissurotomy or split-brain cases in which epilepsy patients who have had their brain's corpus callosum severed have begun to manifest abnormal behaviours. Specifically, a 'strong impression' has been created of 'two *centres of consciousness*, each seeking to pursue its own agenda' (2013, p. 232). In cases of multiple personality, meanwhile, psychiatrists encounter 'the apparent existence of *simultaneously conscious* multiple personalities in the same individual' (2013, p. 234). In view of this evidence, Hasker argues that:

The cases, I maintain, provide strong empirical support for the following conclusion: (C1) In a number of actual cases, the human body/mind/soul supports simultaneously multiple centres of consciousness. But if this is true, it is also true that (C2) it is possible for a single concrete human nature – a single trope of humanness – to support simultaneously two or more centres of consciousness. (2013, p. 236)

While he recognizes that both the split-brain and the multiple-personality phenomena have a 'pathological character' in humans, Hasker maintains that they do at least serve to 'provide important indirect support for the trinitarian possibility postulate' (2013, p. 231). 'What cannot now be said', he argues, 'is that the very idea of a single "soul" with multiple centres of consciousness is incoherent. The phenomena from psychology go a long way towards demonstrating the conceptual coherence of such a view of the Trinity' (2013, p. 236). As Wood has commented, Hasker makes these two psychological phenomena 'function as models' to show 'that the divine "threeness-in-oneness" is epistemically possible, and consistent with everything else we know' (2021, p. 67).[5]

Both strong and weaker social trinitarian models have been subject to criticism from other analytic philosophers and theologians. Aside from the general concern, already noted, that social trinitarian models risk providing an inadequate account of the divine unity (and thereby lapse into tritheism), social trinitarian models also appear to contravene the traditional doctrine of divine *simplicity*. This doctrine is a core component of so-called 'Classical Theism' (held by almost all theologians prior to the nineteenth century), which in its strongest form asserts that God is a non-composite being with no component parts whatsoever – all of his attributes and properties are one. It is easy to see how this doctrine 'does not sit very well with more robust ways of distinguishing the divine persons', as found in social trinitarian models (Crisp et al., 2019, p. 59).

In response, some social trinitarians openly reject this understanding of divine simplicity and therefore do not consider it a legitimate criticism of their models. Hasker, for instance, describes it as 'devoid of biblical warrant' and a 'cognitive black hole that ... needs to be excised' (2013, pp. 55 and 61). Swinburne, in contrast, accepts divine simplicity but believes this applies to the Father alone, rather than the (composite) Trinity he causes. Swinburne writes that 'the simplicity of the claim that there is one divine person is not diminished if it follows from the existence of such a person that he would produce two other divine persons' (2018, p. 15). A third alternative, open to those social trinitarian models with a non-generic divine nature (for example, Moreland and Craig,

2003), is to argue that this feature of the model secures divine simplicity to at least some degree.

A third concern about social trinitarianism arises if the three persons are indeed acknowledged to be three 'parts' of a single 'whole'. This is the worry that it seems to create two different ways to 'be' God. It would seem that one way to 'be' God is to be one of the divine persons, while an alternative way to 'be' God would be by being the Trinity as a whole. As Leftow expresses the problem:

> Either the Trinity is a fourth case of the divine nature, in addition to the persons, or it is not. If it is, we have too many cases of deity for orthodoxy. If it is not, and yet is divine, there are two ways to be divine – by being a case of deity, and by being a Trinity of such cases. (1999, p. 221)

Responding to this concern, Moreland and Craig (2003) draw a distinction between two types of divinity, 'the *full* divine nature, which is possessed by God and implies tri-unity; and a *derivative* divine nature, possessed by each person' (Rea, 2009b, p. 415). An alternative response, as found in Davis (2006), is to affirm that the predicate '... is God' can be used in two different ways. He writes that the

> Godhead 'is God' in the sense of strict numerical identity. The Godhead (which consists of Father, Son and Holy Spirit), as we might say, *exhausts* God. But when we say that the Father 'is God', the Son 'is God', and the Holy Spirit 'is God', we are not talking about strict numerical identity. Here the predicate 'is God' ... is a property meaning something close to 'is divine.' (2006, p. 75)

A final line of response, found in Swinburne and others, is to state that divinity consists in possessing the attributes of omniscience, omnipotence, etc. In this case, each of the persons is fully divine, and so too is the Trinity – but derivatively, since its three members possess these attributes. It is the individual persons rather than the collective Godhead who, 'to speak strictly, would have the divine properties of omnipotence, omniscience, etc; though clearly there is a ready and natural sense in which the collective can be said to have them as well' (Swinburne, 1994, p. 181).

Latin models of the Trinity

For analytic theologians who find the objections to social trinitarianism insurmountable, the so-called 'Latin' conception of the Trinity has offered one alternative avenue to take. Whether or not this approach accurately reflects the historic Western tradition (a debated point, as previously noted), these so-called Latin models of the Trinity are defined by a rejection of both tenets of social trinitarianism described above. In other words, the divine nature is understood in a specific individual sense, not a generic one, and the three persons are not construed as separate centres of consciousness. Rather, there is ultimately only one subject within the divine being. As Crisp writes, 'on the Latin model, will and understanding in God belong to the divine essence, not to the persons' (2019, p. 81). It follows that the challenge for Latin theorists has been to provide an account of the three divine persons that is sufficiently strong to avoid accusations of modalism.

Historically, the most influential Latin account of the Trinity is found in Thomas Aquinas' *Summa Theologiae*, while among modern systematic theologians it has found support in the work of Karl Barth and Karl Rahner. From this Latin perspective, the only distinguishing feature of the three persons are their relations of origin, namely the paternity of the Father, the filiation of the Son and the spiration of the Holy Spirit. In Aquinas' terminology, the Father, Son and Spirit 'are said to be "subsistent relations" within the metaphysically simple Godhead. That is, the divine persons are relations within God that are somehow ontologically independent' (Crisp, Arcadi and Wessling, 2019, pp. 58–9). Barth and Rahner, meanwhile, preferred to refer to the three divine hypostases as 'modes of being' or 'manners of subsisting' (rather than 'persons') to avoid the inference that they are three self-conscious subjects.

Within analytic theology, the most influential and widely discussed Latin model of the Trinity is that of Leftow (2004). On his view, the persons of the Trinity share one single trope of divinity ('God'), since the divine nature is not generic and thus unable to have multiple tropes. Instead, each of the persons represents three different 'life streams' within God's one being:

> God's life has the following peculiar structure: at any point in our lives, three discrete parts of God's life are present. But this is … because God always lives His life in three discrete strands at once, no event of His life occurring in more than one strand and no strand succeeding another. In one strand God lives the Father's life, in one the Son's, and in one the Spirit's. The events of each strand add up to the life of

a Person. The lives of the Persons add up to the life God lives *as* the three Persons. There is one God, but He is many in the events of his life. (p. 312)

For Leftow, therefore, God is ultimately a *single* 'person' (or subject) in the modern sense of the term, but one who always lives simultaneously in the three separate life streams we call Father, Son and Holy Spirit. He illustrates his model of the Trinity by utilizing an analogy from time travel:

> Suppose that one Rockette used a time machine to do all the dancing of an entire chorus line: she dances on the extreme left, runs offstage to the machine, goes back in time, joins herself as the dancer next in from the left, etc. Were this to occur, the audience would see many episodes of her life at once: episodes at distinct times along her personal time-line would occur at once in public time. The Trinity, I've suggested, may involve something broadly similar. As causal relations among her life's episodes are such that one Rockette, Jane, dances many times at once, so perhaps causal relations among episodes in God's life are such that God always lives three episodes of His life at any one public time, one as Father, one as Son, and one as Spirit. (Leftow, 2012b, p. 313)

He believes that his Latin model avoids the charge of modalism, since 'Nothing in my account of the Trinity precludes saying that the Persons' distinction is an eternal, necessary, non-successive and intrinsic feature of God's life' (2004, p. 327). His model has not been immune from challenge, however. McCall, for example, notes that Leftow's account still seems to suggest that God has parts (that is, different life streams), which is at odds with the 'traditional claim that God is simple' (2021, p. 186).⁶ Hasker, meanwhile, suggests that Leftow cannot escape the charge of modalism, since in his model 'there is really only *one* subject of this threefold life' (2013, p. 113). Moreover, the biblical 'idea that the Persons of the Trinity love and commune with each other loses much of its appeal if it is all just a matter of one person, namely God, loving and communing with himself' (2013, p. 114). Indeed, if Leftow's model is correct 'in the Gospels, we have the spectacle of God-as-Son *praying to himself*, namely to God-as-Father ... [but] this just doesn't seem to be what the Gospels are saying' (2013, p. 118).

In *Christ and the Cosmos* (2015), Keith Ward has proposed an alternative Latin account of the Trinity, which goes even further than Leftow in denying any threefold consciousness within the one God. Indeed, Ward is critical of Leftow's model for being too similar to social trinitarianism. For if the three life streams (or streams of consciousness) within Leftow's account can 'think and act' distinctly, then this 'is all you want ... for a social view' of the Trinity' (Ward, 2015, pp. 240–41). Instead, Ward

> denies that the Father and Son are distinct persons in any recognisable sense of the term 'person', and he likewise denies that there is mutual love between Father and Son. There indeed is love between the man Jesus Christ and the Father but this is only 'mutual love between the Father and the human aspect of the incarnate Son'. In his theology, the divine persons are three 'aspects' or 'forms of being' of 'one divine consciousness and will, one personal being'. (McCall, 2021, p. 187)

Ward denies that his account of the Trinity is modalist, since the three 'forms of being' named Father, Son and Spirit in Scripture reflect 'an essential threefoldness of the divine, an "immanent Trinity" which belongs to Being itself' (2015, p. 253). Whether Ward's defence against the charge of modalism succeeds, however, is questioned by both Davis (2016) and Tuggy (2016). McCall critiques Ward from a different angle, however, suggesting that he may be guilty of polytheism. Ward describes God as omnipotent but also says that Jesus is non-omnipotent, despite his being 'in some sense' divine (2015, pp. 164–5).

> But how many senses of 'divinity' are there if there is only one God? How many can there be? If God has an omnipotence-rich divine essence (call it the O-positive divine essence) while Jesus has an omnipotence-deprived divine essence (call it the O-negative divine essence), then we have two divine essences. And if these are instantiated (in Ward's case, one by God and the other by the divine Son), then how do we not have two gods? (McCall, 2021, p. 188)

As with social trinitarian models, we wait (perhaps indefinitely) for a definitive Latin account of the Trinity. Frustrated with the limitations of these two existing paradigms for conceiving of the Trinity, other analytic theologians have begun to mine and explore alternative conceptual frameworks in their attempt to model the doctrine. One approach has led to a 'constitutional' model of the Trinity, while another has produced a 'mysterian' account of the doctrine. We shall consider these two positions in turn.

Constitutional models of the Trinity

In their attempts to resolve the logical problem of the Trinity, analytic theologians such as Peter van Inwagen (1995) and Jeffrey Brower and Michael Rea (2005) have drawn on the philosophical concept of 'relative identity'. This idea affirms that two or more entities may be the same in one respect but differ in another. As McCall explains:

> On relative identity, a question such as 'is x the same as y?' is ill-formed. The proper question is 'is x the same F as y?' Proponents of the logic of relative identity hold that objects may be identical under one sortal concept but distinct under another. Thus things can be said to be the same relative to one kind of thing but distinct relative to another kind of thing. (McCall, 2021, p. 189)

Applied to the Trinity, this concept of relative identity enables van Inwagen to say that if we are counting 'divine beings by beings, there is one; counting divine persons by beings, there is one; counting divine beings by persons, there are three; counting divine persons by persons, there are three' (1995, p. 250). This application of relative identity allows van Inwagen to argue that the apparently contradictory elements of the doctrine of the Trinity can, in fact, 'be shown to be mutually consistent' (2003, p. 97).

In their influential article 'Material constitution and the Trinity', Brower and Rea (2005) utilize what they call an 'impure' version of relative identity to illustrate that two or more things may have 'numerical sameness without identity'.[7] They utilize the Aristotelian distinction between a *hylomorphic* object's constituting *matter* and its visible *form* to argue that each person of the Trinity is similarly constituted:

> For like the familiar particulars of experience, the Persons of the Trinity can also be conceived of in terms of hylomorphic compounds. Thus, we can think of the divine essence as playing the role of matter; and we can regard the properties *being a Father, being a Son,* and *being a Spirit* as distinct forms instantiated by the divine essence, each giving rise to a distinct Person. Each Person will then be a compound structure whose matter is the divine essence and whose form is one of the three distinctive Trinitarian properties. (Brower and Rea, 2005, p. 68, emphasis original)

The conclusion of this analysis is to affirm that Father, Son and Spirit exhibit numerical sameness (of essence) but with distinct identities (as different persons). To illustrate their approach, Brower and Rea utilize the analogy of a marble statue:

> An artistic contractor fashions a marble statue that is to be used as a pillar in the building he is constructing. So he has made a statue; he has also made a pillar. It would be strange to say that he has made two material objects that are simply located in exactly the same spot at the same time (though many philosophers do *in fact* say such a thing). What we are inclined to say is that the statue and the pillar are one and the same material object, not two. And yet they are *distinct*. Surface erosion will destroy the statue without destroying the pillar. Internal corruption that preserves the surface but undermines the statue's capacity to support the weight of a building will destroy the pillar but (if the statue is removed from its position as a load-bearing structure) will not destroy the statue. Thus, we want to say that the statue and the pillar are the *same material object*, even if they are *not identical*. By now the relevance of all this to the Trinity should be clear: almost everything that I just said about the statue and the pillar could likewise be said about the divine persons. In the case of the divine persons, we have three properties – *being the Father, being the Son,* and *being the Spirit* … all had by something that plays the role of matter. [It] is the divine substance, whatever that is, that plays the role of matter. (Rea, 2009b, pp. 418–19, italics original)

Brower and Rea's model is a new approach to the logical problem of the Trinity, which distinguishes itself from social and Latin alternatives. They claim it is 'the most philosophically promising and most theologically satisfying solution on offer' (2005, p. 70). Rea (2009b) does concede, however, that we lack knowledge of exactly what the divine substance is that is analogous to the marble in the statue. Leftow picks up on this point and argues that all the options for what substance constitutes the persons of the Trinity are 'problematic' (2018, p. 374). Hasker also agrees that the divine substance is 'ambiguous' in Brower and Rea's model (2013, p. 137).[8] The exact nature of the divine substance remains a mystery.

Trinitarian mysterianism and divine contradiction

Despite their individual weaknesses and limitations, existing analytic models of the Trinity do at least serve to pinpoint some of the enduring mysteries that surround the doctrine – such as the exact nature of the divine *ousia* or of the *perichoresis* of the three persons. In light of these enduring mysteries, some analytic theologians have adopted new, more minimalist, approaches to the doctrine which seek to acknowledge explicitly the transcendence of God and the cognitive limitations of humanity. For instance, Oliver Crisp has offered his own 'chastened' model of the Trinity. He does so because 'existing ways of conceiving the Trinity fail for a similar reason – namely, *they attempt to say too much about the triunity of God*' (2019a, p. 82). Specifically:

> The Latin Trinitarians think they can give an account of the divine persons as subsistent relations. But it is not at all clear how a relation can be said to subsist – that is to exist independently like a substance. So how can such relations be divine persons? And, in any case, how can a *relation* be a *person* – even in some sort of attenuated or analogical sense of the word 'person'? Despite strenuous efforts to explicate this among Latin Trinitarians, it is still very difficult to see what sense can be made of such a claim. The major concern with social Trinitarians is that their accounts of the triunity of God seem to collapse into tritheism, where the divine persons, like Zeus, Poseidon, and Hades, share in, or instantiate, or exemplify a common property, 'divinity'. This social Trinitarian commitment to a strong sense of distinctions within the Godhead appears to jeopardise the monotheism of Christianity and a commitment to divine simplicity. (2019a, pp. 82–3)

While Crisp is more sympathetic to Brower and Rea's constitutional view of the Trinity, even their model 'depends upon the controversial Aristotelian thesis that one can have numerical sameness without identity' (2019a, p. 83). Instead, Crisp offers his own 'mysterian' account of the Trinity that is consistent with four 'stipulations', namely 'MODEL, MYSTERY, TRINITY and TRANSCENDENCE', which he defines as follows:

> MODEL: A simplified conceptual framework or description by means of which complex sets of data, systems, and processes may be organised and understood.

> MYSTERY: A truth that is intelligible in principle but that may not be entirely intelligible to human beings in their current state of cognitive development.

TRINITY: The conjunction of dogmatic propositions concerning the divine nature, expressing the claim that God is one in essence and subsists in three persons, that are found in the dogmatic deposit of the ecumenical creeds, especially the Nicene-Constantinopolitan Symbol, and that reflect (a particular way of understanding) the teaching of Scripture and the apostolic faith.

TRANSCENDENCE: God is transcendent in virtue of being the creator of all things. (Crisp, 2019a, p. 99)

With these stipulations in place, Crisp proceeds to construct his chastened mysterian model as follows:

(1) The triunity of the divine nature is an instance of MYSTERY because God is transcendent (as per TRANSCENDENCE).
(2) Human beings cannot apprehend the triunity of God absent divine revelation.
(3) In revealing himself to us, God accommodates himself to the epistemic limitations of human beings. (Presumably this includes allowing for the noetic effects of sin.)
(4) TRINITY is a revealed dogma (that is, a doctrine that has a particular canonical form).
(5) TRINITY provides a dogmatic framework for understanding the divine nature that is theologically minimal.[9]
(6) TRINITY does not explain how God is triune; it does not in and of itself offer a particular MODEL of the Godhead; it is metaphysically underdetermined. (For this reason it is consistent with more than one dogmatic extrapolation, including a range of Trinitarian doctrines and MODELS.)
(7) The terms 'person' and 'essence,' and their cognates that demarcate the way in which God is three and the way in which God is one in TRINITY, are referring terms that are placeholders; we do not have a clear conceptual grip on their semantic content. (This is consistent with the claim that we may have a partial, piecemeal, or analogous sense of these terms.)
(8) TRINITY is consistent with MYSTERY. (Crisp, 2019a, pp. 99–100)

Crisp compares the mystery of the Trinity to the situation faced by inhabitants of a two-dimensional world in Edwin Abbott's novel *Flatland*, who cannot conceive of a three-dimensional sphere:

In the case of the Trinity ... the idea that an entity may present itself as one in essence and yet subsisting in three persons seems incredible, paradoxical, and, to many, contradictory. But this makes sense if, like the sphere, God is transcendent. That is, God is beyond our mere human experience in a way similar to the manner in which the sphere is above and beyond the experience of the Flatlander (2019a, pp. 98–9)

Another very recent minimalist response to the Trinity has been offered by J. C. Beall in his *Divine Contradiction* (2023). Beall does not deny that the doctrine appears to us as contradictory, but argues that we should not abandon the doctrine because of this. Instead, given the nature of God, we should abandon the quest for a logically consistent account of divine reality. The transcendent, triune God, he argues, is truly and fully described only with the use of contradictory language.

Trinitarian prospects

The focus of this chapter, and of analytic theological work on the Trinity, has been on responses to the logical problem of the Trinity. Unsurprisingly, no single model of the triune God has received universal consent, and work on this central question will doubtless continue in the years ahead. However, it is important to note that additional areas of trinitarian theology are increasingly becoming subject to analytic investigation, and the field is likely to continue to diversify further over the coming years.

For example, work by analytic theologians has begun to consider the Trinity's relationship with time (e.g. Mullins, 2016), the inseparable operations of the persons (e.g. Vidu, 2016), and their eternal relations of origin (e.g. Hollingsworth, 2023). Coakley (2013a) also represents an important work of feminist trinitarian theology. Going forward, as McCall (2021) notes, valuable future work could be done by analytic theologians on such subjects as the (alleged) eternal functional subordination of the Son to the Father, and the relationship between the Trinity and the associated doctrines of divine simplicity and election.

Notes

1 It is perhaps worth noting that some *a priori* arguments in favour of the Trinity have been offered within the Christian philosophical tradition, without relying on the scriptural evidence. For example, in the ninth book of his *On the Trinity*, Augustine argued that God must be a trinity, since God is love (1 John 4.8) and love is necessarily triune – consisting of the lover, the beloved and the bond of love that exists between them. Richard of St Victor made a similar argument in the twelfth century, which in turn has been adopted and adapted by Richard Swinburne in *The Christian God* (1994).

2 See, for example, Coakley (1999), Cross (2002a) and Hasker (2013). Each of these authors questions the so-called 'Regnon thesis' (named after the nineteenth-century theologian Theodore de Regnon) that the historic Latin tradition took the unity of God as its trinitarian starting point, whereas the Greek tradition always began its trinitarian theorizing with a commitment to the threefold personhood of God.

3 'Modern' in this context means a post-Enlightenment 'Cartesian' or 'Lockean' understanding of a person, as a conscious willing agent.

4 Some critics have seen hints of subordinationism in Swinburne's model at this point, since only the Father exists by (what Swinburne calls) 'ontological necessity', without any prior active cause of his existence. The Son and the Spirit, in contrast, only exist by what Swinburne calls 'metaphysical necessity', since their existence relies upon the Father's active causation. As Moreland and Craig have observed, 'the causal dependence of the Son on the Father is problematic for the Son's being divine. Indeed, given that the Son is a distinct substance from the Father, the Father's begetting the Son amounts to *creatio ex nihilo*, which as Arius saw, makes the Son a creature' (2003, p. 588). Similar concerns would apply to the causation of the Spirit and have been echoed by Leftow (1999), Helm (2010) and others.

5 Hasker's use of these two psychological phenomena has been challenged by Rea (2009b), who suggests that the patients in question are examples of one *fragmented* psychological subject, rather than multiple *distinct* psychological subjects. Rea thus fears that 'modalism looms' over Hasker's psychological analogy for the Trinity (p. 410). Hasker himself denies this, however, arguing that even in the case of a fragmented psychological subject 'it is still the case that we have multiple centres of consciousness, supported by a single instance or trope of humanness' (2013, p. 237).

6 Indeed, Rea wonders whether Leftow's account even secures the consubstantiality of the three trinitarian persons. He writes that 'it is hard to tell' if the different dancing Rockettes in Leftow's analogy are really consubstantial; 'They are events (or event-based things) involving a common substance, but that doesn't guarantee consubstantiality' (2009b, p. 412).

7 Brower and Rea's constitutional account differs from a pure relative identity account because it does not embrace the view that 'relative identity claims are more fundamental than classical identity claims' (Crisp, Arcadi and Wessling, 2019, p. 83n).

8 Despite this weakness (in his view) of Brower and Rea's account, Hasker does employ a very similar constitutional model of the Trinity himself. See Hasker (2013), pp. 238–45.

9 Crisp defines TRINITY as 'theologically minimal in the sense that the tenets of TRINITY are consistent with more than one model of the Trinity' (2019a, p. 100).

Recommended further reading

McCall, T., 2010, *Which Trinity? Whose Monotheism?: Philosophical and Systematic Theologians on the Metaphysics of Trinitarian Theology*, Grand Rapids, MI: Eerdmans.

Hasker, W., 2013, *Metaphysics and the Tri-Personal God*, Oxford Studies in Analytic Theology, Oxford: Oxford University Press.

4

Incarnation: The Person of Christ

For Christians, the Incarnation of the Son of God is the defining event in salvation history. In the person of Jesus of Nazareth, God's work of self-revelation and redemption is believed to have reached its fullest expression. As the prologue to John's Gospel so famously phrases it, 'the Word became flesh and lived among us, and we have seen his glory, the glory as of a father's only son, full of grace and truth' (John 1.14, cited in Crisp, 2007, p. 160). And yet, as with the Trinity, the Incarnation is a doctrine that the early Church could clearly see in Scripture yet struggled to fully comprehend.

In a very real sense this struggle continues to this day (as we shall see below), but it was in AD 451 that the Council of Chalcedon articulated a 'definition' of the doctrine that remains the standard of orthodoxy for most Christians to the present day:

> Following, then, the holy Fathers, we all with one voice teach that it should be confessed that our Lord Jesus Christ is one and same Son, the Same perfect in Godhead, the Same perfect in manhood, truly God and truly man, the Same [consisting] of a rational soul and a body; homoousios with the Father as to his Godhead, and the Same homoousios with us as to his manhood; in all things like unto us, sin only excepted; begotten of the Father before ages as to his Godhead, and in the last days, the Same, for us and for our salvation, of Mary the Virgin Theotokos as to his manhood; One and the same Christ, Son, Lord, Only begotten, made known in two natures [which exist] without confusion, without change, without division, without separation; the difference of the natures having been in no wise taken away by reason of the union, but rather the properties of each being preserved, and [both] concurring into one Person (prosopon) and one hypostasis – not parted or divided into two persons (prosopa), but one and the same Son and Only-begotten, the divine Logos, the Lord Jesus Christ.
> (quoted in Coakley, 2002, p. 143)

As Crisp (2007a) summarizes it, this Chalcedonian Definition affirmed the following tenets of what has become known as 'classical' Christology:

1. Christ is of one substance (*homoousios*) with the Father.
2. Christ is eternally begotten of the Father according to his divinity and temporally begotten of the Virgin Mary according to his humanity.
3. Christ is one theanthropic (divine-human) person (*hypostasis*) subsisting in two natures (*phuseis*), which are held together in a personal union.
4. Christ's two natures remain intact in the personal union, without being confused or mingled together to form some sort of hybrid entity or *tertium quid*.
5. Christ's two natures are a fully divine nature and a fully human nature, respectively, his human nature consisting of a human body and 'rational' soul. (Crisp, 2007, p. 161, italics original)

The Chalcedonian Definition thereby proscribed as heretical a variety of Christological views that had been held over the proceeding centuries. For example, Arians and adoptionists had, in their own different ways, denied the full divinity of Christ. At the opposite extreme, docetists, Apollinarians and others were judged to have denied his full humanity, while monophysites such as Eutyches of Constantinople (c.380–456) were guilty of mixing or merging Christ's two natures in their accounts of his 'hypostatic union'. Finally, those adopting a 'Nestorian' brand of Christology had failed to clarify that the incarnate Christ was one person, a single hypostasis, rather than two.

The circumstances surrounding the Council of Chalcedon and its subsequent reception history have been subject to considerable academic scrutiny – including by those such as Sarah Coakley, Richard Cross and Eleonore Stump who are also active in the field of analytic theology. The church historian Donald Fairbairn (2022) has also recently produced an overview of conciliar Christology written 'in the service of analytic theology'.

For Christians in Roman Catholic, Orthodox and most Protestant denominations, the Chalcedonian Definition continues to set the parameters for any orthodox account of the Incarnation, boundaries that are respected by almost all analytic theologians engaged in Christology. These analytic theologians also share the 'unanimous' consensus of Christian theologians and philosophers over the past two millennia 'that the incarnation is a mystery that we cannot hope to fully grasp' (Rogers,

2010, p. 95). Nevertheless, analytic theologians have also engaged in the enduring task of defending the coherence of the doctrine against those who say that it is 'worse than a mystery: it is an impossibility' (Rogers, 2010, p. 95). As a consequence, analytic theologians have sought to articulate the metaphysics of the Incarnation and demonstrate the logical coherence of Chalcedonian orthodoxy. Before addressing this 'how' question relating to the Incarnation, however, it is worth summarising how analytic theologians have sought to defend the underlying assumption of Chalcedon that Jesus of Nazareth was indeed God incarnate.

Evidence for the Incarnation

Analytic theologians have adopted a variety of approaches in their efforts to argue for the truth of the Incarnation. Some, notably Pawl (2016), have avoided the task altogether, simply assuming the truth of the Church's historic affirmation of the doctrine – often assumed to have been made under the guidance of the Holy Spirit. Others have gone a little further and cited New Testament 'proof texts' in support of the doctrine.[1] Moreland and Craig (2003), for example, introduce their account of the Incarnation with this brief paragraph:

> [T]he New Testament authors affirm that Jesus was God (Jn 1:1–3, 14, 18; 20:26–29; Rom 9:5; Tit 2:13; Heb 1:8; 2 Pet 1:1) and describe him as the fullness of deity in bodily form (Col 1:15–20; 2:9; Phil 2:5–8). The New Testament church called him kyrios ('Lord'), the same word used in the Greek translation of the Old Testament in place of Yahweh, and applied to Jesus Old Testament passages concerning Yahweh (1 Cor 16:22; Rom 10:8, 13). (Moreland and Craig, 2003, p. 597)

Richard Swinburne, however, is an example of those who have offered a more ambitious *a priori* argument for the Incarnation. He begins by assuming that God's motives for becoming incarnate would include 'providing atonement, identifying with our suffering, and providing information and encouragement', before proceeding to ask the following question: 'Let us call a candidate for being God incarnate a prophet. What observable features would we expect a prophet's life to have if it was to be the life of God Incarnate?' (2003, p. 55). Swinburne then proposes the following 'marks' that the life of any such prophet would be expected to display:

> If God is to become incarnate in order to fulfil all the purposes for becoming incarnate ... we would expect his life to show these five marks. His life must be, as far as we can judge, a perfect human life in which he provides healing; he must teach deep moral and theological truths (ones, in so far as we can judge, plausibly true); he must show himself to believe that he is God Incarnate; he must teach that his life provides an atonement for our sins; and he must found a church which continues his teaching and work. (p. 59)

It is Swinburne's contention, 'treating the Bible, and in particular the New Testament, simply as an ordinary historical document written by ordinary human authors', that there *is* good evidence that Jesus of Nazareth fulfilled these prior requirements for being God incarnate (2008, p. 96). For example, Swinburne believes Jesus implicitly taught his divinity by accepting worship, forgiving sins, and teaching with unqualified authority (that is, as if he were God). Swinburne adds one posterior requirement for Jesus of Nazareth (or any other candidate claiming to be God incarnate), namely that they should have some kind of 'divine signature' upon their life. This signature must be a 'super-miracle' which involves 'an evident violation ... of natural laws – for God, who keeps the laws of nature operative, alone can permit them to be set aside' (2003a, p. 62). Swinburne argues that the New Testament documents (again treated merely as historical records) show, on the balance of probability, that God performed the super-miracle of raising Jesus from the dead. The three key pieces of evidence cited by Swinburne are Christ's empty tomb, his appearances to his disciples, and Sunday observance of the Eucharist by the earliest churches in commemoration of his resurrection (see Swinburne, 2013a, pp. 249–52).

Similar arguments in favour of Christ's divinity have been offered by Stephen T. Davis and others. Davis (2009), for example, utilizes these arguments in support of the opening premise of C. S. Lewis' famous 'Trilemma', also known as his 'Mad, Bad or God' (MBG) argument. Davis summarizes Lewis' argument as follows:

> Since Jesus claimed to be the divine Son of God – so the argument goes – then if he was not in fact divine, he must have been either a lunatic or a moral monster. No sane and righteous person can wrongly claim to be divine. But since Jesus was evidently neither a lunatic nor a moral monster – so the argument concludes – he must indeed have been divine. (2009, p. 166)

Davis then sets this argument out in a logical form:

(1) Jesus claimed, either explicitly or implicitly, to be divine.
(2) Jesus was either right or wrong in claiming to be divine.
(3) If Jesus was wrong in claiming to be divine, Jesus was either mad or bad.
(4) Jesus was not bad.
(5) Jesus was not mad.
(6) Therefore, Jesus was not wrong in claiming to be divine.
(7) Therefore, Jesus was right in claiming to be divine.
(8) Therefore, Jesus was divine. (Davis, 2009, p. 168)

Though this MBG argument is deductively *valid* (that is, it contains no errors of logic), Davis and Howard-Snyder (2009a) disagree on whether it is *sound* (that is, whether all its premises are true, or at least plausibly true). Whereas Davis believes that the argument is a sound demonstration of the rationality of belief in the Incarnation, Howard-Snyder holds that the MBG argument is not sound, since premise (3) excludes the possibility that Jesus was 'merely mistaken' in the belief that he was divine (p. 188). To illustrate his point, Howard-Snyder speculates that Jesus of Nazareth could conceivably have been tricked by Beelzebub into believing that he was divine, or he may have sincerely (but erroneously) misapplied Old Testament Messianic passages to himself (2009a, pp. 205–9). Howard-Snyder consequently concludes that we are *not* 'in a position to say that the merely mistaken option is significantly less likely than or plausible than the God option' (p. 210). Davis, however, rejects the 'merely mistaken' alternative to the Trilemma. While one could theoretically 'cook up a scenario' in which a sane and moral person mistakenly took themselves to be divine, in practice it is not 'possible for an otherwise perfectly sane and good person mistakenly to consider herself to be God' (2009, pp. 169–70). Accordingly, premise (3) in the MBG argument does 'seem to have a high degree of plausibility' (p. 170). If Davis's intuition about premise (3) is correct, and if premise (1) can be plausibly shown to be true from the relevant historical (that is, biblical) evidence, then the MBG argument has utility within contemporary Christian apologetics.

The metaphysics of the Incarnation

For any Christian who believes in the reality of the Incarnation – whether based on *a priori* philosophical arguments, biblical evidence or ecclesial tradition – the challenge remains to comprehend *how* it could have taken place. Much work by analytic theologians has therefore focused on the metaphysics of the Incarnation, and whether a coherent account of the Chalcedonian doctrine can be articulated. As Cross (2009a) notes, while some maintain that the Chalcedonian Definition

> gives no more than particular syntactic rules governing the use of the terms 'person' and 'nature' ... it has seemed to most recent philosophical commentators ... that the linguistic rules are secondary to some apparently substantive metaphysical claims: namely, that there is some divine subject of properties – the second person of the Trinity – that gains human properties (a human nature). Clearly the metaphysics leaves open just what a nature is. (2009a, p. 453)

'Abstract' versus 'concrete' Christologies

For example, analytic theologians are divided on the question of whether Christ's human nature was *abstract* or *concrete*, a distinction first highlighted by Alvin Plantinga (1999). He describes the abstractist view as follows:

> When the second person of the Trinity became incarnate and assumed human nature, what happened was that he, the second person of the Trinity, acquired the property of being human; he acquired whatever property it is that is necessary and sufficient for being human. (Plantinga, 1999, pp. 183)

Alternatively, on the concretist view:

> What [the second person of the Trinity] assumed was a human nature, a specific human being. What happened when he became incarnate is that he adopted a peculiarly close and intimate relation to a certain concrete human being, a 'human nature' in the sense of a human being. That is, there is or was a concrete human being – a creature, and a creature with will and intellect – to whom the Logos became related in an especially intimate way, a way denoted by the term 'assumption'. (pp. 183–4)

Historically, a concretist view of Christ's human nature has been more popular than an abstract one, including among Medieval and Reformation theologians. It also continues to have some advocates within contemporary analytic theology (e.g. Oliver Crisp and Andrew Ter Ern Loke). On this concrete view, it was Christ's human and divine natures (rather than his single *hypostasis*) which each possessed the ability to will and act – each of his natures was a 'principle of operation' with the power to cause things 'to happen in the real world' (Baker, 2013, p. 37). The notion that the incarnate Christ had two wills in virtue of his two natures has conciliar support, since *dyothelitism* was affirmed at the Third Council of Constantinople in AD 681, which proclaimed 'two natural volitions or wills in [Christ] and two natural principles of action which undergo no division, no change, no partition, no confusion' (quoted in Fairbairn and Reeves, 2019, p. 152).

The concretist view of Christ's nature, however, is at risk of a Nestorian interpretation. For if Christ had two complete, concrete natures (human and divine), each with the ability to will and act, do we not have *two* distinct conscious 'persons' in our usual sense of the term? In response, Crisp has written as follows:

> One way to resist this [Nestorian] conclusion is to claim that in assuming a concrete human nature God the Son took on the complement of a human person. That is, he took on the thing that would have formed a human person if the incarnation hadn't happened. But because the incarnation did happen at the moment of conception, the human in question (Jesus) never formed a substance independent of a divine person. Instead, God the Son uploaded himself, as it were, into the human nature of Jesus at conception. This means that the human nature of Christ is always 'owned' by a divine person. It never exists as a person independent of God the Son in the way that you and I exist as independent persons. (Crisp, 2019b, p. 6)[2]

The majority of contemporary analytic theologians, however, adopt an abstractist view of what a nature is (that is, a collection of essential properties), which is consistent with the conventional understanding of a nature in analytic philosophy more widely. The challenge facing this view of Christ's human nature, however, is that it struggles to account for his having a human will as well as a divine will, as the Church has traditionally taught. Indeed, this abstract-nature view

> seems insufficient as an account of the incarnation. Is the property of human nature enough to be truly human? Does this include a human mind and consciousness? Some worry that this sort of view is rather like the difference between Clark Kent and Superman. Kent and Superman are one person, the Kryptonian Kal-El. When Kal-El operates in the guise of Superman or in the guise of Kent, he wills as Kal-El in both circumstances. He does not have two wills as such. (Crisp, 2019b, p. 6)

Many defenders of an abstract understanding of Christ's human nature have therefore felt obliged to construct an account of how Christ possessed a human will as well as a divine one. Such efforts (for example Morris, 1986 and Swinburne 1994) may involve positing the existence of two will-bearing 'minds' in Christ's one 'person'. Others, however (for example Moreland and Craig, 2003; DeWeese, 2007), avoid the problem by flatly denying that Christ had a human will in addition to his divine one. Moreland and Craig write that 'dyothelitism, despite its conciliar support, finds no warrant in Scripture ... [and] it is extraordinarily difficult to preserve the unity of Christ's person once distinct wills are ascribed to the Logos and to the individual human nature of Christ' (2003, p. 611).

Pawl (2021), meanwhile, questions whether this concretist-abstractist debate about Christ's human nature is of any real significance:

> Even though there is an ontological gulf between these two theories of the human nature of Christ, in a real sense there is very little fundamental disagreement between the two views. For any traditional Christology will require there to be a flesh and blood thing that the Word is specially related to, and in virtue of which it is true to say things like 'the Word was born' and 'the Son suffered on the cross.' We might call that thing, as I have elsewhere, *Christ's human element*. (p. 198, italics original)

Two- and three-part Christologies

Following Pawl's lead, the question then arises, 'What was the composition of Christ's human nature or element?' Here analytic theologians are divided between *two-* and *three-part Christologies*. Two-part Christologies claim that Christ had two component parts, his divine nature and his human body, with the role of the human soul played by the person of the Son. In other words, this view asserts that at the Incarnation the Son gained a contingent, created part (a human body) that he previously lacked.

Moreland and Craig exemplify a two-part Christology, since they deny that Christ possessed a created human soul. They postulate with Apollinarius (c. AD 310–390) 'that the Logos was the rational soul of Jesus of Nazareth' (2003, p. 608). However, this 'Neo-Apollinarian' view (as they call it) could be deemed unorthodox, since Apollinarius's views were rejected at the Council of Constantinople in AD 381, on the principle that Christ must have assumed a full human nature (i.e. a body *and* a rational soul) in order to redeem it in full. As Gregory of Nazianzus (c. AD 330–390) famously phrased this principle: 'That which is not assumed is not healed.' Aware of this objection to their position, Moreland and Craig defend their view with the assertion that

> the Logos contained perfect human personhood archetypally in his own nature. The result was that in assuming a hominid body the Logos brought to Christ's animal nature just those properties that would serve to make it a complete human nature. As a result of the union Christ did, indeed, possess a complete individual human nature comprised of body and soul. (2003, p. 608)

Swinburne (2011) has promoted a similar two-part Christology, arguing that the divine Logos replaced an ordinary human soul in Christ but, crucially, adopted a 'human way of thinking and acting', which he believes is what the early Church councils meant by affirming that Christ had a rational soul. In the opinion of one historical theologian at least, Swinburne's view avoids the charge of Apollinarianism, since his 'express claim is that the Son began to instantiate human mental states, and this is something that Apollinarius was not prepared to countenance' (Cross, 2009a, p. 470).

However, for analytic theologians unpersuaded of the orthodoxy (or coherence) of such two-part Christologies, there is the alternative of a three-part Christology. This is one in which Christ 'has three part-ish things: (1) the divine nature, and the human nature, which is itself composed of two parts; (2) the body; and (3) the soul' (Pawl, 2021, p. 199). There have been differences within this view, however, for example between those who define the human soul as an Aristotelian 'subsisting form' of the body, or a 'substance in its own right' (Pawl, 2021, p. 200). If Apollinarianism is the danger for two-part Christologies, a danger here is of Nestorianism. For if Christ had a substantive human soul, with its own mind, this intuitively suggests that he contained two persons. As we saw above, Morris (1986) is among those who have sought to argue that a single person can be in possession of two minds or consciousnesses. He cites cases of brain-hemisphere commissurotomy, multiple personality disorder and hypnosis in support of this contention. Morris goes on to explain how the two minds in Christ are related: 'The divine mind of God the Son contained, but was not contained by, his earthly mind, or range of consciousness' (1986, p. 103). There is consequently an 'asymmetric accessing relation' between the divine and the human minds of Christ:

> The divine mind, as omniscient, has full and uninterrupted access to the contents of the human mind. The human mind, on the other hand, only has access to the contents of the divine mind on certain important occasions. So when we read in the Gospel accounts that Jesus foretells the future or sees into the hearts of his friends and enemies, we are to conclude that in these moments the divine mind 'uploads' the pertinent (but otherwise inaccessible) information to the human mind. (McCall, 2015, p. 96)

A more recent three-part Christology has been offered by Loke (2014). He calls his model a 'Kryptic' account of the Incarnation (taken from the Greek word *krypsis*, meaning 'hiding'), since 'in a certain sense the supernatural properties of God incarnate were concealed ("veiled") during the Incarnation' (2014, p. 20). Loke describes his Kryptic Christology using what he calls the 'Divine Preconscious Model' (DPM), in which 'preconsciousness' refers to 'mental contents that are not currently in consciousness but are accessible to consciousness by directing attention to them' (p. 66). His DPM model then states that:

> At the Incarnation, the divine attributes of the Logos (such as the Logos' omniscience, omnipotence, and omnipresence) were pushed into the Logos' divine preconscious, while a human nature was assumed that included a human preconscious. Loke calls the former 'part A' of Christ's preconscious and the latter 'part B' of his preconscious. The two minds of Christ (his divine mind and human mind) share one consciousness. But Christ has a full divine nature ... and a full human nature. So, once the Incarnation occurs, Christ is composed of three parts: (1) the concrete divine nature and the concrete human nature, the latter of which is composed of (2) Christ's human body and (3) Christ's human soul. [Loke's] model is Kryptic because it holds that the divine attributes of the Incarnate Christ are hidden in the divine preconscious, fully accessible (so he still possesses them) but hidden from view in the sense that Christ does not (or rarely does) access them. (Arcadi, 2016, pp. 460–1)

Transformational and relational Christologies

Whether one opts for a two- or a three-part Christology, there remains the question of how the two natures of Christ are united in a single person. One minority report, called the *transformational* view by Hill (2011), claims that the divine Son did not merely unite himself with a human nature, but was 'transformed into a human ... just as a caterpillar becomes a butterfly by being transformed into one' (p. 8). This view finds very little support among analytic theologians, however, since it faces numerous philosophical and scriptural objections (see Leftow, 2015) and violates historic church teaching, notably the following statement by the Council of Ephesus (AD 431):

> For we do not say that the nature of the Word was changed and became flesh, nor that he was turned into a whole man made of body and soul. Rather do we claim that the Word in an unspeakable, inconceivable manner united to himself hypostatically flesh enlivened by a rational soul, and so became man and was called son of man. (Cited by Pawl, 2021, p. 199)

Far more popular (and historically orthodox) is the *relational* view, in which the second person of the Trinity, in becoming incarnate 'came to relate to something else [i.e. a human nature], in a special way' (Pawl, 2021, p. 199). This special way is traditionally known as the 'hypostatic union'. Thomas Flint (2011) has defined two ways of understanding this hypostatic union, which he refers to as 'Model T' and 'Model A' respectively. Flint defines Model T as follows: 'In becoming human, the Son or Word of God ... takes on CHN as a part. This assumption results in a Son who combines both his original divine substance (D) and his created human nature (CHN)' (2011, p. 71).

Model A, meanwhile, asserts that:

> The Son unites himself to CHN in the incarnation. But the composite thus formed is not the Son. The Son remains simply one part of the composite entity that results from him assuming human nature. That composite entity, which ... we can call Christ, is a contingent thing, composed of another contingent entity (CHN) and of a necessary one (the Son). (2011, p. 79)

Model T would appear to have the stronger claim to orthodoxy, since the early ecumenical councils spoke of Christ as 'one person "in" or "of" two natures' (i.e. two natures united in the person of the Son). As Pawl (2021) observes, Model A appears to contradict this, 'since it misidentifies the things united together, claiming one of them is the Word himself' (p. 201). He also notes that 'Model A denies that the Word suffered. True, Christ did, and the Word is part of Christ. But the Word himself did not suffer' (2021, p. 201). Despite these concerns, Model A accounts of the hypostatic union have been defended by Leftow (2011) and Crisp (2011).

Finally, some analytic theologians have proposed analogies for the hypostatic union. One example is Kathryn Rogers' video-game analogy (2010), which has been summarized as follows:

> Imagine an adolescent boy, Rogers calls him 'Nick' (N) and N is engaged in a first-person video game where the entity he controls on the screen is 'Nick's Character' (NC). N uses NC in order to operate in the virtual, video-game world. This state of affairs of N engaging in the video game as NC Rogers denotes 'Nick Playing' (NP). Accordingly, when N is playing the video game as NC, NP obtains. If, per chance, N's mom tells him to go take out the trash and he turns off the game, then NP would not at that time obtain. This illustration maps on to the theological reality we are discussing in the following manner. N corresponds to the divine Word, NC corresponds to the human nature of Christ, and NP corresponds to the Incarnation. On this view, there is only ever one person involved in NP, N. But there are two natures engaged: N's original nature and NC. It is only in the causal activity of N engaging in the game as NC that NP obtains. Likewise, so the illustration goes, it is only in the causal activity of the Word using the human nature that Christ obtains. (Arcadi, 2018a, p. 7)

Rogers is aware of the limits of her analogy, however. 'One obvious disanalogy,' she writes, 'is that Nick is not the creator of the virtual world' inhabited by Nick's Character (2010, p. 106). Nor does Nick's Character 'have an intellect or will. He is a two-dimensional image', which conflicts with conciliar teaching that Christ's human nature had its own will (Rogers, 2010, p. 106). Third, and finally, in this analogy Nick is simply 'manipulating' Nick's Character. But in the Incarnation the Word 'is not just the manipulator for Christ's humanity. The Word really is *being* Christ. He has entered more fully into creation than Nick can enter into the video game' (p. 107, italics original). Another, more recent analogy, proposed by Hasker (2017), is inspired by the 2009 film *Avatar*. In the film 'a human person can enter a machine and have his consciousness transferred to an alien biological organism. So likewise, the Word, through the hypostatic union, can enter the biological human nature' (Pawl, 2021, p. 201).

The 'Fundamental Philosophical Problem' of the Incarnation

Up to this point we have not yet addressed what has been called the 'Fundamental Philosophical Problem' of the Incarnation – a problem that has elicited a wide and varied range of responses from analytic theologians. As defined by Richard Cross:

> The fundamental philosophical problem specific to the doctrine is this: how is it that one and the same thing could be both divine (and thus, on the face of it, necessary, and necessarily omniscient, omnipotent, eternal, immutable, impassible, and impeccable) and human (and thus, on the face of it, have the complements of all these properties). (2009, p. 453)

It would seem that there is an inherent contradiction in claiming that the incarnate Christ could simultaneously possess both divine and human predicates. For example, how could any individual be both omniscient and partially knowledgeable at the same time? Or simultaneously possess both limitless and limited power, or be both passible and impassible, etc.?

Pawl (2021) identifies five broad categories of response that have been made to this fundamental problem, which can be summarized as follows:

(i) Modifying logic;
(ii) Revision of the concepts of divinity and/or humanity;
(iii) Denying Christ's simultaneous possession of divine and human predicates;
(iv) Denying Christ's divine and human predicates are possessed in the same respect; and
(v) Denying that Christ's divine and human predicates are incompatible.

Option (i), *modifying logic*, has involved two alternative approaches. The first is to employ a relative-identity relation between the two natures of Christ. As we saw in our discussion of the Trinity, 'on this view, it is possible that two things, A and B, be the same x, but not the same y' (Pawl, 2021, p. 202). Applied to the Incarnation, this implies that Christ's two natures share the *same* person, but possess *different* powers and other predicates (see Jedwab, 2018). A second approach, defended by Beall (2019) recognizes that according to 'mainstream' accounts of logic the incarnate Christ does appear to be contradictory in his attributes. Beall's response, however, is to 'put the simplest explanation on the theological table: namely, Christ *appears* to be contradictory because Christ *is* contradictory' (2019, p. 400, italics added). Beall's argument is highly technical but, in essence, he 'rejects the validity of the Law of the Excluded Middle. Such a response allows the contradiction but precludes the spread of the contradiction … [i.e.] we cannot derive from that contradiction just anything' (Pawl, 2020, p. 39). Beall is aware that his position is

> … jarring, and even in some ways mysterious; but orthodox Christianity has advanced the role of Christ to be just so: jarring and in various ways mysterious. In this case, the mystery is (at least in part) that there is a being whose very existence entails contradictions – that he is perfect and all-knowing but is imperfect and has limited knowledge (and so on). (2019, p. 418)

Option (ii), *revising the concepts of divinity and/or humanity*, is what Richard Cross calls a 'restriction solution' to the fundamental problem of Christology (2009, p. 463). Such solutions can involve revising certain tenets of Classical Theism to deny, for example, that God 'must be immutable, impassible, atemporal and simple' (Pawl, 2021a, p. 203). Such revised definitions of divinity are variously called 'modified Classical Theism', 'Theistic Personalism' and more, and seek to bring some or all of the divine and human predicates of Christ into alignment.[3] Thomas Morris (1986) has taken a different approach, revising the definition of humanity to draw a distinction between someone who is *fully* human and someone who is *merely* human. On this view, all humans apart from Christ are fully human and merely human, in that they possess all the properties of human nature, and of no other nature. Christ, in contrast, is fully human but not merely human, since he also possesses a fully divine nature. As Morris says, 'The Chalcedonian claim is not that Jesus was merely human. It is rather that he was, and is, fully human in addition to being divine' (1986, p. 66). In his unique case, Christ will possess all the attributes essential to humanity, but those attributes that only apply to mere humans (such as limited power) do not apply to him. Overall, this approach seeks to remove some of the apparently incompatible divine and human predicates of Christ, by revising our definition of one or both of his natures.

The next category of responses to the fundamental problem, category (iii), involves *denying Christ's simultaneous possession of divine and human predicates*. The most common form of this response is kenotic Christology, which claims inspiration from Philippians 2.6–8, where

Christ is described as having emptied himself, taking the form of a slave. Traditional kenotic Christologies of the nineteenth century suggested that Christ voluntarily gave up some or all of his divine attributes at the Incarnation. On this view 'attributes typically attributed to the divine nature (such as, say, omniscience or omnipotence or omnipresence) are actually not necessary to the divine nature' (Arcadi, 2018a, p. 4). Among contemporary analytic theologians, however, a more nuanced approach, known as 'Modified Kenotic Christology' (MKC), has been proposed (e.g. Davis, 2011). According to MKC, Christ gives up his *common* (i.e. non-essential) attributes of divinity, while retaining all the attributes that are *essential* to his divine nature. Problematic divine attributes (from a Christological perspective), such as omniscience or omnipotence, are consequently viewed as common rather than essential attributes, which could be freely surrendered at the Incarnation. MKC states that what is essential to divinity is not omniscience (for example), but 'rather the attribute of *omniscient-unless-kenotically-and-redemptively-incarnate*' (McCall, 2015, p. 100, italics original).

Critics of the MKC view, however, argue that denying the necessity of such divine attributes as omnipotence, omniscience, etc. 'entails a concept of God that might strike one as far too thin to be acceptable' (Moreland and Craig, 2003, p. 607). In addition:

> Ontologically speaking, it is not clear that there even are such properties as being-omniscient-except-when-kenotically-incarnate. These contrived properties are not attributes in the sense of capacities or qualities but are really statements masquerading as attributes. Moreover, it is not clear that the problem of the Incarnation is solved even by postulating such gerrymandered properties of Christ. For it seems that certain divine attributes cannot be temporarily divested in the way envisioned by kenoticists. For example, it seems incoherent to say that Christ had the essential property of being-omnipotent-except-when-kenotically-incarnate, for if, having relinquished omnipotence, he retained the power to get omnipotence back again, then he never in fact ceased to be omnipotent. (Moreland and Craig, 2003, p. 607)

Rogers (2010), meanwhile, believes that kenoticism's 'most important [problem] is this: on the understanding of the activity of the Word assumed by Chalcedon, it is through the Word that all things are sustained in being from moment to moment. If the Word were to set aside his power, the created universe would blink out of being – an unfortunate consequence' (p. 99). Pawl also criticizes the kenotic strategy, since

> ... the doctrine of the exaltation claims that after his resurrection, Christ is glorified to his rightful place, bearing all his divine majesty and attributes. At that point, Christ is still human, yet he is exalted to his former status. If the doctrine of the exaltation is true then kenotic Christology will not provide a universal answer to the Fundamental Problem. For there will be some time, any post-exaltation time, at which Christ has all the attributes humans must have in addition to the attributes of which he supposedly emptied during his earthly mission. (Pawl, 2020, pp. 43–4)

Turning to option (iv) in Pawl's list of responses to the fundamental Christological problem, we encounter views that *deny Christ's divine and human predicates are possessed in the same respect*. This is what Cross calls the 'reduplication strategy', which attempts to 'defuse' the fundamental problem by 'dividing potentially contradictory properties into two groups, associating one with the divine nature, and the other with the human nature' (2009a, p. 455). As Cross himself notes, this approach appears to have some legitimation from the Chalcedonian Definition, which applies his eternal existence to his divinity and his temporal birth to his humanity (i.e. 'begotten of the Father before ages as to his Godhead, and in the last days, the Same, for us and for our salvation, of Mary the Virgin as to his manhood'). As Pawl explains:

> This approach most often employs *qua locutions* – statements of the form 'Christ is immutable *qua divine*' and 'Christ is mutable *qua human.*' The idea here is to find some way of claiming that there is no contradiction, owing to the fact that a necessary condition for a contradiction – the proposition being both true and false at the same time *in the same respect* – goes unsatisfied. (Pawl, 2021, p. 204)

Gorman (2014) and Labooy (2019) offer sympathetic accounts of this reduplicative strategy but, as Pawl notes, this type of response to the fundamental problem has generally 'fallen on hard times in the literature, in large part because it is often not elaborated. One is told that Christ is immutable as God and mutable as man, but one isn't told how this is supposed to show the contradiction to be thwarted' (2021, p. 205).

We come, finally, to option (v), the strategy for addressing the fundamental Christological problem which *denies that Christ's divine and human predicates are incompatible*. Pawl uses the example of passibility and impassibility to argue that 'when properly understood, one and the same thing can be impassible and passible at the same time, in the same respect' (2021, p. 205). He achieves this by defining impassibility as being when something has *at least one nature* that is impassible, rather than defining impassibility as when something has *no nature* that is passible. If impassibility is defined in the former way,

> ... then to be impassible and passible is to have a nature that can be causally affected and also a (different) nature that cannot be causally affected. Christ, on this view, fulfils both of these conditions, and so Christ is both passible and impassible. You and I are passible and not impassible; the Father and the Holy Spirit are impassible and not passible. But in the unique case of Christ, owing to the hypostatic union of two natures in one person, the truth conditions for being both passible and impassible can be satisfied. The same reasoning ... can work for the other allegedly incompatible pairs of predicates. (Pawl, 2021, p. 205)

To illustrate his view, Pawl offers an intriguing cheerleader analogy (2016, pp. 155–7). He asks his readers to imagine a world in which everybody has exactly one arm, and this arm can either be 'bent' or 'unbent'. In such a world, it seems that the idea of a person *simultaneously* having their single arm bent *and* unbent is impossible and inherently contradictory. However:

> Now suppose that into this crazy one-armed world, there comes a cheerleader, a two-armed cheerleader. His left arm is bent 90 degrees, but his right arm is straight. Because he has two arms he can be both arm-bent and arm-unbent. To further the fiction, suppose too that most philosophers and logicians in this world were not convinced of the existence of the cheerleader. (After all, he is literally the only thing in the world that has two arms.) They would probably continue to insist that nothing can be both arm-bent and arm-unbent. Meanwhile, fans of the cheerleader would have to revise the conditions under which the terms 'arm-bent' and 'arm-unbent' truthfully apply. The fundamental intuition is clear enough: when we learn that something previously regarded as impossible turns out actually to exist (a two-armed cheerleader, a God-man), we must revise the way we understand the logical relationships that obtain between predicates we previously regarded as incompatible. (Wood, 2021, pp. 57–8)

Taken together, these five different strategies for responding to the Fundamental Philosophical Problem of Christology show that it is not a watertight demonstration of the incoherence of the Chalcedonian understanding of the person of Christ. These strategies provide an illustration of the apologetic value of analytic theology since, at the very least, they challenge secular assumptions about the implausibility or impossibility of a central Christian doctrine.

New avenues in analytic Christology

As we have seen, much work in analytic theology has focused on explaining and defending the Chalcedonian two-natures doctrine of Christ. However, 'just as it is part of orthodox Christianity that Christ has two natures, one fully divine and one fully human, so it is part of orthodox Christianity both that Christ was really tempted and that Christ was unable to sin' (Stump, 2018, p. 242). One other area that has been subject to a good deal of analytic theological discussion, therefore, is Christ's relationship to sin and temptation.

The traditional teaching of the Church is that Christ is not merely sinless (that is, having never sinned), but also impeccable (that is, unable to sin). However: 'If he is impeccable, does that render him not omnipotent, owing to the fact that there is something – that is, sinning – which Christ cannot do?' (Pawl, 2020, p. 29). The typical response to this question is to deny that being able to sin is a power, so that Christ's 'inability to sin is not the lack of some power had by others' (Pawl, 2020, p. 30). Rather, as Mawson (2018) argues, the ability to sin is best understood as a *liability* rather than a power. Being omnipotent means that Christ's divine nature possesses all powers and zero liabilities. Grössl (2021) examines further complexities created by Christ's impeccability, and canvasses possible solutions.[4]

On the question of Christ and temptation, the Church's traditional view (following Hebrews 4.15) is to affirm that he could be tempted yet, since impeccable, never succumbed to it. There have, broadly speaking, been three accounts of how an impeccable person can be tempted. The first approach, adopted by Crisp (2007c) and others, is to draw a distinction between *internal* and *external* temptations. Christ could be externally tempted, by the devil or another human, but without feeling 'the internal, sinful impulses toward that temptation nor be able to succumb to them' (Pawl, 2020, p. 30). A second approach is called the epistemic approach. On this view, temptation does not require the ability to succumb to it, merely the *belief* that one has the ability to sin (see Pawl, 2019, pp. 139–43). This would require the incarnate Christ to have been ignorant of his divine status and abilities, so that he mistakenly thought he was susceptible to sin. Clearly this view is problematic, so a third 'psychological' view has gained currency. This view defines temptation in such a way that it is compatible with the inability to sin or the belief that one can sin: 'Temptation: An affectively charged cognitive event in which an object or activity that is associated with pleasure or relief of discomfort is in focal attention, yet the object of that desire conflicts with the person's values and goals' (Pawl, 2019, p. 144).

From this perspective, Christ could have experienced a desire for bread in the wilderness, or an aversion to crucifixion while in the garden of Gethsemane, yet regarded such desires as contrary to his goals, respectively, of fasting in the desert and of making atonement for sin. As Pawl (2020) notes, this viewpoint also makes a distinction between 'natural and innocent' passions and those that are not. Natural passions include fear, hunger and thirst, for example, which Christ would have experienced 'and are a blameless basis for temptation' (2020, p. 31). Vicious, evil passions, in contrast (such as for murder or sexual assault), would never have been experienced by Christ, so were not a source of temptation for him.

In addition to Christ's relationship to sin and temptation, other avenues in Christology have begun to be explored by analytic theologians and will doubtless receive further attention in the coming years. Oliver Crisp has been particularly prolific, for example, with his work addressing numerous wider topics in Christology (see Crisp, 2007b, 2009 and 2016). He has considered the election of Christ, for instance, as well as the possibility of multiple incarnations. More recently, he has evaluated the 'incarnation anyway' doctrine (the view in which Christ would have become incarnate even without the fall of humanity) and defended belief in the virginal conception of Christ (see Crisp, 2019a). Pawl (2019) also addresses several wider questions, seeking to reconcile conciliar Christology with the theses that: multiple incarnations are possible; Christ descended into Hell during his three days of death; Christ's human will was free; and that Christ, via his human intellect, knew all things past, present and future. Dumsday (2017), meanwhile, has considered how modern biology can inform our understanding of the Incarnation.

Alongside these explorations of the *person* of Christ, analytic theologians have also paid considerable attention to the atoning *work* of Christ. The following chapter therefore seeks to provide an overview of this topic.

Notes

1 Crisp (2007), for instance, lists passages including: John 1.14; Romans 1.3–4; Galatians 4.4–5; Philippians 2.5–8; Colossians 2.9; 1 Timothy 2.5 and 3.16; and Hebrews 2.14.

2 Crisp's argument here is consistent with the doctrine of *enhypostasia*, first developed by Leontius of Byzantium (AD 485–543). This doctrine states that 'Christ's individual human nature, that body–soul composite which was the man Jesus of Nazareth, did not have its own *hypostasis*, that is to say it did not subsist on its own but became hypostatic only in its union with the Logos. The *hypostasis* of the human nature is identical with the divine person. Thus neither of the individual natures is without a *hypostasis* nor does each possess a *hypostasis* peculiar to it, but they have one and the same *hypostasis* that belongs properly to the divine Logos, the Second Person of the Trinity' (Moreland and Craig, 2003, p. 609).

3 See the opening chapter of Davies (2021) for a summary of the differences between Classical Theism and (what he calls) 'Theistic Personalism'.

4 See also the recent collection of essays on impeccability and temptation edited by Grössl and von Stosch (2021).

Recommended further reading

Crisp, O. D., 2016, *Word Enfleshed: Exploring the Person and Work of Christ*, Grand Rapids, MI: Baker Academic.

Pawl, T., 2020, *The Incarnation*, Elements in the Philosophy of Religion, Cambridge: Cambridge University Press.

5

Atonement: The Work of Christ

Like the Trinity and the Incarnation, the doctrine of the Atonement occupies a central location within the Christian faith. Throughout its history, the Church has held the conviction that, whatever else it achieved, the work of Christ opened the possibility of reconciliation between sinful humanity and a holy God. Beyond this core conviction, however, there exists a plethora of different accounts of how exactly this reconciliation has been achieved by Christ. This diversity of views is in large part due to the absence of a creedal definition of the doctrine:

> In this respect there is a sharp contrast between the doctrine of the Atonement and other central doctrines such as the Incarnation and the Trinity. Under pressure from theological controversy, the early church felt itself obliged to formulate the fairly precise definitions of such doctrines that we find expressed by the familiar Nicene and Chalcedonian formulas. Such definitions have operated as a traditional constraint on theological theorizing. Nothing similar happened in the case of the doctrine of the Atonement, and so the history of theological reflection on it is richly pluralistic. It is a colorful tapestry of scriptural motifs and theological elaborations. (Quinn, 2009, p. 349)

Confronted by such an array of atonement theories, analytic theologians have taken a threefold task upon themselves. These tasks are by no means mutually exclusive, and include: (i) to clarify the concepts and ideas deployed within atonement theology; (ii) to offer a careful philosophical critique of historic atonement theories; and (iii) to offer their own constructive accounts of Christ's reconciling work. Attention to these three tasks is evident, for example, within recent book-length treatments of the Atonement by Stump (2018), Craig (2018, 2020) and Crisp (2022a) and Rutledge (2022). We turn first to conceptual analysis of the Atonement by analytic theologians.

Conceptual analysis of the Atonement

How then is the concept of atonement understood by analytic theologians working in this field? Eleonore Stump applies to divine–human relations the definition of 'atonement' found in the *Oxford English Dictionary*, namely, 'The action of setting at one, or the condition of being set at one, after discord or strife' (2018, p. 7). This idea of reuniting estranged parties is also central to the definition of the Atonement offered by Oliver Crisp, in which it is *'the act of reconciliation between God and fallen human beings brought about by Christ'* (2022a, p. 16, italics original). Implicit in this definition is the biblical teaching that human beings are alienated from God owing to their sin (e.g. Rom. 3.23) and have been reconciled to him by the work of Christ (e.g. 2 Cor. 5.18–19).

In his own writing on the Atonement, William Lane Craig has drawn a distinction between 'broad' and 'narrow' meanings of the word:

> The word 'atonement' is unique among theological terms, being a derivation, not from Greek or Latin, but from Middle English, namely, the phrase 'at onement,' designating a state of harmony. The closest New Testament (NT) word for atonement in this sense is *katallagē* or reconciliation, specifically reconciliation between God and man … But there is a narrower sense of 'atonement' that is expressed by the biblical words typically translated by this English word. In the Old Testament (OT), 'atonement' and its cognates translate words having the Hebrew root '*kpr*.' Best known of these expressions is doubtless *Yom Kippur*, the Day of Atonement. To atone in this sense takes as its object sin or impurity and has the sense 'to purify, to cleanse.' The Greek equivalent in the Septuagint (LXX) and NT is *hilaskesthai*. While the result of atonement in this narrow sense may be said to be atonement in the broad sense, nevertheless the biblical words translated as 'atonement' or 'to atone' need to be understood in the narrower sense if we are to understand the meaning of the texts. Theologically, the doctrine of the atonement concerns atonement primarily in the narrower, biblical sense of cleansing of sin and has traditionally been treated under the priestly work of Christ. (Craig, 2018, p. 3)

Craig's subsequent analysis of the Atonement uses the word in its narrower sense, focusing on how the work of Christ has 'cleansed' humanity of sin. He therefore differs in approach from Stump (2018) who, as noted above, uses the word 'atonement' in its broadest sense. The scope of her writing on the Atonement consequently examines a host of wider issues in soteriology and pneumatology.

Joshua Thurow recognizes the centrality of reconciliation to the idea of atonement but, like Craig, defines the concept more narrowly, articulating five principles of atonement that form a 'highly plausible' common foundation for a wide range of different atonement theories (2021, p. 244). These principles are:

PA1. Atonement aims at reconciliation.
PA2. Adequate atonement should address both past wrongs as well as future character and behaviour.
PA3. At least three kinds of acts contribute to atoning: A) communicating one's dissociation from the wrong action, B) improving morally, C) offering satisfaction, by which I mean acts aimed at either repairing the effects of one's wrong action or 'making up for' what one did.
PA4. The victim has the power to determine (perhaps within certain limits) whether the wrongdoer's atoning attempts constitute adequate atonement.
PA5. The fittingness and adequacy of the manner of performing atonement depends on context. (Thurow, 2021, p. 244)

Thurow adds that the three kinds of acts listed as A, B and C in PA3 'are not the only kinds of acts that can contribute to atonement', since 'submitting to punishment, for example, may also contribute to atonement' (2021, p. 245). Moreover, PA3 'does *not* imply that any of the acts of type A, B and C is required for full and proper atonement. Some cases of wrongdoing (e.g., certain minor or accidental faults), may be atoned for without either reparation or any acts of moral improvement beyond sincere apology' (Thurow, 2021, p. 243). More generally, PA5, 'the fittingness and adequacy of the manner of performing atonement', depends upon 'contextual factors such as the history of the relationship between the offender and victim, the nature of the offense' and so on (p. 245).

A similar understanding of atonement has been articulated by Richard Swinburne. He sees atonement as including four components, namely 'repentance, apology, reparation and penance, not all of which are required to remove … guilt arising from less serious wrongdoing' (2013b, p. 2). Repentance and apology are, respectively, the private and the public disowning of a sinful act. Swinburne understands reparation, meanwhile, to involve removing the harm committed by a wrongdoer. Sometimes the sinner can restore the status quo, but on other occasions he can only make things similar to how they were – so that the victim is equally happy with their new circumstances. Fourth, Swinburne defines an act of 'penance' as a costly 'token of my sorrow' that goes beyond mere compensation (p. 3). Finally, this process of atonement is complete 'when the wronged person ... undertakes to treat the wrongdoer, in so far as he can, as one who has not wronged him; and to do that is to forgive him' (p. 3).

Crisp (2022a) draws a distinction between the *doctrines*, *models* and *theories* of the Atonement offered by Christian theologians. For Crisp, a doctrine is a

> comprehensive account of a particular teaching about a given theological topic held by some community of Christians or some particular denomination. So, on this way of thinking, a doctrine of the atonement is an account of the atonement that has been taught by a particular group of Christians such as Baptists, Anglicans, Mennonites, Orthodox and so on. (2022a, p. 19)

Such doctrinal statements can be found in denominational confessions and catechisms. For instance, the Church of England's doctrine of the Atonement is expressed in article 31 of its *Articles of Religion*: 'The Offering of Christ once made is that perfect redemption, propitiation, and satisfaction, for all the sins of the whole world, both original and actual' (cited in Crisp, 2022a, p. 22).

As this quotation illustrates, however, such doctrinal statements tend to be fairly thin on detail. More information is contained in models of the Atonement, which

> ... thicken up the dogmatic minimalism of atonement doctrines ... so as to provide a fuller explanation of the nature of the atonement and, in particular the mechanism of atonement. On the other hand, models of the atonement do not necessarily attempt to provide a complete or comprehensive view of Christ's reconciling work. (Crisp, 2022a, p. 23)

So whereas a doctrine of the Atonement might be broad in scope but thin on detail, an Atonement model will be 'narrower' in focus but 'conceptually thicker' (Crisp, 2022a, p. 24). Crisp also adds that 'models are often the products of individual theologians, whose particular opinions and arguments are offered up as contributions to the furtherance of our understanding of the atonement' (p. 30).

Theories of the Atonement, meanwhile, are an 'explanation of what we should believe about what did in fact, obtain in the case of [Christ's] incarnation, life, death and resurrection' (Crisp, 2022a, p. 28). According to these definitions, Crisp suggests that

> ... most theologians engaged in the project of providing some doctrinal explanation of the work of Christ as an atonement are attempting to give a *model* of atonement that they find compelling. They are *not* actually engaged in providing a *theory* of atonement. Often the model in question is offered as one, but only one, among several possible models. (2022a, p. 29, italics added)

In practice, historical and contemporary models of the Atonement vary in a number of significant ways. For instance, they vary in their utilization of biblical material pertinent to the Atonement. While the consensus among most biblical scholars is that Scripture 'does not offer a single explanation of Christ's atoning work', it is replete with *metaphors* and *motifs* that can be drawn upon by theologians (Crisp, 2022a, p. 13). Biblical metaphors applied to Christ's atoning work include figurative portrayals of him as 'the lamb of God who takes away the sins of the world, the shepherd who dies for his sheep, the high priest who enters the holy of holies on our behalf, and so on' (p. 17). Motifs, meanwhile, are 'recurring themes or ideas' in Scripture that may or may not be metaphorical in nature. As Crisp notes, 'motifs like sacrifice, substitute, satisfaction, ransom, and so on are important features of particular accounts of the reconciling work of Christ' (p. 17). As a consequence, the manner in and degree to which different atonement models draw upon these metaphors and motifs have provided a basis for analytic theologians to categorize and critique them.

Another way in which atonement models differ is the extent to which Christ's whole life is significant. As Michael Rea writes, 'By all accounts, the death of Jesus on the cross was part of the atonement; but whether the atonement also includes (say) Jesus' obedient life, his suffering in Gethsemane, or other parts of his life is not so universally agreed upon' (Rea, 2009c, pp. 13–14). This question is one important illustration of how atonement models differ in their understanding of the *mechanism* of the Atonement, which Crisp defines as 'the means by which Christ brings about the reconciliation of fallen humanity with God' (2022a, p. 59).

It is also common to distinguish between those accounts of the Atonement that are *subjective* and those that are *objective*. Subjective accounts state that Christ's work 'atones by effecting some crucial change in us – it is a model for our life ... makes us aware of and inflamed with God's love', and changes 'our attitudes, purposes, goals, loves and beliefs' (Thurow, 2021, p. 240). Objective accounts, in contrast, state that Christ's work 'atones by effecting some other, more objective relationship to God, such as remitting guilt or paying a punishment' (p. 241).

However, as Thurow notes, most objective views of the Atonement also think that Christ's work does have a subjective element:

> There's good theological reason for this. In order to atone and bring about reconciliation the wrongdoer must acknowledge her wrong and at least aim at improving herself in the future. So, wrongdoers must contribute something to atonement. When dealing with their sins, people need to confess, repent, and have faith in Christ. Christ's death will at least indirectly bring about these states through grace. Thus, Christ's objective atoning work also brings about the subjective account of atonement. So, the dispute isn't between those who think that Christ's death atones purely subjectively and those who think it atones purely objectively. The dispute is between those who think it atones purely subjectively and those who think it atones both subjectively and objectively. (2021, pp. 241–2)

One area of debate among analytic theologians is the question of whether any act of atonement was essential to reconcile humanity and God, or whether God could simply have forgiven sinners. Swinburne is among those who argue that God could have chosen to 'simply forgive us in response to some minimum amount of repentance and apology' (2013b, p. 6). He claims notable theologians such as Gregory of Nazianzus, Aquinas, Bonaventure and Duns Scotus held this view too. However, Swinburne suggests that God chose to insist upon some form of reparation for sin to ensure that we take our wrongdoing 'seriously' (p. 6). Thurow agrees, and expands upon this insight by writing that:

> First, forgiving the mass of human sin while requiring no punishment or satisfaction does not seem consistent with taking sin seriously ... Second, surely God would want us to be aware of the enormity of human sin as part of repentance; he would want us to treat sin seriously and we couldn't treat it seriously without being aware of its enormity. One excellent way for humans to truly appreciate the enormity of their sin is to pay a cost for it – either by way of punishment or satisfaction. Third, humans who are ideally repentant would want to offer the best satisfaction they could, or perhaps even would want to suffer an appropriate punishment. Fourth, God's ultimate goal for humans is not just to forgive our sins, but to restore us to his image ... and to bring it about that individual humans and the human community function as they should. Simply forgiving us, even if we are genuinely repentant, won't accomplish this goal ... Humans wouldn't

see sin as bad as it actually is, and would be less motivated to actually change their ways. (Thurow, 2015, pp. 58–9)

Crisp (2022a) disagrees, however, arguing (with Anselm) that the divine nature – specifically divine justice – prohibits unconditional forgiveness without atonement. God's just character acts as a self-imposed constraint on his ability to forgive unconditionally, without any act of atonement. In contrast to some other analytic theologians, such as Cross (2009b) and Mihut (2023), Crisp holds that 'retribution is one aspect of divine distributive justice ... in which case not only is it true that God must punish sin; God is not free to not punish sin because it is in God's nature to be just, and a requirement of justice is that sin be punished' (2022a, p. 52). But since mercy and grace are also characteristic of God, he 'elects that the God-man perform an act of atonement of behalf of human sinners' (p. 52).

Crisp also considers the question of whether Christ's atoning work has intrinsic, objective value, or has its value subjectively assigned by God himself. *Acceptilation* views deny that Christ's atoning work has any intrinsic value, only the moral value that God stipulates or imputes to it. *Acceptation* views, meanwhile, state that Christ's atoning work does have some intrinsic moral value, 'but it does not have a moral value sufficient to atone' for the sin of fallen humanity unless God stipulates or imputes to it 'that value in addition to the intrinsic value such an act already possesses' (2022a, p. 42). In contrast Crisp defends a *proportional* view of the Atonement, which holds that Christ's saving work (whatever precise form it takes) does have an intrinsic, objective, moral value 'at least proportional to the sin for which it atones in order to be acceptable to God as atonement for that sin' (p. 46). This position (contra acceptilation) is based on the reasonable intuition, from a biblical perspective, at least, that human actions do have intrinsic moral value. Moreover, contra acceptation views, it would have been unjust for God to assign Christ's work a moral value greater than it actually possessed. Crisp concludes therefore, with Anselm, that 'the atonement of Christ is not just proportional in value to the demerit of human sin. It is necessarily an act of infinite value outweighing the disvalue of all human sin because of the intrinsic dignity, honor, and value of the person who performs it' (2022a, p. 51). In short, Christ's atoning work has the power to save humanity because, as an act of God incarnate, it possesses an infinite objective moral worth.

With these conceptual distinctions in place, analytic theologians feel able to categorize and critique existing models of the Atonement, as well as engage in their own constructive accounts of the doctrine. Following

Crisp (2022a), it is possible to assign most accounts of the Atonement to one of four broad categories. These include: *Moral exemplar* or *moral influence* models inspired by the work of medieval logician Peter Abelard; *Ransom* (or 'Christus Victor') models popularized in modern times by Gustaf Aulen, but with patristic precedents; *Satisfaction* models that follow in the footsteps of Anselm; and *Penal Substitutionary* accounts of the Atonement that gained prominence during the Reformation.

Moral exemplar and moral influence models

Moral exemplar or moral influence models of the Atonement look back to the work of the twelfth-century logician Peter Abelard. In the second book of his *Commentary on Paul's Epistle to the Romans*, Abelard wrote:

> Nevertheless it seems to us that in this we are justified in the blood of Christ and reconciled to God, that it was through this matchless grace shown to us that his Son received our nature, and in that nature, teaching us both by word and by example, persevered to the death and bound us to himself even more through love, so that when we have been kindled by so great a benefit of divine grace, true charity might fear to endure nothing for his sake. (Quoted in Craig, 2018, pp. 27–8)

Views of the Atonement in this genre have been also articulated by Faustinus Socinus, Immanuel Kant and Friedrich Schleiermacher in the centuries since Abelard. And among modern philosophers and theologians, advocates of a moral exemplar or moral influence account of the Atonement have included Hastings Rashdall (1858–1924) and John Hick (1922–2012). While it is commonplace within the Christian tradition to assert that the life of Christ is worthy of imitation (see Cockayne, 2017), or to incorporate his blameless conduct into a wider theory of the Atonement, moral exemplarist models are distinctive in solely ascribing atoning value to his exemplary life and death. It follows that these models are wholly subjective in content, since 'Christ's death achieved our reconciliation with God, not by satisfying divine justice or ransoming us from the devil, but by moving our hearts to contrition and love as we contemplate Christ's voluntarily embracing horrible suffering and death' (Craig, 2018, p. 27).

The least sophisticated forms of this approach, which Crisp has labelled as 'mere exemplarism', hold that 'Christ's work is *merely* an example that should elicit a particular response in individuals who encounter it' (2022a, p. 60). However, this minimalist position is problematic, since it is possible to conceive of many other human lives that have exhibited admirable qualities and inspired others to behave likewise, yet are not believed to have secured humanity's reconciliation with God. As Crisp writes:

> Although a moral example can be a powerful thing – think of modern examples like Saint Theresa of Calcutta, Martin Luther King Jr., or Dietrich Bonhoeffer – someone who is merely a moral example is not a person whose work is salvific ... [since] mere moral examples do not (and given our fallen state, cannot) bring about reconciliation with God. (2022a, pp. 60–1)

Moral examples may well motivate our own ethical improvement, but it is hard to see how they would elicit the spiritual renewal and reunion with God evoked by biblical metaphors such as being 'born again' (John 3.3). As Craig puts it:

> Taken in isolation, the moral influence theory might seem far too thin an account to do justice to the NT data concerning God's wrath, Christ's substitutionary death, justification, and so on. It seems to amount to little more than moral self-improvement inspired by Christ's example. (2018, p. 28)

More sophisticated exemplarist models exist, however, and are defined by Crisp as 'extended exemplarism' (2022a, p. 68). Like the mere exemplarist, the extended exemplarist regards Christ's work as a moral example to imitate. But, in addition, 'the extended exemplarist thinks that this very way of conceiving of the work of Christ provides her with a (thin) notion of reconciliation – that is, with an account of Christ's work as an atonement' (Crisp, 2022a, p. 68). In this extended account of moral exemplarism, one can envisage a scenario in which an individual encounters the work of Christ and

> ... comes to see something of God's grace and love, comes to understand that Christ has shown her divine grace, and comes to think that she is experiencing that love through the report of the atonement in the canonical Gospels that is applied directly and experientially to her through the secret working of the Holy Spirit ... It is a matter of [her] coming to understand Christ's moral example as a means by which she may be reconciled to God that yields the religious transformative experience that constitutes a thin understanding of atonement. (Crisp, 2022a, pp. 69–70)

One example of such 'extended exemplarist' thinking by an analytic theologian is found in Quinn (2009). He offers a 'constructive Abelardian contribution' to discussion of the Atonement, which shares Abelard's conviction 'that divine love, made manifest throughout the life of Christ but especially in his suffering and dying, has the power to transform human sinners, if they cooperate, in ways that fit them for everlasting life in intimate union with God' (Quinn, 2009, p. 360). Unlike Abelard, however, Quinn emphasizes that Christ's passion is more than mere exemplary display of God's love, but also a means through which his supernatural grace is operative in human hearts. Quinn argues that the transformative power of divine love far exceeds that of any inspiring human example of love:

> We should instead affirm that divine love also operates outside the natural order, within what theologians call the order of grace, to produce changes in us. On such a view, the love of God exhibited in the life of Christ is a good example to imitate, but not merely an example. Above and beyond its exemplary value, there is in it a surplus of mysterious causal efficacy that no merely human love possesses. And the operation of divine love in that supernatural mode is a causally necessary condition of there being implanted or kindled in us the kind of responsive love of God that, as Abelard supposes, enables us to do all things out of love and so to conquer the motives that would otherwise keep us enslaved to sin. (p. 361)

Following Johnson, I would argue that Eleonore Stump's recent account of the Atonement (2018) also has a 'moral influence component' (2021, p. 745). Stump articulates a subjective view of Christ's work, whereby it removes human feelings of guilt and shame rather than 'making up to God for the debt or offense of human beings … [or] to enable God's pardon or forgiveness' (2018, p. 342). Her view differs from Abelard's classic position, however:

> On the interpretation of the doctrine of the atonement often attributed to Abelard, Christ saves post-Fall human beings from their sin by modelling for them what a truly good human person is like. His life, passion, and death serve to teach human beings how they should live. On this Abelardian interpretation, Christ counts as nothing more than a teacher; and the purpose of his life, passion, and death are only to provide the basis for persuading a human person to new states of intellect. But, on the interpretation of the doctrine I am arguing for, the main problem for post-Fall human beings lies in the will, not

in the intellect ... The powerlessness, vulnerability, and suffering of Christ on the cross are arguably the most promising means for quieting a person's fear of God's love or for dissolving the willed loneliness in her brought about by guilt or shame in any of their varieties or by the brokenness stemming from the depredations of others ... A person's surrender to God's love in response to Christ's atonement is met immediately by the indwelling Holy Spirit, with all the infused virtues and the gifts and fruits of the Holy Spirit; but the process that is meant to culminate in full and complete union of mutual indwelling is slow. (Stump, 2018, pp. 343–4)

Stump and Quinn notwithstanding, even 'extended' exemplarist views have not found much support among analytic theologians. Both Rea (2009c) and Craig (2018) have noted, for instance, that Abelard's own writings on the Atonement are not confined to a moral influence account. Rather, 'there are various motifs in Abelard's overall theory of the Atonement, one of which, in fact, is penal substitutionary' (Rea, 2009c, p. 18). Moral example does indeed form part of Abelard's account of the Atonement, but even he recognized that other mechanisms were also in play. As Craig writes, 'the moral influence theory makes a valuable contribution to understanding how the benefits won by Christ's death come to be appropriated,' but is only 'one facet of a more complex, multifaceted' account of the Atonement (2018, p. 29).

More substantive objections to exemplarist views are offered by Crisp. He observes, for example, that even extended exemplarist accounts fail to clarify the mechanism of atonement. 'Somehow Christ's loving work generates an appropriate response by means of divine grace that illuminates and changes ... [but] it is still not all that clear *how* Christ's work is an atonement' (Crisp, 2022a, p. 73). A further concern is that moral exemplarist views fail to include 'three important biblical-theological motifs ... These are that Christ's work is *vicarious*, *representational*, and *expiatory*' (p. 74, emphasis original). In other words, moral influence models of the Atonement appear to lack a satisfactory account of how Christ works on behalf of sinful humanity as our representative (e.g. Rom. 5.12–19 and Gal. 3.10–13) and sin-removing Saviour (e.g. Rom. 3.25 and 2 Cor. 5.21). For these and other reasons, analytic theologians largely dismiss moral exemplarism as 'an inadequate account of Christ's work' (Crisp, 2022a, p. 75).

Christus Victor accounts of Christ's work

The *Christus Victor* motif for the redeeming work of Christ was popularized in modern times by Gustaf Aulen (1931), but he argued that it was in fact the 'classic' view of the Atonement held by the Church from the patristic era until medieval times. According to this perspective, Christ's life, death and resurrection constituted a triumphant victory over the evil powers of this world that had hitherto kept humanity in slavery and in suffering. This victory motif finds biblical expression in passages such as Colossians 2.15 ('He disarmed the rulers and authorities and made a public example of them, triumphing over them'). As Craig writes:

> According to this viewpoint, the sacrifice of Christ's life served to deliver mankind from bondage to Satan and from the corruption and death that are the consequences of sin. The Fathers sometimes interpreted Jesus's ransom saying very literally to mean that Christ's life was a payment in exchange for which human beings were set free from bondage. Such an interpretation naturally raised the question as to whom the ransom was paid. The obvious answer was the devil, since it was he who held men in bondage (2 Tim 2.26; 1 Jn 5.19). God agreed to give His Son over to Satan's power in exchange for the human beings he held captive. (Craig, 2018, pp. 22–3)

As this summary illustrates, the idea of Christ paying a ransom payment (cf. Mark 10.45) was often utilized by patristic advocates of the *Christus Victor* motif. Crisp defines this ransom account as the claim that

> Christ's work of redemption is fundamentally about him buying back human beings from the powers of sin, death and the devil. His work is a ransom price that is paid to these powers in order that some number of fallen humanity may be redeemed from destruction and brought to salvation. (2022a, p. 91)

However, this claim is not above criticism from Crisp and other analytic theologians. First, as Thurow observes, the ransom model 'imports the problematic assumption that Satan has some rights against God' (2021, p. 243). Crisp agrees, asking:

> What sound theological reason is there for thinking that human beings sold themselves into slavery to the devil upon commission of original sin, so that they must be bought back from him at such a terrible price? This, it seems to me, is pure sophistry. God does not transact with the devil for human salvation. (2022a, pp. 91–2)

It is equally hard, if not more so, to imagine how Christ could pay a ransom to sin and death, as these are a moral state and a physical state respectively, rather than personal agents (p. 91). Crisp consequently concludes that:

> [R]ansom is no more than an atonement motif. It provides no mechanism for atonement; its language is metaphorical ... However, it may be regarded as an auxiliary claim about the outcome of atonement. The upshot of Christ's work is indeed the release of human beings subject to sin and death. When viewed in these terms his work is a ransom price of sorts: it is the price requisite to bring about human reconciliation, paid by Christ. But it is not a ransom in the sense that it really is a work equivalent in value to the price fixed for the ransom of some number of fallen humanity from another power, whether sin, death, the devil or God. (pp. 92–3)

If the idea of Christ's death as a ransom is nothing more than a motif, this raises a further question about the significance (if any) of Christ's death in his victory over the powers of evil. As Thurow writes:

> These powers are manifested in sickness, demon-possession, personal sin, death, and corrupt social structures. Jesus' healings, exorcisms, teaching and offering of forgiveness, resurrections, and preaching against the rulers all contributed to rescuing humans. But, it is quite unclear what Jesus's death contributes. Perhaps his submission to crucifixion and resurrection together show that not even death will conquer him or his followers. That's quite an impressive manifestation of victory, but it doesn't contribute anything distinctive. He'd already resurrected Lazarus. (Thurow, 2021, p. 242)

These concerns expressed by analytic theologians about *Christus Victor* are not new. As Craig notes, Anselm complained in the twelfth century that this understanding of the Atonement is

> ... inadequate on its own to explain why God would take the extraordinary step of sending His Son to suffer and die in order to redeem mankind. In contrast to *Christus Victor* theorists, Anselm argues that the salvation of mankind is about much more than defeating Satan. It is about making satisfaction to God for man's sins. (Craig, 2018, p. 24)

Satisfaction theories in the tradition of Anselm have received a warmer reception among analytic theologians than either the moral influence or *Christus Victor* accounts of the Atonement, and so to these we now turn.

Satisfaction models

Anselm's satisfaction model of the Atonement appeared in his treatise *Cur Deus Homo* ('Why God became Man'), which was the first truly systematic account of the Atonement in the history of the Church. At the heart of Anselm's understanding of the Atonement is the conviction that human sin has dishonoured our Creator and necessitates either punishment or *satisfaction*. An act of satisfaction (which can also be called *compensation* or *reparation*) is a supererogatory act of meritorious worth offered to God that is sufficient to outweigh the demerit of sin. Anselm's portrayal of God in this account is sometimes caricatured as that of feudal monarch, whose honour is too easily offended and whose character is too proud to forgive. However:

> A careful reading of Anselm reveals that his fundamental concern is with God's justice and its moral demands. Sin is materially bringing dishonor to God, but the reason God cannot just overlook the offense is that it would be unjust to do so and thus would contradict God's very nature ... So, given the moral character of dishonoring God, Anselm asks 'whether it were proper for God to put away sins by compassion alone, without any payment of the honor taken from him?' Anselm responds negatively: 'To remit sin in this manner is nothing else than not to punish; and since it is not right [recte] to cancel sin without compensation or punishment; if it be not punished, then it is passed by undischarged' ... The concern here is not merely with propriety but with its being wrong to leave sin unpunished. The concern is justice. (Craig, 2018, p. 25)

Theologically, one might still object to the idea of God being dishonoured on the grounds that he is impassible and immutable, so not liable to change of emotional state. Anselm shares these convictions of Classical Theism, however, writing that 'God himself is his own incorruptible and immutable honor' (quoted in Crisp, 2022a, p. 100). Rather, Anselm understands sin as 'a derogation *in what the human agent wills*. It is a dishonour to God in the sense that it fails to measure up to the sort of act of obedience that we owe to God' (Crisp, 2022a, p. 100, emphasis original). Humans are too mired in sin and guilt to offer their own satisfaction of sufficient worth, believes Anselm. But Christ, as the supremely virtuous God-Man, can do so on our behalf.

> Just as one might compensate someone who has had something precious stolen by a close relative with some appropriate act of reparation, so in the satisfaction account of the atonement Christ provides an act of compensation to God the Father in place of the punishment due for human sin and dereliction. (Crisp, 2022a, p. 97)

This act of compensation by Christ is the gift of his own life. As Craig explains:

> Since Christ was sinless, he was under no obligation to die. By voluntarily laying down his life, he gives to God a gift of infinite value that he did not owe ... How, then, does the gift of Christ's life win our salvation? Anselm says that divine justice requires God the Father to reward the Son for the gift of his life. But how can a reward be bestowed on someone who needs nothing and owes nothing? The Son therefore gives the reward to those for whose salvation he became incarnate. He remits the debt incurred by their sins and bestows on them the beatitude they had forfeited. (Craig, 2018, p. 26)

Crisp writes that Anselm's 'central claim about the nature of the atonement as satisfaction is, it seems to me, a compelling theological insight that should be taken very seriously by contemporary theologians' (2022a, p. 96). In true analytic style, he then summarizes an 'Anselmian' satisfaction model of the Atonement in the form of a sequential argument:

1. God is essentially just.
2. Divine distributive justice is retributive in nature.
3. Sin is heinous; it derogates from God's honor.
4. The penalty for sin must be sufficient requital for human sin.
5. The penalty for sin may be met in one of two ways: either the punishment of sin or some other supererogatory act of sufficient value that it may be accepted as satisfaction for human sin.
6. The atonement is hypothetically necessary for satisfaction. God cannot forgive sin independent of satisfaction.
7. The atonement 'restores' divine honor; it is sufficient requital for human sin.
8. The benefits of atonement are appropriated by means of the sacramental life of the church. (Crisp, 2022a, p. 97)

Since it first appeared in his work *Responsibility and Atonement* (1989), Richard Swinburne has articulated and defended his own satisfaction model of the Atonement. According to Swinburne, every human sinner owes atonement to God for the sins which he or she has committed. But humanity's guilt before God is so great, and our proneness to sin so strong and pervasive, that we cannot on our own make adequate atonement. While we might manage to repent and apologize, Swinburne believes adequate reparation and penance are beyond our capacity: 'We need help' from outside (2013b, p. 6). Swinburne consequently sees Christ's life and death as a God-given act of reparation that repentant sinners can 'plead' for their personal atonement. Swinburne's logic is that 'since what needs atonement to God is human sin, men living second-rate lives when they have been given such great opportunities by their creator, appropriate reparation and penance would be made by a perfect human life, given away through being lived perfectly' (1989, p. 152). By sending Christ into the world, God provided such a life, 'a perfect life of service to God and humans in difficult circumstances, leading to its being taken from him in crucifixion' (Swinburne, 2013b, p. 8). Christ's life and death can then be pleaded by repentant people in atonement for their sins:

> 'Our life is a failure' we may now say. 'We have made a mess of the life which you gave us, we have made no reparation of our own for our sins, nor have we helped others to make atonement for their sins. But we have been given a perfect life, not owed to you, O God. We offer you this life instead of the life we should have led. Take its perfection instead of our imperfection. We are serious enough about our sins to repent and apologise and to offer you back an offering of this value as our reparation and penance.' (Swinburne, 1989, pp. 154–5)

Swinburne's model of the Atonement has attracted a wide range of responses, from varying perspectives.[1] One important deficiency seen in Swinburne's model is that it does not seem to provide adequate justification for Christ's death upon the cross. Indeed, Swinburne himself acknowledges that Christ's reparation 'is not so much his death, as his actions which led to his death' (2013b, p. 8). As Steven Porter has argued:

> Surely all the good acts of Christ's life as well as the suffering and humility he endured in the incarnation constitute a substantive gift to offer as reparation and penance. Since the goods of reparation and penance can be achieved without Christ's death, it would appear that his voluntary death was either foolish or suicidal. (2009, p. 319)

In response to this concern, Joshua Thurow has proposed a new form of satisfaction model that explains why Christ's death was an essential component of his reparative act. Thurow argues that Christ's death should be viewed through the lens of the Jewish sacrificial system, which provided the theological and cultural context in which he lived and died. In this context, the shedding of blood by sacrificial offerings 'was used as a means of communicating that sin had been wiped away' (Thurow, 2021, p. 253). Jesus' crucifixion thereby enabled

> ... the blood of his pure sacrifice to symbolically represent life covering and washing away death due to sin. Indeed, given the Jewish backdrop, it is hard to see how God could have communicated acceptance of an atoning act for all human sin that didn't involve the blood of a pure sacrifice. (pp. 253–4)

With this insight in hand, Thurow outlines the central ingredients of Jesus' atoning act (JA):

(JAi)   his life, led in preparation for his death, was a substantial reparation for human sin.
(JAii) his moral perfection and holiness richly represents how humanity should have been, thus enabling humanity to richly confess and repent to God by offering a representation of what they should have been, and
(JAiii) the symbolic content of the blood shed at Jesus' death enables God to communicate to humans that he accepts Jesus' death as an act of atonement. (Thurow, 2021, p. 253)

Despite their popularity among many analytic theologians, satisfaction models of the Atonement are not uniformly endorsed. Stump (2018), for example, challenges Anselm's assumption that God cannot simply forgive sin. In her view, divine love necessitates a willingness to forgive without penalty or payment of any kind. As described above, however, Anselm holds the alternative view that divine justice necessitates either punishment or satisfaction for sin. Theologically, Anselm (and other advocates of satisfaction models) are within their rights to believe that 'God's nature is so constituted that it is impossible for God to ignore or forgive sin without failing to be true to Godself in some fundamental sense' (Crisp, 2022a, p. 112). God's love, from an Anselmian perspective, is seen in his willingness to allow his Son to offer his life as satisfaction for our sin.

Cross, meanwhile, has rejected satisfaction theories of the Atonement (specifically those of Anselm and Swinburne) because of the retributive view of divine justice they assume and, more significantly, because he doesn't believe that sins against God require reparation. On the assumption that the gifts God gives to humans 'come at no expense to Himself' (and the implicit assumption that God is impassible?), Cross argues that 'human sinfulness causes God no harm other than a loss of service' (2009b, p. 335). If this intuition is correct, it follows that humans only owe God repentance and apology for their failure to serve him as they ought, not an act of reparation. Reparation is only due to other humans who are harmed or injured by our sinful acts. 'So the gist of all this is that I can deal with the Godward aspect of my sinfulness by apology and … thus do not need to plead Christ's life and death as reparation' (p. 340).

Instead, Cross articulates a 'merit' view of the Atonement, which is both similar to the satisfaction account and endorsed by Anselm himself towards the end of *Cur Deus Homo*, where he writes, 'It is necessary that the Father should compensate the Son … On whom is it more appropriate for [Christ] to bestow the reward and recompense for his death than those for whose salvation … he has made himself man?' (quoted in Cross, 2009, p. 342). According to this model, Christ's sinless life and death earn him merit in God's sight that warrants a reward. The reward Christ asks for is a promise from his Father to forgive all who repent and apologize for their sin. This creates a moral obligation for God the Father to forgive sinners, an obligation he was not previously under. Cross writes:

> On this scheme, Christ's death is a supererogatorily good act that merits a reward from God. The reward is whatever Christ asks for. Christ asks that God forgive the sins of those who repent and apologize to God. God is then obliged to do so. So the redemptive result of Christ's sacrifice is God's being obliged to forgive those who call upon him in penitence and sorrow. (2009, p. 342)

Cross acknowledges that this merit theory 'appears decidedly lacking in scriptural warrant', although he believes it is not inconsistent with biblical references to Christ's death as a precious sacrifice and Christ's promises that he will secure the forgiveness of sins. On the subject of biblical warrant, Craig (2018) and other advocates of penal substitution argue that divine justice and human salvation were secured by Christ's bearing the *punishment* for human sin on the cross, rather than by his offering sufficient *satisfaction* or *meritorious act* to God. This atonement mechanism, they believe, is more consistent with biblical passages that seem to speak of Christ's death in penal substitutionary terms – 'particularly Isaiah 53 and its NT employment' in passages such as 1 Peter 2.22–25 and Hebrew 9.28 (p. 41). And so to this model we now turn.

Penal substitution

Penal substitutionary models of the Atonement rose to prominence during the Reformation, including within the work of Martin Luther and John Calvin. Within contemporary analytic theology the most sustained defence of penal substitution has been made by William Lane Craig (see Craig 2018 and 2020). He defines the core claim of this model of the Atonement as the view that 'God inflicted upon Christ the suffering that we deserved as the punishment for our sins, as a result of which we no longer deserve punishment' (2018, p. 41). It is important to note that penal substitutionary theorists differ on whether God literally punished Christ for human sins, or whether he simply 'afflicted Christ with the suffering which, had it been inflicted upon us, would have been our just desert and, hence, punishment' (p. 41). The former view requires that God somehow 'imputed' human sins to Christ, even though he himself had never sinned. The latter view maintains that Christ bore the *penalty* due for our sins without, strictly speaking, being *punished*.

An underlying assumption behind all penal substitutionary theories is that divine justice is retributive in nature. Retributive theories of justice are those which argue that punishment is justified because the guilty deserve to be punished. A *prima facie* biblical case in favour of retributive divine justice can be made by appeal to texts such as Romans 1.32 and Hebrews 10.29, which suggest that the wicked deserve punishment. Other passages such as Romans 11.9 and 12.19 refer to divine retribution for sins, 'so that God's justice must be in some significant measure retributive' (Craig, 2018, p. 52). Within analytic philosophy, Steven Porter has defended a belief in retributive divine justice, specifically the view that this can (and should) involve punishment in the case of serious wrongdoing – including sin against God. He argues that:

> Due to the fact that [intentional wrongdoers] have deliberately misused certain rights and/or privileges, they deserve to have those rights and/or privileges withdrawn. Retributive punishment, then, is the forcible withdrawal of certain rights and/or privileges from a wrongdoer in response to the intentional misuse of those rights and/or privileges by the wrongdoer ... Assuming that earthly human life is a good and

gracious gift of God and that the opportunity for loving relationship with himself is the highest good bar none, then to [sin] is a clear misuse of the rights and privileges we have been given by God. Granting the above argumentation, it is permissible for God to forcibly withdraw the rights and privileges of human life on earth and the opportunity for relationship with himself ... To put the matter in theological terms, we deserve the divine punishment of physical and spiritual death. (Porter, 2009, pp. 321–3)

But what exactly *is* punishment, and can the sin and guilt that deserve punishment ever be transferred to another? Both of these questions lie behind two common objections to penal substitution among analytic theologians. To be more precise, it is alleged that penal substitution is conceptually incoherent because an innocent person (that is, Christ) can neither be punished nor have another person's liability for punishment transferred or 'imputed' to them (e.g. Murphy, 2009).

The first of these concerns can be laid out in deductive logical form:

1. If Christ was sinless, God could not have condemned Christ.
2. If God could not have condemned Christ, God could not have punished Christ.
3. If God could not have punished Christ, penal substitution is false. Thus it follows from the sinlessness of Christ that penal substitution is false. (Craig, 2018, p. 43)

Premise 2 of this argument is based upon an *expressivist* theory of punishment, popularized by Joel Feinberg, which maintains that harsh treatment imposed upon an individual must express condemnation or censure of wrongful behaviour. If this expressivist theory is correct, God could not have condemned or censured Christ, since he committed no wrongdoing. In response, an advocate of penal substitution has various lines of defence. One response is to deny premise 1 and argue that human sins were somehow imputed to Christ, making him a wrongdoer in his Father's sight and thereby worthy of condemnation and censure. This idea of imputation has ostensible biblical support in passages such as 2 Corinthians 5.21 and 1 Peter 2.24–25. An alternative avenue is to accept premise 2 but deny that God punished Christ. Rather, he merely imposed a penalty upon him without condemnation or censure. As Craig (2018) notes, Feinberg himself draws a distinction between penalties for offences (for example, parking tickets) and punishments, with only the latter expressing condemnation. Another line of defence open to the advocate of penal substitution is to question the expressivist theory of punishment and thereby deny premise 2 of the argument above. For example, Craig cites legal precedents in which punishment is inflicted without being an expression of censure, such as for 'crimes of strict liability'. Such cases 'are far from unusual, there being many thousands of statutory offenses involving elements of strict liability, including crimes like possession of narcotics or firearms and the selling of mislabelled foods or of prescription drugs without a prescription' (Craig, 2018, p. 45).

The second conceptual worry about penal substitution, as described above, is whether sin or guilt can ever be transferred from an individual to Christ. Murphy expresses this concern:

> While we might have some experience of one person's sins really belonging to another (e.g., in cases in which parents raise children to be vicious), we have no such experience of *transfer* of moral responsibility for actions ... With respect to [guilt], again, we have no experience of guilt as such, cut off from its sources; one is always guilty for something done or undone, or some state of affairs realized or unrealized. We can use the words 'the guilt itself is transferred,' but again this will shed no light. (2009, p. 259, italics original)

One response to this argument is to concede the impossibility of transferring culpability and liability from one person to another in normal human affairs, but to affirm that God can (and has) undertaken such a transaction as part of the unique redemptive work of Christ. As Craig writes, 'The proponent of penal substitution might plausibly respond that our want of such experience is hardly surprising, since imputation of sins or guilt is a uniquely divine prerogative. Arguably, God and only God as supreme Lawgiver, Judge and Ruler is in a position to impute the sins and guilt of one person to another' (2018, p. 47).

Craig proceeds to argue, however, that there are precedents within human legal systems for the imputation of sin and guilt to someone other than (or as well as) the wrongdoer. For example, so-called 'legal fictions' involve 'something that the court consciously knows to be false but treats as if it were true for the sake of a particular action' (2018, p. 17). Such fictions are in widespread use and have a long pedigree. Craig cites, for example, the case of *Mostyn v. Fabrigas* in 1774 when a London court adopted the legal fiction that the Mediterranean island of Menorca was part of London (and so within its jurisdiction), in order to secure justice for a man (Mr Fabrigas) who had been subject to false imprisonment on the island. Analogously, it can be argued that, for the salvation of sinful humanity, God adopted the legal fiction that Christ had committed our sins (p. 47). A further legal precedent identified by Craig is that of 'vicarious liability', in which a wrongdoer remains guilty but their guilt is 'replicated' and imputed to another individual or corporate entity as well as themselves. For instance:

> An employer may be held liable for acts done by his employee in his role as employee, even though the employer did not do these acts himself ... It needs to be emphasized that the employer is not, in such cases, being held liable for other acts, such as complicity or negligence in failing to supervise the employee. Indeed, he may be utterly blameless in the matter. Rather, the liability incurred by his employee for certain acts is imputed to him in virtue of his relationship with the employee, even though he did not himself do the acts in question. The liability is not thereby transferred from the employee to the employer; rather, the liability of the employee is replicated in the employer ... Both the employer and the employee may be found guilty for crimes that only the employee committed. (Craig, 2018, p. 50)

This is a valid analogy for the Atonement, claims Craig: 'For the defender of the doctrine of imputation does not hold that when my guilt is imputed to Christ, it is thereby removed from me. Guilt is merely replicated in Christ' (2018, p. 49).

Unpersuaded by such arguments, Murphy (2009) has advocated a subtly different atonement model, called 'vicarious punishment', which he believes avoids the conceptual difficulties of penal substitution. In this account of the Atonement, sin and guilt remain ascribed to the human wrongdoer. But the punishment upon the wrongdoer is not their own physical suffering, but to witness hard treatment visited upon someone with whom they are in a special relationship. Consequently, the punishment experienced by the wrongdoer is psychological rather than physical in nature. Applied to the work of Christ, this model states that:

> We human beings have sinned, have violated the divine law, in egregious ways. We thus merit punishment; and until this ill-desert is requited, there is an obstacle to proper union with God. In order to exact retribution and requite this ill-desert, God chose to punish us vicariously. Because Christ accepted this scheme freely, and with awareness that he would indeed be called upon to undergo the suffering constitutive of the punishment, it does Jesus neither injustice nor cruelty that he was to suffer in the carrying out the punishment on sinful humanity. So, on this view, the way that each of us is punished for our transgressions of divine law is that *his or her Lord is killed.*

Each of us, for his or her sins, is subjected to the hard treatment of having his or her Lord made to suffer and die. What makes this hard treatment imposed on us sinners is that the relationship of *being Lord of* is a special relationship that makes the misfortunes of the Lord constitutive of bad for the subject. This is very hard treatment indeed. (Murphy, 2009, p. 265)

Conceptual difficulties aside, another frequent concern about penal substitutionary models is the apparent injustice of God punishing an innocent party. Stated deductively, Craig presents this argument as follows:

1. God is perfectly just.
2. If God is perfectly just, He cannot punish an innocent person.
3. Therefore, God cannot punish an innocent person.
4. Christ was an innocent person.
5. Therefore, God cannot punish Christ.
6. If God cannot punish Christ, penal substitution is false.
   (Craig, 2018, p. 52)

As Craig notes, one way in which the soundness of this argument can be challenged is to deny premise 6, specifically, to deny the claim that God *punished* Christ. As we saw above, it is possible for an advocate of penal substitution to hold that Christ merely suffers the 'penal consequences' of human sin, rather than punishment for them. As Crisp observes, this strategy ameliorates the apparent injustice of penal substitution, since it 'certainly seems less problematic ... than to claim that he suffers the punishment of human sin – given that he himself is without sin and, therefore, (plausibly) an inappropriate target for punishment' (2022a, p. 132). As both Lewis (2009) and Strabbing (2016) have pointed out, there are examples in ordinary human life when one person consents to pay a penalty on behalf of another – such as a parking fine, for example. An alternative strategy is to assert that liability for human sin can be vicariously imputed to Christ without injustice, because he has freely consented to this transfer taking place. As Craig asks:

When would the imposition of vicarious liability be even prima facie unjust? Arguably, it could be only in cases in which it is nonvoluntary. If an employer, out of personal concern for his employee, wishes to act mercifully by voluntarily being held vicariously liable for his employee's wrongdoing, how is that unjust or immoral? In the same way, if Christ voluntarily invites our sins to be imputed to him for the sake of our salvation, what injustice is there in this? Who is to gainsay him? (Craig, 2018, p. 58)

A further argument in favour of the uniqueness (and moral permissibility) of Christ being punished in place of sinners rests on an alleged divine legal prerogative and the doctrine of the Trinity. God has the right, so it is argued, to decide to punish a particular innocent party when that person is himself, namely Christ, the second person of the Trinity.

> As Grotius observed, even if God has established a system of justice among human beings that forbids the punishment of the innocent (and, hence, substitutionary punishment), He Himself is not so forbidden ... [If] He wills to take on human nature in the form of Jesus of Nazareth and give His own life as a sacrificial offering for sin, who is to forbid Him? He is free to do so as long as it is consistent with His nature. And what could be more consistent with our God's gracious nature than that He should condescend to take on our frail and fallen humanity and give His life to satisfy the demands of His own justice? (Craig, 2018, p. 54)

Moreover, this extraordinary exception to the normal demands of justice may be justified when it serves a greater good, that is, the redemption of humanity. As Craig argues, a penal substitution advocate could 'claim that God, by waiving the prima facie demands of negative retributive justice and punishing Christ for our sins, has mercifully saved the world ... and was therefore acting compatibly with moral goodness' (2018, p. 56).

Joshua Thurow is sensitive to the apparent injustice of penal substitution, and has offered a revised account of the Atonement which is *communal* in nature. According to this communal substitution account, Christ is a member of humanity and therefore justly qualified to be an atoning representative of fallen humankind. Thurow argues that it is 'entirely morally permissible for a member of a community to suffer punishment or offer satisfaction on behalf of the community; this is precisely what Jesus does, according to the Communal Substitution Theory' (2015, pp. 53–4). Although Christ 'is innocent of sin, he is nevertheless appropriately causally connected to the human community's sinfulness. Furthermore, as a human, Jesus fulfils the requirement that at least one member of the guilty community do something to atone for their sin' (p. 55). According to Thurow's model, individuals' sins can also be forgiven through Christ's atoning work: 'This is because, at a general level, individual and communal human duties are identical. Insofar as an individual human violates the two greatest commandments, the community of which he is a member also violates the two greatest commandments' (pp. 56).

New approaches to the Atonement

Thurow's model is just one of several new accounts of the Atonement that have been offered by analytic theologians in recent years, seeking to overcome perceived deficiencies within existing models. Oliver Crisp, for instance, has recently offered an account of the Atonement that attempts to steer 'a middle way' between penal substitution and satisfaction models. In Crisp's view, the mechanism of the Atonement is best expressed as 'a vicarious, reparative, and penitential act of soteriological representation, whereby a part (Christ) may stand in for the whole (fallen humanity) and act on behalf of the whole' (2022a, p. 189). Christ's work is *vicarious* in the sense that it is an act performed for the benefit of others, *reparative* in that it makes amends (or compensates) for some wrong done by one party to another, and *representative* in that one individual acts or speaks on behalf of another individual or group. Crisp is careful to distinguish representation from substitution. Representation involves someone belonging to or embodying a wider group, whereas substitution involves someone replacing another person or group. In Crisp's view, 'Christ as the God-man stands in for the rest of humanity, representing and thereby providing salvation for humanity' (2022a, p. 192). But to save us, Christ must be more than a mere human, 'he must also be a human being without sin in order to represent humanity soteriologically. And he must be divine in order for [his work] to have the right kind of value requisite for the atonement' (p. 199). Christ's incarnation, life, death and resurrection are to be understood as a vicarious penitence, constituting 'one complex performative act by means of which he offers an apology on behalf of fallen humanity' (Crisp, 2022a, p. 199).

> In sum, the atonement is a vicarious, reparative, and penitential act of soteriological representation. Like the literary trope of synecdoche, Christ stands in for the whole of humanity in his act of reconciliation. But he is not a substitute for humanity, and he does not bear the punishment or guilt for human sin. Thus, penal substitution is excluded. His act does satisfy the standard of God's moral law. He does pay the penalty for human sin that includes death and alienation

from God on the cross. But the payment of this penalty is an aspect of his penitential act on behalf of fallen humanity. Moreover, because he is the God-Man, his vicarious action has the value sufficient to atone for the sin of all humanity. (p. 202)

Bayne and Restall (2009) and Hill (2018), meanwhile, have outlined a 'participatory model of the Atonement' (PMA) inspired by the apostle Paul's idea of 'participation' in or 'union' with Christ. This metaphor, found in passages such as Romans 6.3–8, expresses the new identity that Christians possess, by faith, as they become part of the new humanity inaugurated by the Risen Christ. Hill has outlined the core components of the PMA as follows:

(1) Sin is an ontological reality that binds human beings, corrupting their nature, destroying their relationships, and leading them to disobey God. This results in each person suffering from a sinful identity: they are not simply people affected by sin, they are sinners.
(2) The only way for sinners to escape sin and cease being sinners is to die and lose this old, sinful identity.
(3) Through participation in Christ via faith and the sacraments, human beings can share his death and 'die' to their old identities.
(4) They can also share his resurrection and gain new identities.
(5) As a result, human beings can be remade with new identities, free from the power of sin and the guilt that it brings. (Hill, 2018, p. 176)

Hill acknowledges that this model requires further development and, in particular, has sought to clarify the idea of participation by using metaphysical ideas found in the work of Jonathan Edwards. This leads him to conclude that participation 'might involve becoming similar to Christ through the action of the Holy Spirit, to such a degree that a person might be called identical (in some sense) with Christ' (2018, p. 175).

Jonathan Rutledge, finally, has recently offered an account of the Atonement that takes as its 'primary concept of analysis the most prominent metaphor scripture applies to the death, burial, resurrection, and ascension of Christ: namely, his death as a *sacrifice*' (2022, p. 3). He then proceeds to outline a model of the Atonement analogous to three pivotal sacrifices in the Old Testament, namely:

... a new Passover offered on the cross through which a new covenantal relationship between God and humanity is inaugurated, a *yom kippur* sacrifice offered on the heavenly altar as depicted in the letter to the Hebrews and by which that newly inaugurated covenant is maintained, and a *yom kippur* scapegoat ritual that poignantly reaffirms the reality of divine forgiveness for sin.

Rutledge is very sympathetic to Thurow's communal understanding of the Atonement, asserting that 'as fully human, Jesus is a member of humanity, and in virtue of his perfect life accrues a rightful representative status within humanity' (p. 152). This enables Christ to bear humanity's punishment for sin 'as our representative', such that 'when Christ is punished, humanity is punished as well' (p. 152). In Rutledge's account, Christ's death is understood as 'the first part of a sacrificial, ritual process that culminated with the resurrected Christ ascending to the heavenly temple ... and offering his perfectly lived human life as a sacrifice for humanity' (p. 187). The Passover and scapegoat dimensions of Christ's sacrificial work, meanwhile, communicate to humanity the forgiveness now available from God, as well as the new covenant that has been established by his Atonement.

As this chapter has sought to illustrate, much conceptual analysis and constructive model-building work on the Atonement has been undertaken by analytic theologians, with clear scope for more. But we now move to review the newest avenues of enquiry for analytic theology as a discipline – its work on the life and worship of the Church, and on the spirituality and sanctification of individual Christians. To this so-called ecclesiological and liturgical 'turn' in analytic theology we do indeed now turn.

Notes

1 For instance, McNaughton (1992) denies the need for any Swinburnian reparation for sin and argues that the moral exemplar approach is a morally and logically superior account of Christ's atoning work. Aspenson (1996) has criticized Swinburne for failing to explain the 'mechanism' by which Christ's perfect life can be 'transferred' to someone else in reparation for their sin. Reichenbach (1999), meanwhile, has offered an 'Inclusivist' reinterpretation of Swinburne's theory, which denies the need for a sinner to consciously 'plead' Christ's act of reparation in order to benefit from it.

Recommended further reading

Craig, W. L., 2018, *The Atonement*, Elements in the Philosophy of Religion, Cambridge: Cambridge University Press.

Crisp, O. D., 2022, *Participation and Atonement: An Analytic and Constructive Account*, Grand Rapids, MI: Baker Academic.

Stump, E., 2018, *Atonement*, Oxford Studies in Analytic Theology, Oxford: Oxford University Press.

PART THREE

Analytic Theology and the Life of the Church

6

Ecclesiology, Liturgy and the Sacraments

Analytic theology need not be conceived of as an abstract theological discipline, with little practical relevance. In recent years the scope of analytic theology has broadened, with the tools of analytic philosophy applied to areas of Christian praxis as well as doctrinal belief. In this chapter we shall examine the contribution of analytic theologians to our understanding of the corporate life of the Church, including issues in ecclesiology, liturgical theology and the sacraments. The sort of questions analytic theologians have sought to answer have included: What is the identity of the Church? What happens when Christians engage in acts of worship? And what is the nature and purpose of the sacraments of baptism and the Eucharist? As shall be seen, particularly notable contributions to this field have been made by individuals such as James Arcadi, Joshua Cockayne, Terence Cuneo and Nicholas Wolterstorff.

Ecclesiology

Belief in the 'one, holy, catholic and apostolic Church' is a core confession of the Christian faith, and forms part of the Nicene-Constantinopolitan Creed of AD 381. Yet ecclesiology is a subject that until recently, at least, contained many 'underdeveloped areas of enquiry' for analytic theologians (McCall, 2015, p. 151). The first foray into the field of ecclesiology by a self-confessed analytic theologian was undertaken by William Abraham (2010). After acknowledging that 'little has been' written on ecclesiology by Christian philosophers, he avers that this 'omission ... cannot be allowed to stand', since 'no topic in Christian theology should be off limits to philosophical investigation' (Abraham, 2010, p. 170). Ecclesiology, as defined by Abraham, is concerned with the 'identity, nature, structures, ministry, sacraments and mission of the church', and he himself sought to initiate further work in the field by attending to a couple of introductory, conceptual issues (p. 170).

Abraham's first insight is that the meaning of the word 'church' is an 'essentially contested concept' (p. 174). The idea of an essentially contested concept was first coined by W. B. Gallie, and refers to a concept 'the proper use of which inevitably involves endless disputes about their proper use on the part of their users' (p. 174). The Church is one such concept, because (in Abraham's view) neither etymological analysis, biblical exegesis nor contemporary Christian usage produces an unambiguous definition of the term. So while etymology might suggest that the Greek word *ekklesia* means 'the called out people of God', it is used to translate the Hebrew word *qahal* in the Septuagint, which means 'assembly' or 'gathering'. The use of the term is also 'uneven in the New Testament. It shows up in Matthew and Acts but not in Mark, Luke or John; in Paul but not in 1 and 2 Peter' (p. 171). The word is applied to local groups of believers as well as wider Christian communities.

> Regrettably modern usage does not offer any additional help. The range and sense of reference for 'church' is bewildering. The term can refer to a building, a local Christian community, a modern Christian denomination, and the whole body of Christians worldwide. Even then, this common usage is deeply contested by various groups of Christians ... There is no neutral conceptual analysis of the term church. (Abraham, 2010, p. 171)

Given its essentially contested nature, Christian analytic philosophers and theologians 'cannot dogmatically assert that this or that constitutes the essence of the church' (p. 174). If Abraham's insight is correct, then dialogue, gracious disagreement and a dose of humility are essential ingredients of ecclesiological analysis. Abraham's second observation is that any account of the Church must 'do full justice to the work of the Holy Spirit' within Christian communities (p. 174). From this perspective, ecclesiology is an offshoot or subset of pneumatology – the Church is that group of people in whom God's Spirit is at work.

The Church as the interpreter of revelation

In contrast to Abraham, Richard Swinburne's account of the Church is a subset of his understanding of revelation, rather than of pneumatology. For Swinburne, the Church is above all else the organization founded by Christ to ensure the plausible interpretation of divine revelation. He writes that:

> Any revelation needs an interpreting body, a Church, which can draw out its consequences for new cultures in new circumstances. Without a

Church, it would gradually become obscure whether and in what way God had become incarnate ... [and] without a Church to make his work available (for example by providing baptism and the eucharist) and interpret his teaching for new generations and cultures, all that too would be lost. (Swinburne, 2008, pp. 75–6)

Given this understanding of the Church, 'the critical question becomes that of determining the criteria for identifying which one or more ecclesial bodies is the whole or part of the Church Jesus founded' (Abraham, 2010, p. 176). Swinburne seeks to answer this question by deploying two criteria derived from his analysis of other human 'societies', namely continuity of aim and continuity of organization (2007, p. 174). In the case of the Church, 'continuity of aim amounts to continuity of doctrine ... an ecclesial body must teach what Jesus did and taught and what the Apostolic Church taught about what Jesus did' (Swinburne, 2008, p. 136). The second criterion, meanwhile, requires an ecclesial body to have continuity of organization with the Apostolic Church, which

> ... involves its members being admitted in similar way (by baptism) and its leaders being commissioned with similar powers in similar ways (by ordination) to those of earlier leaders, and so on back to the Apostolic Church, any differences arising only from gradual development. It also involves having similar procedures for determining which interpretations of doctrine ... are the correct ones. (p. 137)

Swinburne consequently engages in historical analysis to determine which ecclesial bodies today can lay claim to being 'the' Church – or at least an authentic part of the Church. His historical enquiries suggest that:

> All ecclesial bodies, except for some Protestant bodies, have preserved connectedness and continuity of organization in the respect of recognizing baptism as the method of entry into the church, and recognize the eucharist as the central Christian act of worship. Clearly, both the Roman Catholic church and the Orthodox church, and (to a lesser extent, because of its denial of the authority of Councils) the Anglican church, have significant claims to continuity of organization also in all other respects. (Swinburne, 2007, p. 213)

Similarly, despite 'differences between Protestants and other Christians, for the past thousand years almost all ecclesial bodies ... satisfied the criterion of continuity of doctrine to a very large extent ... [so] maybe we must say that the Church is divided' (Swinburne, 2008, p. 139). If this is the case, Swinburne believes it represents 'a highly unsatisfactory situation, because we need continuing interpretation of revelation, and so a church with a mechanism for providing it; and Christians must work to reunite the broken body of Christ' (2007, p. 215).

The Church as the body of Christ

This last theme – the unity of the Church and its identity as the 'body' of Christ – is the key focus of Joshua Cockayne's *Explorations in Analytic Ecclesiology* (2022). This work represents the most extensive treatment of the subject by an analytic theologian to date. Inspired by Jesus' prayer in John 17.22 'that they may be one', Cockayne's stated aim is to provide an account 'of the Church's unity in Christ through the Holy Spirit' (p. vii). Adopting Crisp's definition of a model as 'a simplified account' of a theological doctrine, Cockayne seeks to offer 'a model of ecclesiology which serves to make clear what it means to think of the Church as one in Christ through the power of the Holy Spirit, but one which never pretends to get to the full truth of the matter' (p. ix). Cockayne's subsequent analysis of the Church and its unity passes through three stages, beginning with a defence of the view that the Church can be a diverse set of individuals yet also considered a meaningful whole, before moving to explore the Church's 'unity through the Spirit' and its 'unity as the body of Christ' (p. 21).

The first stage, then, of Cockayne's work is to defend the claim that the unity of the Church is not at the expense of individual identity and personal responsibility. He rejects a dichotomy between individualism and holism, drawing on theological work by Dietrich Bonhoeffer (1998) and insights from the political philosophy of Philip Pettit (1996). The unity of the Church is a work of the Holy Spirit not a human imposition, a divine creation that neither suppresses nor denies the individuality of its members. In his critique of Hegelian idealism, Bonhoeffer affirmed the Hegelian belief in the existence of 'objective social realities' (such as the Church) but wrote that 'the tragedy of all idealist philosophy was that it never broke though to personal spirit' (quoted in Cockayne, 2022, p. 9). The Hegelians' error, according to Bonhoeffer, is that they

> ... do not affirm the importance of the individual in the community to a sufficient degree ... thereby leading to an absorption of the I into the Thou, in which individuals are no longer separable as individuals. In contrast, Christian thought, Bonhoeffer contends, affirms the em-

phasis on the communal without losing the individual in the crowd. (Cockayne, 2022, pp. 9–10)

Without the notion of the individual 'I', says Bonhoeffer, it is hard to make sense of the Christian belief in a vertical God–human relationship or in the horizontal I–Thou relations that exist within the communal life of the Church. Cockayne draws on Pettit's philosophical insights, meanwhile, to distinguish between *individualism* and *atomism*. Whereas the latter denies the objective reality of holistic social entities, individualism is compatible with a belief in individual identity *and* group realism. Pettit's view is therefore called *individualist holism* and claims that while 'individuals are the most basic building block of social reality, it does not follow ... that social realities *reduce* to claims about individuals' (Cockayne, 2022, p. 15). Applying this insight to ecclesiology enables Cockayne to affirm the reality of the Church as a social entity *and* to defend the distinct identities and responsibilities of the individual agents that comprise it – 'so long as "the agents that comprise it" include both divine persons and human persons' (p. 18). This caveat leads on to the second stage of Cockayne's project, namely the unifying work of the Third Person of the Trinity within the communal life of the Church.

Drawing on contemporary analytic philosophical work on the nature of social groups, including List and Pettit (2011), Cockayne defends a *functionalist* ontology of the Church. Functionalist ontologies define entities by 'what they do rather than by their physical make up' (p. 55). Unlike a person, the Church is not made of a single conscious mind but, like a person, functions 'as an agent with representational and motivational states and is capable of acting on these states' (p. 118). This is the heart of what Cockayne has called his Modified Functionalist Model (MFM) of the group agency of the Church (p. 118).

Cockayne also adopts terminology coined by Stephanie Collins (2019) to describe the Church as a type of '*Collective* ... constituted by agents that are united under a rationally operated group-level decision-making procedure that can attend to moral considerations' (2022, p. 26). He offers the Cabinet of the UK government as an example of a secular collective, since it possesses decision-making structures that enable it to 'perform actions (such as 'getting Brexit done') or hold to certain attitudes (such as the government's stance on which kind of Brexit is preferable for the public), which are not the mere summation of the members' actions and beliefs' (p. 27). Collective groups differ from other types of group (such as 'Coalitions' and 'Combinations' in Collins' terminology), which lack a joint decision-making procedure and so do not qualify as agents. A key difference between the Church and a secular collective, however, is the unseen, guiding hand of the Spirit in its decision-making processes. The Spirit leads the Church through its members by the 'guiding and shaping of their will and desires in conformity with Christ's will' (p. 71). He can even be described as a 'Benevolent Dictator' as he performs this role (p. 38).

> Thus, the task of ecclesiology, on the ground, so to speak, is that of discernment. That is, the Church must discern the will and instructions of the Spirit as they relate to the will of Christ and seek to live faithfully in light of this discernment. (p. 46)

In practice, Cockayne believes this task of discernment is undertaken via prayer and the reading of Scripture and 'by relating to the other members of the Church' also seeking to follow the Spirit's lead (p. 40).

The third and final element of Cockayne's ecclesiological model is to explain the sense in which the Church is Christ's 'body' (e.g. 1 Cor. 12.27). He recognizes that clearly the Church and Christ are not a 'numerical identity ... since the Church is not at the right hand of the Father' (p. 188). Instead, Cockayne adopts the philosophical concept of *bodily extension* to model the relationship between the Church and its Head. He summarizes the general criteria for bodily extension as the following:

> (i) The enabling entity must be readily available and typically relied on by the extending entity.
> (ii) The enabling entity must be easily accessed by the extending entity.
> (iii) The enabling entity must be identified by the [extending] entity as part of their bodily system. (p. 62)

These criteria for bodily extension might apply to the relationship between an amputee and their prosthetic limb, or between a cyclist and their bike, for instance. Cockayne also cites a fictional illustration of bodily extension from the animated film *Ratatouille* (2007), in which a chef named Linguini is helped to produce delicious cuisine thanks to the intervention of Remy, a culinarily proficient rat:

> Wanting to utilize Remy's talents, but scared of bringing a rodent into the kitchen, Linguini hides Remy under his hat, developing a system by which Remy can move Linguini's body by pulling the relevant strand of hair in a specific direction. By manipulating Linguini's body, Remy produces beautiful and original dishes, impressing the critics of Par-

is along the way. Remy is the primary agent at work, at least in the moment of cooking, even if Linguini's agency is not replaced. Thus we might think, Linguini has the mind of Remy, or Remy is the head of Linguini. (Cockayne, 2022, pp. 70–2)

Applied to ecclesiology, Cockayne's view is that the Holy Spirit creates an 'intimate instrumental union' between Christ and his Church, sufficient to describe the latter as an extension of Christ's body (p. 74). It is through his extended body that Christ acts within the world today. Using the terminology above, Christ is an 'extending entity' and the Church is his 'enabling entity', so that:

(i) The Church is readily available and typically relied on by Christ, since the Holy Spirit moves in and through the Church such that the Church is the body of Christ.
(ii) Through the work of the Spirit, the Church is easily accessed by Christ.
(iii) Christ identifies with the Church as his body. (Cockayne, 2022, p. 73)

A similarly shaped ecclesiology to Cockayne's is found in Crisp (2022a). Crisp summarizes his view of the Church as 'The Mystical Body of Christ' since the relationship that exists between members of the Church and their Head 'is not something that we can fully fathom this side of the grave' – it is a 'mystical' work of God (p. 209). And yet Crisp is convinced that the Holy Spirit has a significant role in both forming and sustaining this union. Applying animation models of group theory to the Church, he describes the Holy Spirit as the 'divine agent' who both animates and binds together Christ's people (p. 226). The Spirit is a 'mysterious "force" at work uniting the different members of the church together as a whole … without whose agency the church would not exist as a group at all' (p. 226). He continues:

Although the church *qua* church does not have agency as such, it is able to act together by means of the agency of the Holy Spirit as the members of the church seek to be conformed to the image of God in Christ, to whom they are mystically united. (p. 227)

Perhaps the most recent contribution to ecclesiology by an analytic theologian is from Derek King (2023). His objective is to provide an ecclesiological response to the so-called Problem of Divine Hiddenness. Drawing on insights from Scripture, Gregory of Nyssa and his own personal observations, King argues that the Church 'helps explain why God is hidden in the way he is. She helps explain this because she is revelatory of God – or is how God is making himself known to all people – including non-believers' (2023, p. 3). King thereby seeks to refute the arguments of philosopher J. L. Schellenberg, who claims that God's hiddenness provides good evidence for atheism.

For our present purposes, the most important part of King's thesis is his account of the nature of the Church. Like Crisp, King favours an animation model of group agency in the Church, which he calls his 'Modified Animation Model' (MAM). According to MAM, atomism is rejected and the reality of the Church as a group agent is affirmed. And it is the work of Christ (via his Spirit) that animates and unites the Church's individual members as a group, since he works 'through' them (King, 2023, p. 62). He continues:

> Individuals may palpably experience Christ working through them but [his work] can go unrecognized. Either way, MAM insists that Christ works through the Church such that the words and actions of the Church can be interpreted as those of Christ. ... If MAM is a good way to think about the Church's agency, then the Church is a mediator of divine revelation. A problem almost too obvious to name lurks, however: The Problem of Sin. The problem is that individuals in the Church, or entire Church communities, participate in sinful (i.e., un-Christ-like) dispositions or actions. This presents a problem not only in practice, but in theory for MAM by posing this dilemma: either Christ performs sinful actions or the Church sometimes acts apart from Christ. What can MAM say in return? (pp. 62–3)

The theoretical answer King offers to this problem is to describe sin as 'an example of rogue agency' (p. 64). Individual church members 'or even entire Church denominations' go rogue when they 'temporarily fail to participate in Christ's agency' (p. 64). In practice, meanwhile, discernment is required to identify which words and actions in the Church belong to Christ and which do not. In answer to this question, King contends that the work of Christ in the 'gathered' life of the Church can be most clearly discerned in her liturgy and the sacraments (p. 141). Through its communal prayers, preaching, Scripture reading and provision of the sacraments, Christ is at work: a work that enables the hidden God to be encountered and experienced by human beings. And so to these topics we now direct our attention.

Liturgy

Liturgy and ritual feature prominently in most of the world's religions, not least within the Christian Church. Indeed, 'historically, it seems that ritual has played an enormous role in sustaining and shaping Christianity' (Taliaferro, 2010, p. 186) and recent years have seen significant growth in interest among analytic theologians in this important aspect of church life. Writers including Sarah Coakley, Joshua Cockayne, Terence Cuneo, Eleonore Stump and Nicholas Wolterstorff have all begun to examine the nature of Christian liturgy, which Wolterstorff has described as 'one of the most challenging and fascinating fields for philosophical inquiry' (cited in Cockayne, 2021, p. 478). But, if true, this raises the question of why the subject had previously received such little attention from Christian philosophers. Charles Taliaferro has offered some possible answers, including the observation that:

> From the mid-twentieth century to the 1970s, philosophers focused on the analysis and critique of religious beliefs that seem to be presupposed by religious rites. If there are good reasons to think that our language and concept of God are incoherent or we have compelling reason to think there is no God, then there seems little to be gained in the philosophical exploration of ritual involving God. (Taliaferro, 2010, p. 184)

Wolterstorff, meanwhile, suggests that the neglect of liturgy by analytic philosophers may reflect the fact that the major theological disputes in the history of the Church have concerned other doctrines (such as the Trinity and the Incarnation in the patristic era). The focus on such topics in philosophical theology may therefore reflect the historical 'prominence' of such doctrines (2018, p. 2). But this is just a thesis, and Wolterstorff confesses that he ultimately finds the historic neglect of liturgy by analytic philosophers 'inexplicable' (p. 5).

The first task facing an analytic account of Christian 'liturgy' is to define the term itself. The word 'liturgy' comes from the Greek *leitourgia*, which literally means 'work of the people'. Within philosophy, the word 'has been used broadly to denote all goal-orientated practices or rituals in human life' (Cockayne, 2021, p. 478). But for the purposes of analytic theology, liturgy can be defined more narrowly as those activities performed (that is, enacted) within Christian worship, usually following a prescribed order or 'script' (Wolterstorff, 2018, p. 13). Such scripts establish 'right and wrong ways of worshipping' in different contexts and cultures, without necessarily taking written form (Cockayne, 2021, p. 479).

Christian liturgies may also be described as 'religious rites', which Taliaferro defines as 'repeatable symbolic actions involving God' (2010, p. 181). Wolterstorff also emphasizes this Godward orientation of liturgy, since it is 'by enacting a liturgy we engage God directly and explicitly' (2018, p. 27). King, meanwhile, offers a typical summary of Christian liturgical activities when he writes that 'I have in mind practices like the communal confession of sins, reading Scripture, the sermon, and reciting Creeds' (2023, p. 80). Administration of the sacraments of baptism and the Eucharist also appear in most lists of liturgical activities, as well as 'occasional offices' such as marriage and funeral services. As Cuneo observes, the range of bodily acts undertaken within different Christian liturgies is enormous, and may include 'kissing, standing, bowing, prostrating, chanting, singing, anointing, processing, praying, kneeling, sensing, reading, listening, eating, washing, vesting ... and even spitting' (2016, p. 154). Although the performance of such actions may appear random and disconnected 'to the untrained eye', they are in fact shaped and ordered by the liturgical script being followed at the time. Moreover, for Cuneo such 'bodily acts do not merely *accompany* the linguistic acts prescribed by the liturgical script', but themselves 'count as cases of engaging God by blessing, petitioning and thanking' him (p. 156).

The virtues of liturgy

Taliaferro (2010) offers an account of the virtues (and associated liabilities) of Christian religious rites. He draws on the work of philosophers Franz Brentano and Roderick Chisholm, who argued that 'value can be magnified by being imitated or loved; they held that if something is good, then loving it or imitating it counts as a further good' (Taliaferro, 2010, p. 187). Taliaferro refers to the virtues of 'reference, expression and embodiment' that can be found within Christian liturgy (p. 188). The *virtue of reference* affirms the intrinsic value of referring to a good such as friendship, justice, beauty or God. The *virtue of expression* recognizes the value of expressing a good 'through gesture or action', while there is a further virtue 'we may call the *virtue of embodiment* in which the good is so referenced and expressed that the persons involved may be said to embody or display the good even more fully' (p. 188). Taken together, a rite that expresses the virtues of reference, expression and embodiment may be said to 'magnify' the good in question (p. 188).

Applied to the Church's liturgy, 'Christian rites involve the goods of reference, expression, and embodiment insofar as prayer, praise, and the acknowledgement of a relationship with God are, themselves, a good, even a supreme good' (p. 188).

Taliaferro identifies a further virtue that can be expressed within liturgies, the *virtue of repetition*, since 'repeating (from time to time) that you love your beloved can be a way of renewing the reference, expression, and embodiment of your love' (p. 189). Christian liturgies express this fourth virtue because they 'are explicitly aimed at renewing one's relationship with God' (p. 189). The danger, of course, with repetition is that it can 'drain the meaning of almost any word simply by engaging in a mind-numbing repetition of it' (p. 188). More generally, Taliaferro recognizes that Christian liturgies 'can be tainted when not carried out with reverence, intentionality, balance and wisdom' (p. 191).

Apt liturgical acts

Identifying the circumstances in which a liturgical act is (or is not) carried out appropriately or successfully is a question that has been pursued further by Cuneo (2016) and Wolterstorff (2018). Cuneo, for example, argues that just as in normal social situations there are appropriate and inappropriate forms of behaviour towards other people, there are also apt and inapt ways of engaging with God. He suggests that a liturgical script 'provides us with the opportunity not only to engage God *simpliciter* but also to engage God appropriately' (quoted in Cockayne, 2021, p. 480). Wolterstorff draws an analogy between a liturgical script and a composer's musical score. An orchestra can be said to have performed a piece appropriately when the score is correctly followed. In a similar way, a liturgical script 'specifies a set of rules for a correct liturgical enactment' of an act of worship (Cockayne, 2021, p. 480). A written script cannot prescribe every detail of a liturgical enactment, however, 'nor by a text supplemented by oral directives. Always some of the prescriptions constituting the script are embedded within the social practice of the particular religious community' (Wolterstorff, 2018, p. 20). To worship appropriately in any given context, therefore, an individual needs to learn by experience, observing the liturgical practice of the church community, denomination or tradition they inhabit.

As well as correctly following a script to worship appropriately, Cuneo and Wolterstorff have also argued that for an individual to worship successfully they need to have the right *intentions*. As Wolterstorff writes, 'if it is the *intention* of the participant, when performing the prescribed verbal and gestural acts, that he *not* thereby perform the prescribed acts of worship, then he has *not* performed them; otherwise he has' (2018, p. 108, emphasis added). On this view, intention *not feeling* is what matters for the successful enactment of a liturgy. As Cuneo illustrates this principle: 'To thank someone at some time, one needn't be feeling gratitude at that time' (2016, p. 157). Wolterstorff similarly stresses that a strong personal faith in God's existence is not essential for successfully performing a liturgical act. Rather, it is the desire to worship God that is significant. For example,

> Wolterstorff suggests that in the instance of someone who utters, 'thanks be to God,' 'on the off-chance and in the hope that God does exist and is the sort of being who can be thanked and who is worthy of being thanked,' if such a God does exist, then this person has thanked God. (Cockayne, 2021, p. 480)

Continuing this theme, King (2023) has considered the value a non-believer without any faith in God may derive from participating in liturgical acts. King believes that such a person 'can interact with God' through liturgical actions, 'even if she does not recognise her actions as carrying that significance':

> The easiest example is Scripture proclaimed in the service. Through the reading of Scripture, the nonbeliever can acquire both propositional and personal knowledge. She might acquire propositional knowledge from the propositions she hears about the nature of God or God's dealings with humanity. She might acquire personal knowledge because the Scriptures, read and proclaimed, are God's communication and revelation to us. The nonbeliever can also participate in communal prayers. In confessing her sins or asking God for protection along with the rest of the community, she lends her voice to the one voice of the community and is a part of that prayer despite her non-belief. (King, 2023, pp. 87–8)

Liturgy as a communal act

Understanding the communal dimension of liturgical acts has been another prominent feature of contemporary analytic writing on the subject. As Cockayne observes, the collective nature of most liturgies 'can be seen straightforwardly by attending to the fact that most liturgical scripts use the second-personal pronoun throughout' (2021, p. 481).

Cuneo and Wolterstorff have each provided accounts of collective intentionality in liturgy to explain the communal dimension of Christian worship. Cuneo makes use of John Searle's work on joint actions to speak of 'we-intentions' as the defining feature of groups engaged in collective action in pursuit of a common goal. A church choir is one such group, since 'group singing clearly ... requires the requisite "we intentions" to produce a harmonious sound' (Cuneo, 2016, p. 138). Wolterstorff, meanwhile, draws on Michael Bratman's insight that successful performance of joint intentions necessitates the 'meshing or interlocking' of individual intentions. He writes that:

> When the participants in some liturgical enactment come together they don't do any such thing *as come to agreement with each other* over their actions. Joint action automatically results from each participant intending to fill his or her role in together following the script. Shared joint-action intentions that interlock emerge automatically. (Wolterstorff, 2018, p. 63)

As well as possessing shared or joint intentions, Cuneo and Wolterstorff also both note that successful joint action requires a 'mutual responsiveness' between the individuals involved (Wolterstorff, 2018, p. 64). For example, Cuneo writes that a choir's harmony 'requires that I adjust my singing to yours and you adjust your singing to mine in "real time," often in ways that are not dictated by the score that we are following' (2016, p. 138). Wolterstorff makes a similar point when he writes that 'if one person ... says the creed very slowly and another says it very quickly, they are not saying the creed *together*' (2018, p. 64). Cockayne, however, has expressed concern that 'the kind of intuition meshing and mutual responsiveness described in Wolterstorff's and Cuneo's accounts' of successful collective worship risks excluding 'neuro-atypical individuals' who find such acts difficult (2021, p. 483).

Cockayne's own account of how liturgy unifies a church congregation and enables it to participate in the body of Christ takes its cue from the work of Anglo-Catholic theologian Evelyn Underhill. Underhill identified 'three modes of liturgical participation: joint action, representative action, and corporate silence' (2022, p. xiv). Cockayne draws on insights from contemporary analytic philosophy to flesh out each of these modes. His account of *joint action* has many similarities with those of Wolterstorff and Cuneo above, but he also alerts his readers to the fact that 'acting as one community through joint action is not the same as participating in the body of Christ, even if it can be a *means* of participation' (p. 144). He stresses that:

Acts of shared agency allow us to engage with God as a community, but it is also easy for such acts to become stale and lifeless repetition, with no attention paid to the work of the Holy Spirit. [It] is only through the work of the Holy Spirit that we participate in the ministry of Christ as members of his body. Even in the most formal and scripted forms of liturgical action ... joint action must be responsive to the leading of the Holy Spirit. Thus, we need shared agency not only with our fellow congregants but also with the Holy Spirit. (pp. 144–5)

Turning to *representative action*, Cockayne (following Underhill) defines this as 'actions performed on behalf of the community by a small number of representative individuals' (2022, p. 147). If, as we saw in our discussion of ecclesiology, the Church and individual congregations can be thought of as group agents, then it follows that liturgical actions performed by a minister, priest or other authorized individual 'count as the actions of the group in some important way' (p. 148). By situating representative liturgical acts, such as praying on behalf of a congregation, 'within an account of group agency we can see how all of those who are considered members of a church can in some way be a part of these liturgical acts, even if they are not directly acting, or perhaps not even present' (p. 148). Again, Cockayne cautions that any authorization of an individual to undertake liturgical acts on behalf of the ecclesial group needs to be attentive to the guidance of the Spirit, so prayerful 'discernment is crucial for the task of representative action' (p. 154).

Finally, Cockayne considers the role of *corporate silence* in group liturgical action. Such silences may take place between components of the liturgy, such as after the sermon or Bible reading. As Cockayne describes it, 'corporate silence provides a space in the liturgy for individual reflection, through which the Holy Spirit works in uniting these individual acts of devotion to constitute a group action' (p. 154). Cockayne reviews a couple of philosophical accounts of silence. Roy Sorensen's *realist* account of silence says that 'there are objective absences of sound that can be subjectively experienced by our capacity to hear' (Cockayne, 2022, p. 155). But he favours Ian Phillips' *contrast* view of silence. On this view, silence 'is not directly perceived, as Sorensen supposes, but rather, it is perceived *indirectly* as the contrast between two or more auditory bookends ... singing and speaking for example' (2022, p. 157). Such silences create an auditory 'hole' within a liturgy which provides an occasion 'for the Spirit to unite our actions in imperceptible ways', as well as providing 'an opportunity to respond to the promptings of the Spirit', since it creates space for us to listen to him 'more attentively' (p. 158). Cockayne concludes that corporate silence 'speaks powerfully of the truth that we are secondary agents in the liturgy of the Church, thereby allowing the Spirit to do the work of drawing together the diversity of participants that have gathered to worship God together' (p. 160).

Knowing God through liturgy

If the ultimate purpose of liturgy is to facilitate an engagement with God, how does it achieve this? Analytic theologians have suggested that God is known in a *practical, propositional, personal* and *participatory* way through liturgical acts, and that these kinds of knowledge are not mutually exclusive. For instance, Cuneo (2016) has described the way in which liturgical acts provide *practical* knowledge of how to engage with God. He argues that knowing God 'consists in (although is not exhausted by) knowing how to engage God' (p. 149). By scripting ways in which God can be corporately blessed, thanked and petitioned:

> Liturgy provides the materials for not only engaging but also knowing how to engage God. Or more precisely: the liturgy provides the materials by which a person can acquire such knowledge and a context in which she can exercise and enact it ... [To] the extent that one grasps and sufficiently understands these ways of acting, one knows how to bless, petition, and thank God in their ritualized forms. One has ritual knowledge. (p. 163)

Liturgy also provides *propositional* knowledge about God, to the extent to which it explicitly or implicitly communicates truths about him. Coakley (2013b) has written about truth in liturgy, suggesting various ways in which it might communicate propositional truth about God, even if that is not its main aim. As Cockayne notes, Wolterstorff has similarly argued that liturgies 'typically have an implicit understanding of God ... and repeated exposure to what is theologically implicit in liturgy can play a role in shaping those things an individual takes for granted about God, and thereby in what a person knows about God' (2021, p. 485). Wolterstorff has also drawn attention to the way in which liturgy can provide *personal* knowledge of God. 'For Wolterstorff, liturgy shows us what God is like – e.g. God is a person, a listening person, worthy of praise, etc. – so that we acquire personal knowledge of God' (King, 2023, p. 84). Sarah Coakley has also written of the way in which liturgy facilitates gradual 'acquaintance' with God 'through the repetition of certain practices, which train an individual [to] rightly relate to God and to ... "perceive" God' (Cockayne, 2021, p. 484). Eleonore Stump (2015) has drawn particular attention to the narrative features of liturgy (especially eucharistic liturgy), which she believes are particularly effective at communicating personal knowledge.

King, meanwhile, has written about the capacity of liturgy to facilitate *participatory* knowledge of God. He writes that: 'Participatory knowledge emphasises not only how we engage God, but especially how God engages us. Our participation in the liturgy becomes a manner we participate in God. More than speaking to God, we are actually united to him' (2023, p. 84). As Coakley puts it, liturgy trains 'one's sensibility to the presence of Christ' (2013b, p. 134). This leads King to conclude that

> Cuneo and Wolterstorff are correct in their assessment that the liturgy can yield propositional, ritual, or personal knowledge of God, but I add that, on the basis of Christ's unity to the Church, participatory knowledge is also possible. By our participation in Christ through the liturgy, we form, as Coakley argues, spiritual senses that unite us to God through the sensory realities we experience. (King, 2023, p. 85)

Finally, Cockayne and Efird (2018) have highlighted how an individual's knowledge of God can be enhanced through participation in communal liturgies and corporate worship:

> First, we argue, corporate worship can alter our perception of God – just as experiencing our friends in different social scenarios changes our perception of what they are like, experiencing God alongside other people, with different histories, beliefs, and issues can provide us with a broader and deeper knowledge of what God is like, by allowing us to experience different aspects of God. Second, we suggest, worshipping alongside others plays a causal role in what we attend to – thus, in worshipping alongside another person, we are able to be drawn to aspects of God's character and to come to a broader perception of what God is like than we would by worshipping alone. (Cockayne, 2021, p. 486)

Arguably the two most important liturgical acts in the communal life of the Church are the dominical sacraments of baptism and the Eucharist. Unsurprisingly, these two 'signs and seals' of the redemptive work of God have become objects of study by analytic theologians, and merit particular attention.

Baptism

Broadly speaking, baptism can be described as an initiation rite, a liturgical act that (in some sense) marks an individual's entry into the Church. More specifically, Christians believe that the water of baptism 'somehow enacts divine action, exhibiting a state of affairs of enormous significance for the recipient: remission of sins, an effectual regeneration, an entrance into God's covenant community and so on' (Sutanto, 2021, p. 457). Given its alleged significance, it is surprising that 'philosophers have paid almost no attention to the baptismal rite. Indeed, one would be hard pressed to identify a single article written on the topic by a philosopher in the last fifty years' (Cuneo, 2014, p. 279). This lack of philosophical interest in the subject is particularly striking given the long-standing and contentious debates among theologians concerning baptism's proper mode, recipients, soteriological efficacy and so forth. Happily, analytic theologians, notably Cuneo (2014 and 2016), Sutanto (2021) and Cockayne (2022), have begun to remedy the philosophical neglect of the subject. Cuneo and Sutanto have addressed the question of baptismal regeneration from Eastern Orthodox and Reformed perspectives respectively, while Cockayne's work has considered in what sense this sacrament confers membership of the Church.

Baptismal regeneration and the 'intelligibility puzzle'

In their work on baptismal regeneration, Cuneo and Sutanto have focused on what Cuneo has called the 'intelligibility puzzle' surrounding baptism (2014, p. 280). In Cuneo's own Eastern Orthodox tradition (and others), audacious claims are made about the effects of baptism on its recipients, claims that seem implausible and unintelligible at first sight. For example, Cuneo points to the following prayer of thanksgiving within the Orthodox baptismal liturgy:

> Blessed are You, O Lord God Almighty, Source of all good things ... who has given to us, unworthy though we be, blessed purification through hallowed water, and divine sanctification, through life-giving Chrismation; who now, also, has been pleased to regenerate your servant that has newly received illumination by water and the Spirit, and granted unto him/her remission of sins, whether voluntary or involuntary. (Cuneo, 2014, p. 280)

This prayer appears to promise purification, sanctification, regeneration, illumination and remission of sins to the blessed recipient, which Cuneo summarizes as 'the regenerate states' (p. 280). The intelligibility puzzle he sees created by this Orthodox baptismal text is this:

> How could a person be illumined or enlightened as a result of being baptized? And isn't there good empirical evidence that the imposition of the regenerate states is not in fact accomplished in the vast majority of cases? After all, more often than not, those who are baptized tend not to behave much differently from those who are not baptized; those belonging to the former group seem no more illumined or enlightened than those belonging to the latter. Moreover, when one considers the further fact that the regenerate states are typically predicated of infants and young children who are baptized, the predications are paradoxical, even unintelligible. In what sense could an infant be sanctified, illumined, or enjoy remission of her sins? On a straightforward reading, the text appears to make a series of category mistakes. (Cuneo, 2014, p. 280)

Cuneo believes this puzzle can be resolved, however, by drawing a distinction between a *product-state* interpretation of the passage and a *process-state* one (p. 288). Whereas a product-state reading of the baptismal prayer of thanksgiving suggests that the recipient of baptism has now undergone regeneration (in a past-perfect tense sense), a process-state interpretation suggests that baptism has merely initiated the recipient's regeneration. In a process reading, therefore, 'the one baptized is now *being* purified, *being* sanctified, *being* regenerated, *being* illumined, and *being* released from sin' (2016, p. 178). Cuneo argues that this process-state interpretation of the Orthodox baptismal prayer is credible linguistically, since the original Greek text of the liturgy 'indicates that something like a process-interpretation is along the right lines' (2014, p. 289). A process reading of the baptismal liturgy also receives 'qualified support from the writings of figures such as Mark the Monk and Gregory of Nyssa' (p. 289). If it is indeed correct, this reading of the liturgy resolves the intelligibility puzzle by creating space for a baptised person's regenerate states to come to fruition over time. We should not expect to see evidence of their regenerative states immediately after the baptismal rite. Rather, the regenerative process is only instigated at baptism and thereafter sustained by the individual's co-operation with the interior work of the Holy Spirit and by their participation in the communal life of the Church – including the eucharistic rite (p. 293).

In contrast to Cuneo's Eastern Orthodox account of baptismal regeneration, Nathaniel Gray Sutanto advocates a 'Pneumatic-Reformed response' to the intelligibility puzzle (2021, p. 459). At the outset he notes that Cuneo's solution to the puzzle

> ... is not available to adherents of confessional Reformed theology. That is, Reformed theologians cannot admit that regeneration is a *process*, for, in their theologies, regeneration – much like justification – is a punctiliar moment that effects conversion and is the irreversible act of God that makes possible the daily acts of repentance and the moral progress of the believer. Effectual calling decisively calls the sinner from the spiritual darkness into the light. (Sutanto, 2021, p. 459)

Nevertheless, Sutanto believes that the intelligibility puzzle can be avoided by those who adopt a Reformed perspective on baptism. This is because, unlike the Eastern Orthodox view, they deny that there is 'a direct causal link between baptism and regeneration' (p. 459). The Reformed do not believe that baptism automatically effects regeneration in the recipient. 'Rather,' he writes, 'the Reformed argue that the sacraments merely sign and seal the internal graces rather than actually *effecting* these graces ... which is the exclusive work of the Holy Spirit' (p. 459). The water of baptism is, in and of itself, powerless to regenerate individuals' hearts.

> In other words, adherents of Reformed theology would happily agree with the potential objection that the rite of baptism does not seem to be able to produce the regenerate states ... for it has never claimed that baptism *would* cause the acquisition of those states, and certainly not regeneration itself. The Spirit freely works apart from baptism and can affect the things signified in baptism before, during, or after the baptismal rite itself. Hence there is no puzzle to be resolved here – or at least this puzzle is not one that should trouble the Reformed. (p. 460)

This Reformed view of baptism does not 'trivialize its significance', however: 'For, the *product* of baptism, whether applied to infants or adults, is the entrance into the covenant community of God by way of membership' (p. 460).

Baptism and church membership

It is this communal dimension of baptism, by which it incorporates individuals into the Church, the body of Christ, that is the focus of Joshua Cockayne's work on the sacrament. Cockayne takes as his cue the apostle Paul's words in 1 Corinthians 12.13, which appear to explicitly link baptism to inclusion in the body of Christ: 'we were all *baptized* into one body – Jews or Greeks, slaves or free – and we were all made to drink of one Spirit' (2022, p. 75).

Cockayne begins by looking at recent philosophical writing on the nature of promises, particularly the work of Margaret Gilbert on 'joint commitments' (2022, p. xiii). He observes that in Anglican and many other baptism liturgies, 'the promises of the baptismal candidate ... are public acts of declaration and submission to the beliefs and values of a community. Moreover, the community also promises to uphold and support the faith of those being baptized' (p. 79). In Gilbert's view, making a promise is an example of a joint commitment, which she defines as a commitment of 'two or more people to some way of acting, which is rescindable only with the concurrence of all' (p. 80). Crucially, anyone entering into a joint commitment by making a promise thereby establishes an obligation to other members of the group to act in a certain way. Cockayne believes that this insight has obvious applications to the promises made by baptism candidates, since they establish 'a kind of joint commitment with God in which they are now accountable for living up to their baptismal vows' (p. 82). Moreover:

> Not only does one make a joint commitment to God in the baptism liturgy, but one also makes a joint commitment with the other members of the Church. That is, one promises to enact a set of actions and beliefs not only as an individual but also as a group. It is the 'faith of the Church' one professes. In virtue of her very public commitment as well as the joint commitment of all those present in the baptism service, one is obligated not only to God as promisee but also to the other members of the Church as a kind of corporate promisee. Put simply, the commitments involved in baptism stand one in a new relation to the community of the Church. (p. 82)

In Cockayne's view, Gilbert's joint commitments account clarifies how small social groups may form and establish mutual accountability in the absence of a formal organizational structure. It therefore has some application to a local congregation, but her model is 'surely not sufficient for giving an account of membership in the one Church' (p. 83).

In the case of a large ecclesial group, such as the global Church or a national denomination, 'it seems unreasonable to think that one could make one's commitment common knowledge to the other members of the group, thereby ruling out the possibility of jointly committing to some course of action with them, at least straightforwardly' (p. 83). Moreover,

> the Church is not the result of the joint commitments of its members, but the work of the Holy Spirit. So, whilst Gilbert's account captures something intuitive about the commitments of individuals and tells us something important about the obligations of those who have been baptised, it falls short of providing us with an account of group membership in baptism. (p. 84)

Cockayne therefore concludes that the promises made in baptism liturgies clarify 'what a commitment to the community of the Church entails for the baptized as they belong to a covenant community. However, problems emerge when we try to think of promising *itself* as the means of membership' in the Church (p. 85). Adopting Calvin's definition of baptism as a 'sign and seal' of God's sovereign work, Cockayne therefore argues that the words of the baptismal liturgy merely 'recognize and acknowledge something that God has done, rather than bringing about a change of affairs' (p. 91). It follows that baptism, though desirable, is neither a necessary nor a sufficient condition for an individual to enter into membership of Christ's Church. 'In fact, without the work of the Spirit drawing us into the community of the Church it is entirely redundant' (p. 92).

Applying insights from speech-act theory, Cockayne defines the words used in baptism liturgies as examples of *assertive illocutionary* and *perlocutionary* speech-acts. They are assertive illocutionary acts in that they proclaim what God has done for an individual, and perlocutionary to the extent that they seal membership of the Church within the heart of the baptized person. In short, baptism provides us with 'confidence in our identity in Christ and our belonging to the one Church through the work of the Spirit' (p. 94).

Cockayne concludes his analysis by defending the practice of infant baptism, which he believes to be consistent with his 'Calvinian' understanding of the sacrament, since if baptism 'serves to mark out those who are members of the community of the Church, and to seal this identity on their hearts, then there is no in principle reason to exclude the young from the life of the community' (p. 98). Moreover:

> Empirical research has shown that children's perception of their identity in a social group has a significant effect on their development ... Thus whether or not we treat children as fellow members of the Church has implications for how they develop a sense of belonging to the group and how they learn from other members of the Church. (Cockayne, 2022, p. 99)

He continues:

> By being brought into the community, which is disposed towards God, one creates an environment in which personal faith can flourish. It is for these reasons, I think, that Calvin is insistent that baptism is for children of believing parents; for in such households, the seeds of faith which God implants in even the very young can be exposed to the benefits of grace God reveals through the Church. (p. 103)

Therefore, whether its recipients are young or old, Cockayne's understanding of baptism sees it as a sacrament 'in which we assert the reality of God's one Church and mark the life of the individual who is identified with this community' (p. 104).

The Eucharist

The Eucharist (also known as 'The Lord's Supper', 'The Mass' or 'Holy Communion') is regarded as the central act of corporate worship in most, if not all, Christian traditions. But this sacrament has a mystery at its heart. What did Jesus really mean when, on the night before he died, he shared bread and wine with his disciples and told them, 'This is my body' and 'This is my blood'? (see Matt. 26.26–28; Mark 14.22–24; Luke 22.19–20 and 1 Cor. 11.23–25). In what sense can it be said that Christians 'eat' Christ's flesh and 'drink' his blood (cf. John 6.53) when they celebrate the Eucharist in their church gatherings today, especially since the Nicene-Constantinople Creed asserts that his risen body ascended into heaven and is now 'seated at the right hand of the Father'?

Just as the 'threeness-oneness' question preoccupies analytic theologians' study of the Trinity, understanding the nature of Christ's presence at the Eucharist has dominated their study of this sacrament. In their answers to this question, analytic theologians have articulated a wide spectrum of views. James Arcadi (2021b) has helpfully subdivided this spectrum into three broad schools of thought, namely the *corporeal*, *pneumatic* and *ordinary* ways (or modes) of understanding Christ's eucharistic presence. He defines the corporeal (or 'Real Presence') perspective as one in which 'the bread becomes so connected to the body of Christ that the predication, "This is the body of Christ" is literally true when said of that object' (2021b, p. 464). Pneumatic viewpoints, meanwhile, hold that Christ's connection to the eucharistic elements is in some sort of 'spiritual fashion' (Arcadi, 2021b, p. 464). Third, Arcadi classifies ordinary (or 'Memorialist') views of the Eucharist as those which

> ... do not hold there to be any connection between the bread and the body of Christ. Here the Biblical/liturgical utterance is to be understood as 'there is no metaphysical connection between this object and the body of Christ, but one should think about Jesus Christ when one sees or eats it.' (Arcadi, 2021b, p. 464)

Before attending to these three perspectives in turn, it is worth noting that the nature of Christ's eucharistic presence is no longer the only aspect of eucharistic theology that has been scrutinized by analytic theologians. Joshua Cockayne, in particular, has recently considered the ways in which the eucharistic rite strengthens the unity of the Church, and his work is summarized below.

Corporeal accounts of Christ's 'Real Presence'

In Arcadi's typology, *corporeal* accounts of the Eucharist 'posit a robust metaphysical connection between the bread of the Eucharist and the body of Christ' (2021b, p. 468). He further divides corporeal accounts into 'Roman' and 'German' versions respectively.

Roman views of the Eucharist affirm the Roman Catholic Church's official teaching on the nature of Christ's presence at the Eucharist. On this view, the substance of the bread and wine are *transubstantiated* at the moment of consecration to become instead the substance of Christ's body and blood. However, the outward appearance, taste and texture of the eucharistic elements remain unchanged after consecration. In other words, the *sensible qualities* (or *accidents*) of the eucharistic elements are preserved at the moment of consecration, even though their underlying substance changes. The substance of Christ's body and blood becomes really and wholly 'present', just as the substance of the bread and wine becomes really and wholly 'absent'. One important implication of this view would seem to be that Christ's body is simultaneously located in heaven and on multiple earthly altars whenever and wherever the Eucharist is celebrated.

Several analytic theologians have sought to offer a philosophically robust defence of this Roman Catholic understanding of the Eucharist, including Alexander Pruss (2009), Patrick Toner (2011) and Joshua Sijuwade (2022). Space prohibits a detailed account of all the philosophical possibilities canvassed by Pruss, but one important theme is his rejection of 'the claim that the same place cannot be on two altars or on an earthly altar and in heaven at the same time' (2009, p. 524):

> This claim seems quite plausible, but is not clearly true. Observe first that a person might be wholly located in two buildings at once. Thus, the Royal British Columbia Museum contains a wooden house ceremonially belonging to the descendants of Chief Kwakwabalasami, and someone within that house would be in two buildings at once. Moreover, then the *place* where the person would be would itself be in two houses. But if a place could be in two buildings at once, it seems plausible that a place could be on two altars at once.

In search of a more precise solution to the conundrum, Pruss outlines a range of philosophical 'strategies' that could be followed, including *partial presence, placeless presence, curved space* and *multi-location* arguments (2009, p. 515). In a more recent paper, Pruss also defends the multi-location of Christ's body by appealing 'to the notion of internal time coming from considerations of time travel' (Pruss, 2013a, p. 60). Martin Pickup (2015) has also utilized the idea of time travel to explain the simultaneous presence of Christ's body at multiple locations:

> If time travel is possible, then it could be the case that Christ enters a cosmic time-travel machine and simply ports his body to multiple locations throughout time and space ... For Pickup, Christ could just multiply-port his body to the location of each of the particular pieces of the consecrated elements (each morsel of bread, each sip of wine). Thus, the whole of his body is present, via time-travel, at every morsel of bread or sip of wine. (Arcadi, 2021b, p. 470)

Pruss has also sought to explain the Roman Catholic belief in the 'real absence' of the eucharistic bread and wine after the act of consecration, despite the endurance of their physical appearance and other 'accidental' features such as their taste and smell. He draws analogies to hearing the sound of thunder after a bolt of lightning and seeing the light from a distant star that has long since ceased to exist. Pruss infers that 'if the sound of the lightning strike and the sight of the star count as accidents, then it seems accidents can exist while their subjects no longer do' (2009, p. 534). On this basis, the idea that the accidents of the bread and wine can continue to exist after their substance has gone 'does not seem all that absurd' (p. 534). Toner (2011) also defends the coherence of the real absence view, arguing that if a piece of bread has a set of essential characteristics, it could be the case that, after consecration, God 'miraculously holds the cluster of characteristic properties together independent of a subject [i.e. a piece of bread] that has those properties' (Arcadi, 2021b, p. 469). A similar account of transubstantiation, also adopting a form of essentialist ontology, is offered by Sijuwade (2022).

In contrast to 'Roman' views of the Eucharist, meanwhile, 'German' corporeal views of the sacrament are characterized by a belief that the substances (and accidents) of the bread and wine remain present after their consecration, but become in some sense connected to the substance of Christ's body and blood (Arcadi, 2021b, p. 470). In the traditional Lutheran account (inspired by Martin Luther, Andreas Osiander and others), the substance of Christ's body and blood is co-located 'in, with and under' the substance of the bread and wine. Hence this is often described as a *consubstantiation* view of the sacrament. However, as Arcadi observes, 'There has not been, so far as I know, an attempt in the analytic literature to advocate for the intelligibility of the German-consubstantiation view' (2021b, p. 471). More popular has been what Arcadi defines as the German *impanation* view, which holds that the relationship between the bread and the body of Christ in the Eucharist goes beyond a mere co-location. Rather, it is a *union* akin to the hypostatic union that occurred at the Incarnation (p. 471).

Arcadi has himself offered the most developed analytic account of impanation in his 2018a work, *An Incarnational Model of the Eucharist*. This account argues that, just as the human nature of Christ was the 'vehicle or enabling device for the body of Christ ... the bread can be seen in like manner as a vehicle or enabling device for the body of Christ' (p. 472). This idea of *enabling externalism* is ultimately derived from Clark and Chalmers' 'extended mind thesis' (1989), which held that not all cognitive processes are done in the head (we may use a notebook to record information we wish to remember, for example). The idea of enabling externalism was first applied to the Incarnation by Cross (2011), who argued that Christ's human nature enabled the Word 'to act within the created sphere as a human, something the Word as divine cannot do' (Arcadi, 2021b, p. 473). Applying the same principle to the Eucharist, Arcadi writes:

> Think of the bodily activity of cutting with a knife. I am unable, by my organic hand alone, to slice through a juicy apple. However, an

adequately sharp knife enables me to extend my bodily power to perform my desired activity. In the Eucharist, the properly demarcated bread enables Christ to extend his body to be in a location in which he is not organically located. Although he is not organically located, we might say he is artifactually located, located by means of an artefact *qua* enabling device. (p. 473)

But is this enabling externalist account sufficient to describe the eucharistic bread as Christ's *body*? In response, Arcadi cites the testimony of amputees who regard their prosthetic limbs as genuine (albeit non-organic) parts of their body. He concludes that:

If a prosthetic user personally attests to her prosthesis as being a part of her body, phenomenologically and artefactually, I suggest we ought to be willing to allow for a conception of body that moves beyond the organic to include certain artefacts. And if Christ similarly attests to an artefact being part of his body, we ought to as well. (p. 473–4)

Pneumatic perspectives on the Lord's Supper

Arcadi's *pneumatic* category represents the mid-point on the spectrum of eucharistic views. As a result, it is 'more challenging to characterize than the views on its flanks' but includes those writers 'that do not posit a metaphysical connection between the elements and the body of Christ, but that also posit more than a cognitive recollection as at the heart of the meaning' of Christ's words of institution (Arcadi, 2021b, p. 465). He goes on to suggest that advocates of this intermediate position understand the Eucharist as 'spiritual' in either a) specific (that is, 'Holy Spirit') or (b) colloquial (that is, 'the semblance of') senses (p. 465). Those who fall into the first category include historic theologians such as Martin Bucer, John Calvin and Thomas Cranmer, who emphasized the work of the Holy Spirit at the Eucharist. The second category refers to those who 'attempt a literal explication of Christ's words without recourse to an explication of a metaphysical connection to the body of Christ' (p. 465).

To date, it is only the (b)-type pneumatic viewpoint that has found advocates within analytic theology. For example, Baber (2013) makes use of recent analytic philosophical work on social ontology to argue that the 'change' that takes place in the eucharistic elements is a change in the 'institutional conventions' with respect to them. Baber says this change is analogous to the act of writing a cheque. As Arcadi explains:

By all empirical counts, a rectangular piece of paper with numbers and letters on it literally is worth no more than a piece of paper. Yet, given certain conditions constituted by particular social and institutional conventions, a [cheque] one writes for $200 is, according to social ontology, $200. The meaning of the object goes beyond its metaphysical makeup. (p. 466)

Similarly, through the liturgical act of consecration the meaning of the eucharistic elements is changed so they become Christ's body and blood from the perspective of the Church. As Baber puts it, 'the presence of Christ in the Eucharist is ... secured by the collective intentionality of an institution, viz. the Church' (2013, p. 26). Unlike corporeal views, this account does not require any metaphysical connection between the eucharistic elements and the ascended Christ, nor any substantial change in the bread and wine.

Arcadi also classifies the argument of Cockayne et al. (2017) as a (b)-type pneumatic model of the Eucharist. On their view, the eucharistic elements are *iconic*, in that they facilitate a relational encounter between Christ and the recipient without changing metaphysically. In their own words, 'Christ is derivatively, rather than fundamentally, located in the consecrated bread and wine, such that Christ is present *to* the believer *through* the consecrated bread and wine, thereby making available to the believer a second-person experience of Christ' (Cockayne et al.).

Richard Cross's (2002b) *action-at-a-distance* view of the Eucharist is a third example of a (b)-type pneumatic model. Cross argues that Christ's body can be *definitively present* in the eucharistic elements, even if spatially located at the right hand of the Father. He defines definitive presence as occurring when a substance 'directly or immediately causes an effect at [a] place without being spatially present at that place' (2002b, p. 303). On this view, Christ's body is present at the Eucharist so long as he 'performs some immediate action at the location of the elements' (Arcadi, 2021b, p. 468).

An 'Ordinary' view of the Eucharist

Turning to the third of Arcadi's categories, *ordinary* or *memorialist* views of the Eucharist,

> ... do not think that there is any unique or special relationship between the bread of the Eucharist and the body of Christ. This is, of course, not to say that adherents to this family of views necessarily think the

Eucharist inconsequential or trivial. On this view, the intelligibility of the Eucharist stems from another utterance of Christ's: the mandate to celebrate the Eucharist in remembrance of him. In a manner similar to a good sermon, the Eucharist serves the cognitive function of bringing to mind Christ and his work. (2021b, pp. 464–5)

Within church history the most well-known exponent of this position is the sixteenth-century Swiss Reformer Huldrych Zwingli. Until very recently, however, this view had no advocate among analytic theologians. This has now changed with the publication of Steven Nemes' work *Eating Christ's Flesh: A Case for Memorialism* (2023). Nemes argues in favour of an understanding of the Eucharist in which:

> To eat Christ's flesh is to take joy in his person and work. The bread and wine of the eucharistic meal provide the disciples of Jesus with an opportunity to engage in this kind of eating in a sacramental manner by representing his person and work to them as symbols. The Eucharist is thus the symbol left by Jesus in the church by which his presence to his disciples is made actual and their union with him in mutual love is strengthened. (Nemes, 2023, p. 183)

Nemes' case for memorialism is a prime example of the analytic theological method, being built upon a combination of biblical exegesis, examination of church tradition (especially patristic sources), and philosophical argument. Jesus' recorded words at the institution of the Lord's Supper, for example, must be interpreted figuratively rather than literally, since there is

> ... the obvious contradiction between the *quod dicitur ad litteram* (what is said taken literally) and *quod videtur* (what is seen). This is a principle by which figurative language is intuitively discerned. The bread and wine do not manifest as body and blood, and this is how one can easily and quite naturally appreciate that Jesus was speaking figuratively. (p. 184)

Nemes also examines very early Christian texts on the Eucharist, including *The Didache* and the writings of Ignatius, Tertullian, Justin Martyr and Irenaeus, and concludes that they are more amenable to 'symbolic or phenomenological' interpretations than 'metaphysical' ones which imply Christ's Real Presence (p. 184). Moreover, he argues that a memorialist understanding of the Eucharist 'better accords with the principles of phenomenological philosophy' and the evidence of our senses, since:

Phenomenologists argue that the strict correlation between appearance and being is the necessary presumption of the possibility of knowledge. Only if appearance and being are strictly correlated can knowledge as the experiential confirmation of one's opinion about a thing on the basis of that thing's manifestation be possible. But the Real Presence paradigm requires that this correlation be broken in the case of the Eucharist and thus be contingent in principle. What appears is bread and wine but what is really there is the body and blood of Jesus. It must be possible in principle for appearance and being to come apart. It therefore becomes possible to argue against the Real Presence paradigm on phenomenological grounds that it entails skepticism. Memorialism does not suffer from this problem because it does not require that one divide appearance and being in any way. (pp. 185–6)

In summary, Nemes believes that 'memorialism proposes a conception of the Eucharist that is parsimonious, intuitive, and does not require speculative metaphysical theses without a clear basis in experience or the biblical *loci classici*' (p. 187). In his view, therefore, memorialism is to be favoured over its corporeal and pneumatic alternatives.

The Eucharist and church unity

Although the bulk of analytic theologians' attention to date has focused on the metaphysical question of Christ's presence at the Eucharist, a wide range of additional questions remain to be explored in relation to this sacrament. For example, Pruss (2009) suggests that the following 'philosophically charged' questions are worthy of examination in the future:

The Eucharistic event appears triggered by certain physical actions by the priest ... or by the congregation and its presider. Are the actions of the human agents given a supernatural power of producing such an effect or does God produce the effect entirely by himself on the occasion of these actions? Likewise, is the reception of the Eucharist a cause of the occurrence of grace, or does God simply happen to choose to provide grace on the occasion of the receiving of the Eucharist? And if it is a means, then in what way does this causality work? (pp. 512–13)

One new area that has already begun to be addressed by Cockayne (2022) is the question of the Eucharist's role in promoting church unity. He begins by drawing on accounts of social bonding in psychology to explain how this sacrament fosters 'the human-to-human unity of those gathered to share the Eucharistic meal together' (p. 106). Cockayne cites William McNeill's argument that synchronous movement, such as dancing, can produce a kind of 'boundary loss', a 'blurring of self-awareness and the heightening of fellow-feeling with all who share in the dance' (p. 108). Cockayne observes that McNeil's claims have found support from empirical studies on synchronous movement and group ritual. Moreover, communal meals and other shared experiences have 'been shown to foster a sense of closeness and social cohesion' (p. 109). He concludes:

> It is not a stretch to claim, then, that the ritual acts involved in the celebration of the Eucharist – eating together, reciting liturgy together, moving together synchronously by sitting, standing, kneeling, and drinking alcohol together – play a significant role in the sense of closeness with those we participate alongside. Whatever else we might say about the Eucharist, it seems clear that the ritual movement involved in its practice has potential to significantly increase the sense of unity and social cohesion within a group. (p. 110)

Cockayne goes on to argue that another feature of the Eucharist, namely its emphasis on remembrance, has 'a unitive function' (p. 112). Drawing on philosophical and psychological work on memory, Cockayne argues that the Eucharist serves to create a form of 'episodic' memory (p. 113):

> Put simply, the sense of remembrance involved in the Eucharist is not to be confused with mere fact recollection. Rather, memory is rich, involving our bodies and our imaginations in important ways. In participating in the events of the past we are united with those with whom we are remembering. An analogous practice can be seen in the use of reminiscing in family groups through the telling of stories and sharing of memories, particularly in groups that have gathered after long periods of time. There are even occasions where people report having a sense of memory about an event at which they were not present, because of the centrality of this reminiscing in the life of the family. This seems especially pertinent for thinking about the Church's gathering each week to remember the events of the Passion. (p. 115)

Cockayne therefore conceives of the Eucharist as a form of collective remembrance that increases not only the cohesiveness of a local congregation, but also their connectedness 'to the wider body of the Church over time, and our relation to God as a community' (p. 117). However, while such psychological and philosophical insights may help us understand how the Eucharist fosters Christian unity, the unique contribution of God's Spirit should not be overlooked:

> If Christ is actually present in the Church and in the sacrament, then we need not think of the Eucharistic meal as a mere human ritual that produces psychological harmony in the community. While it may produce these unitive psychological effects, the Eucharist is primarily an encounter with the only source of unity which will be efficacious: the body of Christ through the power of the Holy Spirit. (p. 120)

He also recognizes that human sinfulness is a significant barrier to unity in the Church and unity with Christ. While most eucharistic liturgies include a public confession and absolution prior to reception of the elements, something more than an assurance of God's forgiveness is required to overcome the divisive effects of sin. What is needed, claims Cockayne, is what Terence Cuneo has called *remission*, namely 'being released or liberated from the grip of sin' (2016, p. 189). We need remission, says Cockayne, from subjective feelings of guilt and shame that keep us from full unitive engagement with God and other members of the Church. Repeated participation in the Eucharist helps to achieve our much-needed remission since God uses this sacrament 'for the purpose of eroding our resistance to the unity offered to us in Christ. This process is best thought of as a shift in perception. Slowly ... we are able to see who we truly are in Christ' (2022, p. 125).

To help understand this process, Cockayne draws on Michael Maher's work on Old Testament 'communion' sacrifices (such as the thanksgiving offering, the votive offering and the freewill offering) to identify parallels with the Eucharist. Significantly, the communion sacrifices were not atoning sacrifices; rather their function was 'unitive; in eating the animal they have sacrificed; the community are united to God and united to one another' (p. 127). Communion sacrifices were also used, says Maher, to 'inaugurate or ratify a covenant' as in Exodus 24 (Cockayne, 2022, p. 127). In similar ways, the Eucharist serves a unitive function as Christ's sacrificial body and blood are consumed by a Christian congregation, and as the new covenant relationship with God inaugurated by his death and resurrection is recalled.

Finally, Cockayne observes that participation in the Eucharist is 'both a bodily and interpersonal encounter. And we know that embodied, physical interaction with another person is qualitatively different to interaction lacking such features' (p. 129). This insight is confirmed by 'numerous psychological studies', and leads to the following conclusion:

In the Eucharist then, we are invited not only to allow the consuming of consecrated elements to heal our propensity from sin but to relate to Christ intimately and bodily ... In encountering Christ's body through our own bodies, we allow Christ to transform our minds, our bodies and our wills. Just as in the aftermath of a disagreement or argument, the loving touch of a friend might bring about greater reconciliation than any words were capable of; in taking Christ's body into our own (as strange as this may seem), we are united to him in ways we may not always comprehend. (Cockayne, 2022, pp. 129–30)

Cockayne's final point is to note that, though it may seem overly individualistic, the 'breaking down of our resistance to Christ's will ultimately leads to our closer unity with one another as Christ's body' (2022, p. 130). Nevertheless, Christian discipleship does have a legitimate individual as well as communal dimension, including personal spirituality and prayer. The following chapter thus seeks to provide an overview of analytic theologians' emerging insights on these additional topics.

Recommended Further Reading

Cockayne, J., 2022, *Explorations in Analytic Ecclesiology: That They May be One*, Oxford Studies in Analytic Theology, Oxford: Oxford University Press.

Cuneo, T., 2016, *Ritualized Faith: Essays in the Philosophy of Liturgy*, Oxford Studies in Analytic Theology, Oxford: Oxford University Press.

7

Spirituality and Prayer

Christian spirituality is concerned with cultivating the personal relationship with God which the finished work of Christ has made possible. As one analytic theologian, Kyle Strobel, has put it: 'Christians do not enter the presence of God on their own terms, or in their own "name," but in the name of another. Their access is given by grace ... in the name of Jesus' (2022, p. 168). As adopted children of God, individual Christians throughout church history have sought to know their heavenly Father better through such spiritual disciplines as prayer, meditation, fasting, Scripture reading and theological study. By faithful observance of such practices, Christians also hope to see their characters progressively conformed to the likeness of Christ. In this chapter we will review the emerging work within analytic theology on personal spirituality in general, most notably Efird (2021). Particular focus will then be on analytic theologians' writing on prayer, which has been their most thoroughly explored aspect of personal spirituality to date.

Spirituality

Spirituality has not been a major focus of analytic philosophical enquiry over the last 50 years. Indeed, other than some discussion of petitionary prayer (e.g. Stump, 1979; Phillips, 1981; and Basinger, 1983), it has been largely neglected as a subject. And yet the intrinsic value of a personal relationship with God has been affirmed by Christian analytic philosophers in the context of other debates. For example, Richard Swinburne's *Providence and the Problem of Evil* (1998) devoted a chapter to the topic of worship, in which he asserts that:

> A good God, for his sake and for theirs, will seek to have creatures rightly related to himself. He will seek for those creatures who have the capacity to do so to know him, interact with him, and love him ... As our creator, God will seek to interact with us. He will want us to

feel his presence, to tell him things and ask him to do things; and he will want to tell us things. (Swinburne, 1998, pp. 111–13)

Such assertions naturally raise the question, '*How* can God be known, and known well?' In other words, how can individuals enjoy the type of interactive relationship with God that Swinburne describes in this passage? This question has been explored by Efird (2021), the first foray into spirituality *per se* by an analytic theologian. Efird approaches his task by looking at analytic philosophical work on human-to-human interpersonal relations, before doing some 'conceptual engineering' to apply it to divine–human relationships (2021, p. 440).

Efird begins by citing Bonnie Talbert's statement that knowing another person 'depends on (at least) two things: direct, face-to-face interaction and an understanding of who that person is in the world' (p. 441). Moreover, truly knowing another individual in Talbert's sense includes a 'second-personal' type of knowledge, which includes knowledge of their 'mental states' and 'who [they] are in the world' (p. 441). As Eleonore Stump has highlighted, such knowledge can only come through 'personal interaction' with someone, of a 'direct and immediate sort' (2010, pp. 75–6). Reading a book about a person will not suffice to provide second-personal knowledge of them – it requires what psychologists call 'dyadic joint attention' (Efird, 2021, p. 442). Dyadic joint attention occurs when two persons give their conscious attention to each other, so that one person can 'reveal' themselves to the other and the second person can 'accurately perceive' what is being revealed (p. 442).

As we all know from experience, knowledge of another person can come in degrees. We know our immediate family and friends 'better' than our more distant acquaintances. According to Talbert, we know someone, A, well, when

(1) we have had a significant number of second-person face to face interactions with A, at least some of which have been relatively recent;
(2) the contexts of those interactions were such as to permit A to reveal important aspects of her/himself, and A has done so;
(3) A has not deceived us about him/herself in important respects;
(4) we have succeeded in accurately perceiving what A has revealed, that is, we are not 'blinded' by his/her own biases or other impairments. (Talbert, 2015, p. 194)

The frequency and duration of the interactions between two people will therefore determine the extent to which they grow to know each other well. As Efird notes, it will also depend on how skilled we are at such interactions with another person, including 'the skill of recognising them, the skill of detecting their mental states, and the skill of communicating your own mental states to them' (2021, p. 443). These skills are developed through experience, as we 'learn from our successes and failure, so that, over time, and after many interactions with someone and in a variety of contexts, we effortlessly, and largely unconsciously, interact with them successfully' (Efird, 2021, p. 443).

Efird has sought to apply these insights to the divine–human relationship. He begins by noting that, in principle, there is nothing preventing a human individual coming to know God in a second-personal sense, so long as it is possible to interact with him and share joint attention with him. However, 'an obvious difficulty' in applying Talbert's analysis to knowing God well is that her analysis emphasizes the importance of face-to-face interaction, but 'given that God is incorporeal, he does not have a face, at least not in a literal sense' (Efird, 2021, p. 444). To apply Talbert's insights to the divine–human relationship, Efird therefore engages in some conceptual engineering, 'modifying the concept' of what it means to know someone well (p. 445). The importance of face-to-face interactions in Talbert's model is that (in human relationships) they facilitate joint attention. Alternative types of interaction with God, which facilitate joint attention, therefore need to be identified. Efird suggests various possibilities, including a model of prayer popular in the Vineyard movement, in which an individual attends to their thoughts and seeks to detect 'which ones God has placed in your consciousness', thereby allowing you 'to share attention with God, as by attending to these God-implanted thoughts you attend to God himself' (p. 446). Dyadic joint attention with God might also be facilitated through religious experiences, such as those described by Michael Rea:

> It is not uncommon for people to report having a sense of God's presence in the midst of a church service, or around a campfire singing hymns or praise songs; nor is it uncommon for people to experience the love and forgiveness of Christ in the Lord's Supper, or at various other points in a Christian liturgy ... Similarly, people often report apparently non-mystical, non-numinous experiences of God's presence, love, majesty and the like in nature – out in the woods, on the beach, climbing a mountain, and so on ... People sometimes experience God speaking to them through the Scriptures or through a sermon, or through the words of a friend. (Rea, 2018, p. 116)

Assuming God does disclose himself through such experiences, a human seeking to know God well will need to develop 'the skills of accurately recognizing God in our experiences and accurately interpreting those experiences as revealing what God intends to reveal of himself to us' (p. 447). Developing such skills is a key purpose of the traditional spiritual disciplines of prayer, fasting, Bible reading, study and so forth, since each of them provides

> ... a mode of, and an occasion for, experiencing God second-personally and sharing attention with him, and, through many such experiences, and in many contexts, over a sustained period of time, developing the skills necessary for knowing God, that is, recognizing him in our experience and interpreting them accurately, that is, as revealing what God intends to reveal of himself in them. (p. 447)

As a case study in the spiritual disciplines, Efird considers the devotional study of Scripture. He argues that reading the Bible can help us know God personally in at least two ways. First, 'because of God's omnipresence, we can share attention with God, mediated by the text of Scripture':

> For example, we might imagine ourselves in a biblical story, such as when we read the Sermon on the Mount, we can imagine Jesus speaking the beatitudes directly to us. Practices of reading scripture, such as *Lectio Divina*, encourage just this sort of imaginative engagement with the text. In this way, reading scripture can be a mode of sharing attention with God. (p. 448)

A second way in which Scripture can facilitate a personal encounter with God is by alerting us to God's presence with us (p. 448). Some of the Psalms, for instance, could be said to serve this function, by directing our attention to God, especially in difficult circumstances. The study of Scripture doesn't just facilitate one-off encounters with God, however. Efird stresses that, over time, Bible reading helps us to develop the skills we need for successful engagement with God, since 'we come to know something of who God is and how he reveals himself to us. We can then better recognize God in our own lives and better interpret our experiences as revelatory of God' (p. 449).

Inman (2022) shares Efird's conviction that, undertaken with the right attitude, the study of Holy Scripture facilitates a second person ('I-Thou') encounter with God. Drawing on Wolterstorff's understanding of Scripture as divinely appropriated human discourse, Inman commends 'a reciprocity of orientation' by its Christian readers (p. 126). At the very least, such an orientation involves a 'prayerful openness' to what God is saying to us personally through the biblical text (2022, p. 127).

Prayer

Alongside Scripture reading, prayer is arguably the most widely practised spiritual discipline, and certainly the one which has received the most treatment by analytic theologians. For example, Scott Davison has published frequently on prayer, and a recent multi-author volume edited by Oliver Crisp, James Arcadi and Jordan Wessling (2022) contained a dozen articles on various aspects of the subject. Davison offers a helpful definition of prayer as 'an attempt to communicate with the divine, usually with a particular purpose in mind' (2021, p. 489). These purposes can include expressions of gratitude and thanksgiving, confession and repentance, adoration and praise, petition and intercession, lament and complaint. Prayers of petition have received the most attention from analytic theologians, but each of these genres of prayer is worthy of some consideration.

Prayers of adoration and praise

In his work on Christian liturgical acts, Nicholas Wolterstorff has defined the praise (or 'worship') of God as 'a particular mode of Godward acknowledgement of God's unsurpassable greatness. Specifically, it is that mode of such acknowledgement whose attitudinal stance toward God is awed, reverential, and grateful adoration' (2015, p. 154). Publicly and privately, Christians regularly praise God for one or more of his great qualities, such as his unsurpassed goodness, holiness, mercy, grace and wisdom. But since God possesses such attributes necessarily, some analytic philosophers (e.g. Howard-Snyder, 2009b) have questioned whether he deserves to be praised for them. In response to this concern, Davison writes that:

> One might challenge the claim that God must have a choice about being perfectly good before it makes sense to praise God. In fact it sometimes seems that we praise people precisely because they are unable to do anything else ... There also seems to be an inherent asymmetry between praise and blame: we seem to find it more acceptable to praise people for things beyond their control than to blame them for things beyond their control. (Davison, 2021, p. 489)

Davison concludes that praise is appropriate for anything (including God) that displays excellence, 'regardless of whether such excellence results from a choice' (p. 490).

James Arcadi has recently undertaken an analysis of the act of 'blessing' God. Utilizing the tools of Speech-Act Theory, particularly the conceptual insights of Alston (2000), Arcadi concludes that when Christians speak of blessing God they are 'pledging allegiance' to him, rather than engaging in praise (p. 160). Words of blessing, when addressed to God, satisfy the criteria of a 'Commissive' illocutionary act (akin to making a promise), rather than those of an 'Expressive' illocutionary act, such as thanking or praising someone (p. 161). By making such a pledge of allegiance, Christians who bless God place themselves under an obligation to 'participate' in God's kingdom, for instance by 'loving God and neighbor, meeting together to hear Scripture, pray, fellowship, and celebrate the Eucharist, believing *that Jesus is God* and *that God is Trinity*, etc.' (Arcadi, 2022, p. 162).

Prayers of thanksgiving

Richard Swinburne is one Christian analytic philosopher who has defended the propriety of humans expressing our thanks to God in prayer. Individuals have obligations to their benefactors, especially 'to those who have given to us and conserved in us that gift which is the precondition of all other good things – the gift of life itself' (1989, p. 123). It follows from this principle that children have an obligation to thank and obey their parents, and that all humans have a duty to express our thanksgiving to our Creator. As Swinburne writes:

> God is our supreme benefactor: we owe our existence from moment to moment, and our powers and pleasures, our knowledge and desires, to his sustaining power. And everything that everyone else does for us they can do only because God sustains in them their power. We owe him so much by way of expression of gratitude and service. (Swinburne, 1998, p. 112)

However, a similar objection could be levelled at this argument as to the argument for praising God. If God's perfect goodness necessarily means that he will be creative and generous, do we really have an obligation to thank him? Davison suggests that one potential line of response is similar to the case of praise, namely 'one might question whether a benefactor's having a choice is required for gratitude, in general' (2021,

p. 490). Moreover, God's goodness is 'the ultimate explanation of God's actions, and we ought to be grateful for good things' (p. 490).

But a stronger objection to prayers of thanksgiving has been offered by Nicholas Everett (2003). Given God's omnipotence, his generosity to us costs him nothing, so why should we express any gratitude to him? This question is sharpened yet further when we consider the evil and suffering in the world, which 'on the face of it God could have prevented' (p. 130). In such circumstances resentment rather than gratitude seems 'the more appropriate emotion' (p. 130). Responding to this concern requires, in part at least, an analytic response to the problem of evil – as found, for example, in Loke (2022). But Davison also disputes whether 'Everett's argument shows that it would be mistaken to be grateful to God to any degree' (2021, p. 491). After all, in practice we typically remain grateful to wealthy human benefactors, even if their generosity to us involved very little personal sacrifice on their part.

Prayers of complaint and lament

Prayers of complaint and lament are two similar types of prayer that are both addressed to God in circumstances of trial and tribulation. Crisp (2022b) draws a distinction between these two related genres of prayer as follows:

> COMPLAINT-PRAYER: An expression of dissatisfaction in a communicative act directed toward God that normally includes a reason for the dissatisfaction stated in the form of some kind of grievance.
>
> LAMENT-PRAYER: An expression of grief or sorrow in a communicative act directed toward God, often involving mourning over great loss or hardship. (p. 86)

As these parallel definitions illustrate, Crisp sees the expression of grievance as a distinctive feature of prayers of complaint, understood as a reason for some dissatisfaction. 'Sometimes the grievance of the complainant is expressed in the complaint; sometimes it is only implied or intimated elliptically, so to speak, in the way in which the complaint is articulated' (p. 84). The most well-known biblical examples of prayers of complaint appear in the book of Job, whereas individual and corporate laments are common in the Psalms. Crisp suggests that a further distinction can be made between different types of complaint, by applying Rea's terminology of 'pious' and 'impious protest' forms of prayer.

Rea notes that, while Job's complaints are not endorsed by God, they are accepted and 'validated' by God 'as a reasonable response to Job's circumstances on the part of someone who loves goodness and justice, but whose understanding of goodness, justice, and the relation between particular goods and evils is occluded by familiar human limitations' (2020, p. 196). Impious protest, in contrast, may come from sinful, selfish motives. Crisp then moves to reflect on the purpose of prayers of complaint. His commitment to a classical theistic understanding of the divine attributes, including a strong conception of God's immutability, means that Crisp rules out the possibility that prayers of complaint can change God's attitude or actions towards the individual concerned. The complainer

> is not attempting to change God's mind. Rather, knowing that God ordains what comes to pass, is immutable, omniscient, and loving, the complainer addresses herself to God in the hope that God may help her to reconcile herself to the tragic and difficult circumstances in which she finds herself. (p. 89)

Moreover, if prayers of complaint are indeed about aligning an individual's will with God's, they will also 'foster a sense of dependence on God' (p. 94).

Turning to prayers of lament, Kevin Timpe has recently analysed the nature of lamentation and sought to offer an account of 'lamenting well' (2022). Timpe reviews the plethora of prayers of lament within Scripture (from both Old and New Testaments), and adopts Rebekah Eklund's definition of biblical lament as 'a cry for help to God from within a situation of distress, arising from trust that God is faithful to hear and respond to cries' (2015, p. 7). He notes that biblical prayers are 'impassioned' and often 'call out to God concerning his absence, his inaction, his silence' (Timpe, 2022, p. 105). At other times laments are more confessional in tone, acknowledging sin and requesting God's mercy. Timpe also observes that laments typically presuppose 'a particular view of God's character, His commitments, His care, as well as a particular view of what justice demands of God' (p. 105). A crucial element of lamentation, in Timpe's eyes, is the element of hope that they include. Underlying an authentic Christian prayer of lament is not despair, but a hope 'that God, who is faithful, will respond appropriately' (p. 107). As an act motivated by faith and hope, prayerful lament can 'help orient us toward those goods that are not yet possessed, and to actively live into a life aimed at securing those goods that God ultimately intends for us' (p. 108).

Timpe concludes by offering an account of what it means to lament well. Acknowledging a philosophical debt to 'Aristotle, Aquinas, and – more recently – Anscombe, Foot, MacIntyre, and Roberts', Timpe defines a moral virtue as a rationally informed disposition 'to feel, desire, or act appropriately given the details of a particular situation, and to take proper pleasure or pain in doing so, in a way that contributes to the good of the individual and her community' (2022, p. 110). Given this definition of virtue:

> We might think that a person is virtuous to the degree that she, guided by right reason, laments about the proper things at appropriate times, and feels the proper pain (in the object of lament) and pleasure (in the hope within which lament is framed). (p. 110)

At its most virtuous, lament 'gives voice to those who have been oppressed, harmed, or otherwise treated unjustly' (p. 111). Timpe suggests that lament can be sinful, in contrast, if it 'calls into question God's goodness and faithfulness … [or] when it overvalues the importance or nature of the good whose loss or uncertainty one is lamenting' (p. 111). One may also lament 'falsely' if one laments over a state of affairs that doesn't exist, or by failing to lament sufficiently in situations when it is appropriate (p. 111). Finally, Timpe concludes that good lamentation has 'formative' elements, not least by cultivating the related virtues of faith, hope and love (p. 113).

Petitionary prayer and its problems

Petition and intercession are two closely related forms of prayer widely practised by Christians, which appear to have biblical warrant in passages such as Matthew 7.11 ('If you then, who are evil, know how to give good gifts to your children, how much more will your Father in heaven give good things to those who ask him!'). Prayers of petition are offered to God for our own needs, while prayers of intercession are made on behalf of others. As Harriet Harris observes, 'Both types of prayer seem to be impetratory, "impetrate" being a theological term meaning to obtain things by request. The conviction behind impetratory prayer is that God gives us some things not only as we wish, but because we wish and ask for them' (2010, p. 217).

However, many analytic philosophers of religion have found such prayer deeply problematic, as it appears incompatible with traditional beliefs about the nature and attributes of God. More precisely, they have argued that 'if we consider carefully God's attributes, we will realise that petitionary prayers cannot make a difference to God's actions. These arguments are challenges to the efficacy of petitionary prayer' (Davison, 2021, p. 491). A number of analytic theologians have therefore set themselves the task of defending the efficacy and value of petitionary prayer, both for ourselves and for others, by explaining how it is compatible with God's nature, knowledge, power and goodness.

One initial problem with petitionary prayer is its apparent incompatibility with divine immutability and impassibility. If God is unchanging (that is, immutable) in such things as his character and will, how can petitionary prayer possibly alter his plans and purposes? And if God is unable to be affected by anything external to himself (that is, impassible), what possible effect could human intercessions have on him? Such questions play into an important debate within systematic theology between what Brian Davies (2021) calls 'classical theists' and 'theistic personalists'. Classical Theism has traditionally affirmed strong definitions of God's immutability and impassibility, which do indeed appear to exclude any efficacy for petitionary prayers. Oliver Crisp, for example, denies that petitionary prayers change God's attitudes or actions, because God is strongly immutable. Instead, Crisp suggests that the purpose of such prayers may be 'to change the petitioner, bringing her desires and will into alignment with God's desires and will' (2022b, p. 88). However, it is increasingly common for theologians to weaken (or even deny) God's immutability and/or impassibility. These theologians hold that strict classical definitions of immutability and impassibility are inconsistent with the biblical portrait of a God who is responsive to the actions and prayers of his people. Further discussion of the debates around divine immutability and impassibility can be found in Leftow (2016) and Matz and Thornhill (2019) respectively.

A further set of challenges to petitionary prayer spring from God's less controversial attributes, notably his omnipotence, omniscience and omnibenevolence. As conventionally understood, omniscience refers to God's exhaustive knowledge of the past, present and future (including all possibilities), his omnipotence refers to his power to do anything logically possible, while his omnibenevolence refers to his perfect goodness. These attributes create what John Peckham has termed the 'Influence Aim Problem' of petitionary prayer:

> As I define it, the influence aim problem of petitionary prayer (IAP) is the problem of whether one can consistently affirm that petitionary prayer might influence God to bring about some good he otherwise would not have brought about, while also affirming that God is omniscient,

omnibenevolent, and omnipotent. It seems that an omniscient, omnibenevolent, and omnipotent God would know all preferable goods he could bring about, would prefer to bring about such goods, and would be capable of doing so. How then could it make sense to believe that petitionary prayer might influence God to bring about some good he otherwise would not bring about? (2020, p. 413)

One line of response to the IAP is carefully to define (or redefine) the nature of God's omniscience. For analytic theologians sympathetic to 'Open Theism' (e.g. Hasker, 1989 and Swinburne, 2016), God does not have exhaustive foreknowledge. This 'attenuated' sense of omniscience is based on the assumption that humans possess libertarian free will and that God exists within time (Swinburne, 2016, p. 196). If these assumptions are correct, God is unable to foresee humans' future free actions. Moreover, Open Theists would 'say that if our prayers are free, or God's decision whether or not to answer them is free (or both), then those things are undecided, and so petitionary prayer can make all the difference in the world' (Davison, 2021, p. 492). An alternative, Molinist (or 'Middle Knowledge') account of God's omniscience states that God knows how people will behave in all possible future situations, and which of those possible futures will be actualized. Within analytic theology, Molinism is advocated by Craig (2000) and Flint (1998), among others. According to this understanding of God's omniscience:

> Petitionary prayer can make a difference because God can consider prayers that will be freely offered in the future when God plans how to create the world. The fact that God knows the future in all of its detail does not mean that this future is determined, according to the Middle Knowledge view, since God's knowledge depends upon what we would choose to do freely. (Davison, 2021, p. 492)

Third, a 'Timeless Eternity' view of God's knowledge holds that he knows all of history from his unique atemporal vantage point. Analytic theologians who hold this view (including Helm, 2010) argue that 'God's single act of creation from outside of time has many effects that play out in time, including answers to petitionary prayers that God anticipated from the point of view of eternity' (Davison, 2021, p. 493). Lastly, Alexander Pruss (2013b) has argued that God's 'omnirationality' needs to be affirmed alongside his omniscience. God's omnirationality means that when he acts, he does so in accordance with all 'unexcluded' good reasons. By an unexcluded reason, he means a reason that has not been excluded 'by some higher order reason, such as an authoritative command or a valid promise' (Davison, 2022, p. 13). If Pruss is correct, 'when a person prays for something good and it comes to be, then God has answered that prayer – or at least we can say that the offering of the prayer was among God's reasons for bringing about that thing' (Davison, 2021, p. 491).

A wholly different type of strategy sometimes employed in response to the IAP is to argue that, in some circumstances at least, God's omnibenevolence requires him to act in response to petitionary prayers rather than independently. Peckham has summarized this strategy as follows:

> God's providence is ordered in such a way that there is some good that God perfectly knows about, prefers to bring about and possesses the sheer power to bring about, yet God has some reason(s) compatible with his perfect goodness such that he will not bring about that good without the 'influence' of petitionary prayer. (Peckham, 2020, p. 416)

Adopting the terminology of Davison (2022), analytic philosophers and theologians have proposed *relationship-based*, *responsibility-based*, and *request-based* reasons for the necessity of petitionary prayer. Relationship-based arguments, for example, affirm that there is 'some good that arises in relationship with God that requires ... petitionary prayers' (Davison, 2022, p. 20). For example, Stump (1979) argued that petitionary prayer is needed for a relationship with God that avoids our being 'spoiled by God if all our prayers were automatically answered, and ... overwhelmed if God provided everything good for us without waiting for us to ask first' (Davison, 2021, p. 493). Murray and Meyers (1994) also made the observation that, by making certain goods contingent on our petitions, God helps us to avoid a sinful sense of self-sufficiency. More recently, Brummer (2008), Smith and Yip (2010), Cohoe (2014) and Choi (2016) have all made similar arguments to the effect that an authentic two-way relationship between humans and God requires petitionary prayers to be offered and answered. Responsibility-based arguments, meanwhile, suggest that God makes the provision of some things conditional on imprecatory prayers in order to increase individuals' responsibility for the wellbeing of others and for the general state of the world. Richard Swinburne (1998) and Daniel and Frances Howard-Snyder (2010) are three advocates of this view that 'if God did not make the provision of certain things dependent upon the offering of petitionary prayers, human beings would not have as much responsibility for the world as they do' (Davison, 2022, p. 17).

Request-based defences of petitionary prayers are characterized by the idea that they 'furnish God with unique reasons for performing certain actions, which would (sometimes) seem to raise the probability that God will bring about certain events' (Wessling, 2022, p. 27). This line of argument claims 'that human requests by themselves make a difference in terms of the values at stake in a given situation. God might have lots of reasons for bringing about something, but when we ask for it, that provides an additional reason for doing so – and sometimes that additional reason might make all the difference' (Davidson, 2022, p. 20). This view was articulated by Daniel and Frances Howard-Snyder (2010), for example, who argued

> ... that being asked to do something can change the moral landscape. If you see me by the side of the road, you may stop to offer me a ride, or you may drive on. You're not morally obligated to stop. But once I start waving my arms and running after you, it gives you a reason to stop. There may still be countervailing reasons to you stopping, but they have to be more weighty than my request. Similarly, when we ask God to do something, that gives him reason to do it. (Parker and Rettler, 2017, p. 181)

A more recent variant of this request-based argument is found in Peckham (2020). Peckham offers a 'Cosmic Conflict Approach' response to the IAP. He recognizes that his proposal may initially 'seem outlandish to some', but 'the view that there is a cosmic conflict wherein the devil has some significant degree of temporary rulership is quite at home in Scripture and the Christian tradition' (2020, p. 425). He cites various biblical passages that describe an ongoing spiritual conflict between God and evil supernatural powers, with the latter having their own (temporary) spheres of dominion (e.g. Luke 4.5–6). Peckham then posits the following scenario, in which petitionary prayer changes the moral landscape and enables God to act in a way he otherwise would not:

> Suppose there is a cosmic conflict with rules of engagement ... which grant some limited jurisdiction or domain to the devil and his cohorts, while correspondingly limiting (morally) the parameters within which God acts in the world. Suppose, further, that such rules of engagement are set up such that petitionary prayer might increase God's (moral) jurisdiction to intervene in ways that, absent such prayer, would not have been morally available to God. (Peckham, 2020, p. 424)

Another recent contribution to the request-based genre of arguments has come from Jordan Wessling (2022). He articulates an 'Extended Charity Defence' to explain why God requires (and responds to) intercessory prayer requests on behalf of other people. Wessling argues that intercessory prayer is 'immensely valuable', since:

> Such prayer is good for the petitioner as the practice of praying for others is, certainly, a means by which one is conformed to the loving image of Christ. In addition, this mode of prayer gives the petitioner the immense privilege of helping others in ways that would not otherwise be possible ... The proposal then, is this. It would be good for God to answer weighty other-directed petitions because it is a way of God's taking our requests for such matters seriously, and because it provides a framework for a valuable kind of other-directed prayer. (p. 31)

One final category of arguments justifying God's responsiveness to petitionary prayers is known as the *deontological* defence. According to deontological arguments, God occasionally 'makes the provision of some good thing dependent on the offering of petitionary prayers because somehow this is right or fitting or appropriate' (Davison, 2020, p. 22). For instance, Choi (2016) argues that 'whereas petitionary prayers express praiseworthy attitudes, a lack of petitionary prayer often expresses morally culpable attitudes. So God's answering some petitionary prayers (and not providing things when petitionary prayers are not offered) is part of [a] just system of punishments and rewards' (Davison, 2020, p. 23).

As Davison and others have noted, each of these varied lines of defence against the IAP has its limitations, and none offers a comprehensive solution to the problem. For example, Davison observes that both relationship-based and responsibility-based arguments struggle 'to justify God withholding significant goods that could have been provided, especially for third parties' (2022, pp. 18–19). Request-based arguments also fail to explain why God does not meet individuals' serious needs, even if they 'do not (or cannot) request it' (Davison, 2020, p. 20). Nevertheless, it is possible to see that in certain circumstances one or more of these defences of petitionary prayer may have logical force, undermining the *prima facie* strength of the IAP.

The benefits of prayer

So what are the fruits of prayer, at least as analytic theologians see it? Perhaps most obviously, prayers of an imprecatory nature hold out the promise of obtaining good things from God, either for our benefit or for others'. And as Crisp (2022b) has noted, even if petitionary prayers fail to change God's attitudes or actions towards us, they may effect a beneficial change in our own psychological condition or spiritual maturity. Davison has also suggested that petitionary prayer 'unites people in a common cause, and communicates important values to others' (2017, p. 7). We saw too that Timpe's account of virtuous lamentation suggests it can cultivate a concern for social justice and nurture the virtues of faith, hope and love.

Adam Green is an analytic theologian who has argued that 'prayer provides us with a unique and privileged path to self-knowledge, one whose strengths complement and contrast nicely with introspection' (2022, p. 183). In reaching this conclusion, Green draws both on the spiritual writings of Teresa of Avila and on Richard Moran's philosophical and psychological work on self-knowledge. He argues that as we seek to relate to God and others through prayer, 'these more familiar foci for prayer imply an evolving relationship with oneself as well and that indeed growth in self-knowledge is bound up with spiritual growth generally' (p. 201).

Jason McMartin, meanwhile, has surveyed recent analytic philosophical writing on meaningfulness in life. This work has identified both 'objective frameworks' of meaning and their 'subjective appropriation' as necessary conditions for an individual to live a life with meaning. An objectively meaningful framework (or 'worldview') is one that offers satisfying answers to 'questions relating to how life should be understood in light of such things as existence, purpose, value, worth, suffering, and death' (2022, p. 206). Unsurprisingly, McMartin assumes that the Christian faith 'is the best candidate for an objective framework' of meaning (p. 210). It is a worldview in which, among other things, human beings are seen as creatures made in the image of God, with all the associated privileges and responsibilities. But McMartin then proceeds to argue that prayer is a very promising mechanism for the subjective, self-conscious appropriation of this Christian worldview:

> Prayer may be thought of as a uniquely human response that is deeply congruent with human nature. It instantiates the gift and task of being human. First, our reception of God's blessing rightly results in response … [The] natural reaction of the human person and the activity that is meant to be typical for us is that of blessing God in gratitude and praise for the goodness of the world … Second, petition is at the heart of prayer, mirroring human-as-recipient. Gratitude and worship are also important components. Each of these reflects the dependence of the human person on the grace of God and the human vocation to respond. (p. 213)

In short, McMartin writes, 'Prayer aligns our internal states with reality ... [it] puts us into the relationship for which we were created and is the fulfilment of our nature. The "being with" component of prayer is essential to it' (p. 215).

This reference to the 'being with' component of prayer leads to the most important benefit of prayer as many analytic theologians see it, namely the joy and privilege of relational communion with God. Indeed, as Harriet Harris has suggested, philosophically prayer need not have any further 'point' than simply to 'abide' with God (2010, p. 217). Kyle Strobel has recently drawn attention to the biblical claim that in prayer God makes himself 'relationally present' to Christians through the internal ministry of the Holy Spirit. Drawing on work by Stump (2010) on interpersonal relationships, Strobel argues that the Spirit-mediated presence of God within Christians is deeper and more 'significant' than God's omnipresence within the world at large (2022, p. 174). Prayer is then understood as a reciprocal act, in which the Christian offers back to God their own attention and 'significant personal presence' in response to his (p. 174). Strobel concludes that on his 'modelling of prayer the Christian must intend to be with God, giving herself to the closeness available to the Father, in the Son, and by the Spirit (Eph 2:18), and should do so in truth. This is "drawing near" to God by faith' (p. 182).

The trinitarian dimension of prayer described by Strobel is, of course, a distinctively Christian perspective on the topic, and one that has begun to be explored within analytic theology. Harris (2010) and Sonderegger (2022), for instance, both point to biblical passages that describe the Son and Spirit of God at prayer – prayers in which one divine person prays to another. Christ, of course, prayed frequently to his Father throughout his earthly ministry, not least in the Garden of Gethsemane and on the cross of Calvary. Equally, the apostle Paul describes the intercessory prayer life of the Holy Spirit in Romans 8.26–27 (see Gal. 4.4–7 and Eph. 2.18). If Christians do indeed pray 'in' the Son and 'by' or 'through' the Spirit (as Strobel suggests above) then this may have important implications. Harris suggests, for example, that 'if in prayer God speaks to God, most of the problems raised regarding impetratory prayer are changed. We no longer need to consider that we somehow inform God, influence God, or empower God. God is the subject of prayer' (2010, p. 236). She also adds that a trinitarian perspective may 'avoid us being transactional or individualistic in our accounts of prayer. Prayer is not for wrestling some good out of God, nor merely for conforming our lives to God's, but for sharing in the [triune] life of God' (Harris, 2010, p. 236). In her recent essay entitled 'Does God Pray?', Katherine Sonderegger (2022) suggests that the prayers of the divine persons seen in Scripture are a valuable window into the inner life of the Godhead, and provide a model for how we might praise God ourselves.

As I conclude, this chapter has surveyed analytic theologians' contributions to date on the subjects of Christian spirituality and prayer. More work remains to be done on each of the areas covered, as well as on entirely new topics. For example, analytic theologians may yet give more attention to wider senses of prayer (such as contemplative, or even mystical, prayer), as well as to a broader range of spiritual disciplines such as meditation, fasting, simplicity and service. Spiritual disciplines are, in part at least, aimed at personal sanctification and moral improvement as well as communion with God. Emerging work by analytic theologians on ethical issues (e.g. Dunnington, 2021) can therefore also be expected to contribute to this field.

Recommended Further Reading

Crisp, O. D., Arcadi, J. M. and Wessling, J. (eds), 2022, *Analyzing Prayer: Theological and Philosophical Essays*, Oxford Studies in Analytic Theology, Oxford: Oxford University Press.

Davison, S., 2022, *God and Prayer*, Elements of the Philosophy of Religion, Cambridge: Cambridge University Press.

8

Conclusion – The Apologetic Value of Analytic Theology

Analytic theology adopts the tools and methods of analytic philosophy to address important and enduring questions in Christian belief and practice. In many respects analytic theology is simply a rebranding of Christian philosophical theology, a new name for the type of work long since undertaken by philosophers such as William Abraham, Eleonore Stump, Richard Swinburne and Nicholas Wolterstorff, among others. But analytic theology has increasingly drawn *on*, and drawn *in*, the contributions of scholars from other fields of theological enquiry too. It represents an increasingly diverse field of academics, united by a common intellectual culture and a shared commitment to producing logically coherent, biblically grounded and creedally shaped accounts of the riches of the Christian faith. It has arguably brought a new degree of argumentative rigour and conceptual clarity to contemporary systematic theology, fulfilling some of the hopes and aspirations for the discipline articulated by Reno (2006) and Abraham (2009), among others.

As Chapter 2 of this book sought to show, analytic theology (at its truest and best) recognizes and respects the parameters for authentically 'Christian' theology established by Scripture and the ecumenical creeds. It is not, and ought not to be, a hyper-rationalist 'ivory tower' exercise, detached from the traditions of the Church, from the insights from other disciplines, or from the life and worship of ordinary Christians. Without doubt, exegetical errors and historical omissions will continue to be made in particular cases, but analytic theology as a discipline surely deserves its place among the recognized and respected schools of Christian theology.

Analytic theology and the future

As I hope Part Two of this book illustrated, analytic theologians (and their forebears in philosophical theology) have made valuable contributions to our understanding of central Christian doctrines, including the Trinity, the Incarnation and the Atonement. New models, such as the constitutional account of the Trinity, have shed new light on some of the most perplexing and mysterious dogmas of the faith, without ever claiming to offer *the* definitive account of a doctrine or the final word on the subject. Indeed, there is an admirable humility seen in the writing of many analytic theologians, a recognition that their models (at best) only offer a partial, piecemeal glimpse of divine realities.

Alongside this humility, however, there is also ambition. As Part Three of this book sought to demonstrate, analytic theologians have progressively broadened their fields of enquiry and covered new ground. The ecclesiological and liturgical 'turns' seen in the discipline in recent years testify to this ambition, as writers like James Arcadi, Joshua Cockayne, Terence Cuneo and Nicholas Wolterstorff have explored what is really going on when the Church gathers to worship and celebrate the sacraments as the one 'body of Christ'. What applies corporately also applies individually. The late David Efird has left us with an initial analytic account of spirituality, while insights from Eleonore Stump, Scott Davison and others have clarified how God might be especially 'present' to his people as they read Scripture and say their prayers.

New frontiers still being surveyed by analytic theologians include contextual and non-Christian theologies. Contextual theology proceeds from the conviction that all theological work is inevitably rooted in a particular cultural, geographical and historical location. Much analytic theology to date has been Western (indeed, Anglo-American), ethnically white and predominantly male in origin, but the discipline is starting to recognize its need to diversify and incorporate hitherto marginalized voices. Indeed, Sameer Yadav has proposed an 'analytic theology of liberation', which calls upon the discipline to aim 'not merely at truth, but also at justice for the socially and politically oppressed' (2020, p. 54). At his time of writing, Yadav noted regretfully that there was 'no discernible strand' of analytic theology contributing 'to the current state of black or womanist theologies, more critical and revisionist feminist theologies, queer theologies, or any other radical social and political theologies' (2020, pp. 48–9). In a welcome move, therefore, analytic theologians have begun to produce work on race (e.g. Yadav, 2021), disability (e.g. Yancey, 2021) and gender issues (e.g. Griffioen, 2021; Panchuk, 2021). Tobin and Moon (2020) and Hebeth (2020) consider LGBTQ and transgender experiences from an analytic perspective too. The analytic method is also beginning to gain ground within Jewish and Islamic theology. For instance, the 2022 edition of the *Journal of Analytic Theology* was dedicated to Jewish analytic theology, with nine different contributors. Early works of Islamic analytic theology, meanwhile, include Nordby (2018) and Saemi and Davison (2020).

All in all, analytic theology can rightly be described as what Crisp, Arcadi and Wessling (2019) call a 'generative research program' in theology, namely:

> ... one that provides new ways of thinking about the body of doctrinal, and particularly dogmatic, material that has been generated by the sources of theological evidence and reflection on those sources of evidence, and that offers a better, that is, more satisfactory account of the various sources and the concepts and doctrines that they have generated than alternative explanations. (2019, p. 57)

The body of analytic theological literature can therefore be expected to continue growing in breadth as well as in depth, offering new insights into an increasingly wide range of topics from an increasingly wide range of perspectives. Before closing, however, I wish briefly to make the case that analytic theologians' work may have a particularly valuable application to the task of Christian apologetics.

Analytic theology and apologetics

Christian apologetics can be defined as the task of 'defending and commending the faith' (Beilby, 2011). This definition implies that apologetics has two aspects, one responsive and the other proactive. As Beilby defines it, the 'goal of responsive apologetics is to demonstrate that objections to Christian belief are not successful' (p. 15). The aim of proactive apologetics, in contrast, is to take 'the initiative by giving arguments for Christian belief, arguments intended to show that Christian belief is perfectly rational or, perhaps, that Christian belief is intellectually superior to other worldviews' (p. 15). McGrath adds a third dimension of the apologetic task, which is to clearly explain theological terms and ideas, translating them into a vocabulary that can be understood by a contemporary audience. The use of analogies is also part of this work of translation, utilizing 'familiar or accessible images' to illustrate complex doctrinal claims (McGrath, 2016, p. 20).

Apologetics has traditionally taken as its governing principle the apostle Peter's exhortation to 'always be ready to make your defence to anyone who demands from you an account of the hope that is in you' (1 Peter 3.15). One might also cite Paul's words in 2 Corinthians 10.4–5 in this context too: 'We destroy arguments and every proud obstacle raised up against the knowledge of God, and we take every thought captive to obey Christ.' In the increasingly secular, post-Christendom climate of the Western world at least, the need for effective apologetic arguments and methods seems as great as ever. It is important to recognize, however, that the 'target audience' for contemporary apologetics is not solely those who reject or oppose the Christian faith. Christians also experience difficulties with their faith, and so there is a role for what Beilby calls *'internal apologetics ...* to reinforce faith, to remove intellectual barriers, to help clarify issues and in so doing dispel doubts' (2011, p. 28). Wood concurs, writing that 'many people, including many "ordinary" Christians, really do have questions about the meaning, logical coherence, and truth of Christian doctrines ... [so] it is good that there is a mode of inquiry that explicitly foregrounds such questions' (2021, p. 11). Crucially, the 'mode of inquiry' that Wood has in mind here is *analytic theology*. Works of analytic theology have, I would argue, an important contribution to make to the threefold apologetic task of explaining, defending and commending the Christian faith.

Analytic theology seems particularly well placed to serve apologetics in its most intellectually rigorous, 'academic' form. Beilby defines 'academic apologetics' as follows:

> This form of apologetics is almost always written rather than verbal, and, by its nature, it operates at a very high level of complexity. Typically, the audience for academic apologetics is not specific. Consequently, the focus of academic apologetics is typically not on how the argument will be heard but on whether the arguments are sound. This feature of academic apologetics has caused some to question its usefulness or even its appropriateness. However ... [a]cademic apologetics helps refine apologetic arguments in the fire of academic debate, and academic debate is very useful at exposing the potential weaknesses of arguments. Christian apologetics (either public or private, around the water cooler or from the pulpit) is much better off if the arguments being used have received thorough scrutiny. (Beilby, 2011, pp. 26–7)

Beilby, however, laments the fact that work in the philosophy of religion has been of only limited apologetic value, since it confines itself to arguments for the existence of God, theodicy and other defences of generic monotheism. 'Apologetics, on the other hand, is always pursued from the perspective of a particular religious tradition – Buddhist apologetics or Christian apologetics' (p. 32). The fruits of analytic theology are therefore potentially of far greater use to (academic) Christian apologetics than those of the philosophy of religion, given its focus on distinctively Christian doctrines.

If this inference is correct, it is no accident that two of the most respected academic Christian apologists, namely William Lane Craig and Richard Swinburne, are among the most prominent forefathers of analytic theology. Both men have published works of Christian apologetics (e.g. Craig, 2008; Swinburne, 2008), which draw upon and summarize their extensive prior academic work in philosophical theology. Church history also teaches us that there is often a close relationship between robust forms of systematic theology and apologetics. As William Abraham notes, from the patristic era onwards:

> Theologians have rightly been concerned with the truth of their claims rather than simply their authenticity or Christian identity. They have operated at the level of the normative and the prescriptive, seeking to articulate what we ought to believe rather than simply what has been believed. In other words, the task of apologetics and proof ... has always been in the neighborhood. (Abraham, 2009, p. 56)

It is no great surprise, therefore, that in our own generation analytic theologians have begun to deploy the 'skills, resources and virtues' of analytic philosophy to argue 'for the truth of the Christian Gospel' (Abraham, 2009, p. 69). As noted previously, Crisp, Arcadi and Wessling have described much analytic theology as a contemporary expression of medieval 'declarative theology', an approach to the theological task which has strikingly similar aims to the explanatory, defensive and proactive goals of contemporary apologists. According to Crisp et al., the aims of declarative theology include: first, to explain the 'meaning of the terms used in an article of the faith'; second, to respond to alleged 'defeaters' of Christian belief; third, to offer 'examples, confirming arguments, or analogies related to belief'; and, finally, to provide 'probable arguments' in support of Christian faith (2019, pp. 23–5). William Wood has also recognized the methodological similarities between medieval defences of the faith and the contemporary analytic method, which means it can aid the Church's apologetic task today:

> Many people really do want to know whether core Christian doctrines make sense, how they could be even possibly true, and how they could be consistent with the natural sciences and other things we take ourselves to know. Analytic theology can help answer these kinds of questions. Answering them well requires the kind of technical appara-

tus that flourished in the scholastic period and flourishes again in the modern dress of analytic theology. (2021, p. 298)

This 'technical apparatus' includes the work of conceptual clarification, the use of logical argument and empirical evidence, model-building and more. Together, these tools can help to explain, defend and commend the Christian faith, thereby strengthening the Church's apologetic witness to the outside world *and* its discipleship of Christians wrestling with doubts.

Explaining the faith: Conceptual clarification and analogy

Conceptual clarification is a central component of the analytic theologian's vocation. Much work in analytic theology seeks to define and explain the meaning of complex and controversial theological terms. As we have seen in this present volume, analytic theologians have striven hard to clarify the meaning of key words and concepts in theology, such as 'satisfaction' and 'substance', '*homoousios*' and '*hypostasis*', '*perichoresis*' and 'person'. In so doing, analytic theologians have generated much material that can be usefully deployed in what McGrath (2016) calls the 'translation' mode of apologetics.

A similar apologetic function is served by analytic theologians' frequent use of analogies to help clarify and communicate some of the most perplexing and paradoxical articles of the faith. As Wood observes, such analogies help us understand Christian doctrines 'in a way that coheres with other things we take ourselves to know' (Wood, 2021, p. 76). Think, for example, of Hasker's (2017) avatar analogy for the Incarnation, Moreland and Craig's (2003) use of Cerberus as an analogy for the social trinity, or Brower and Rea's (2005) account of a marble statue to illustrate their constitutional model of the triune God. One might also cite Brian Leftow's use of 'scuba gear' as an analogy for the human nature of Christ, since it 'is the Son's environment suit, letting him manoeuvre in time yet stay dry' (2002, p. 292). As we saw in Joshua Cockayne's ecclesiology, even a Disney animation such as *Ratatouille* has been harvested for its illustrative potential. Analytic theologians (like any good preacher) recognize that no illustration or analogy is perfect, but their creativity and imagination in this area can be of service to the Church as it seeks to communicate the faith once delivered to the saints.

Defending and commending the faith: Analysis and argument

The tools and techniques of analytic theology also serve to defend Christian doctrines from accusations of incoherence or impossibility. Their use of both conceptual and argumentative analysis means they are well placed to help Christian apologists defend the logical coherence and epistemic possibility of the articles of the faith. For instance, analytic theologians following Rea's fifth stylistic prescription ('P5') will treat conceptual analysis 'as a source of evidence' (2009a, p. 5). If they can demonstrate that a non-Christian concept contains a contradiction within it, this is very good evidence for its falsity. Conversely, showing that a concept at the heart of the Christian creed is internally consistent helps to refute an opponent's claim that the doctrine in question is unintelligible or impossible. Analytic theologians' conceptual analysis of the Trinity and of Chalcedonian Christology immediately springs to mind in this regard, as does the work of those defending corporeal conceptions of the Eucharist.

More generally, analytic theologians expend huge effort examining the logical validity of deductive arguments, identifying fallacious reasoning and evaluating the empirical evidence for competing theological claims. As Wood has noted, this analytic approach is well placed to defend Christian beliefs in the secular arena, since they appeal to 'generally accessible evidence and arguments', rather than 'solely with appeals to authority or private revelatory experiences' (2021, p. 297). Analytic theologians make use of publicly available evidence from history, science and the social sciences when evaluating arguments for and against the faith, and utilize 'common standards of rationality and commonsense notions about truth' (Wood, 2021, p. 297). Arguments constructed by analytic theologians can therefore be usefully deployed in apologetic encounters with our non-Christian contemporaries. For example, as Richard Swinburne has noted, in our 'age of religious scepticism ... the historical truths of the Christian religion need to be backed up by inductive arguments beginning, in part, from historical data recognized by theist and atheist alike' (2005, pp. 91–2).

To illustrate this approach, Baker-Hytch summarizes the way that both Swinburne and William Lane Craig have defended belief in the Resurrection:

> Roughly, the strategy of these authors is to argue that a bodily resurrection of Jesus is the best explanation for a range of occurrences reported in Paul's epistles and the Gospels, such as the burial of Jesus, the subsequent discovery of his tomb empty by his women followers,

and the experiences had by the disciples of seeming to see Jesus after his death. Further argumentation is offered on behalf of the trustworthiness of each of the scriptural passages at issue, [but] that argumentation doesn't itself assume the trustworthiness of scripture or any portion thereof. (Baker-Hytch, 2016, p. 358)

As this quotation illustrates, the methods employed by analytic theologians can just as easily be used to positively *commend* Christian truth claims as well as *defend* them, thereby serving the third ambition of contemporary apologetics. By demonstrating the logical coherence of Christian doctrines, and offering deductive or inductive arguments in their support, the work of analytic theologians can strengthen the faith of the faithful and give non-believers pause for thought. If contemporary apologists know where to look, analytic theology can furnish them with intellectually rigorous material to commend, as well as defend, the Christian worldview. Of course, this is not to say that analytic theology is the only valuable source for contemporary apologetics, nor even to argue that the use of logically coherent, reasoned argument is the only appropriate apologetic method (see Davison, 2011 and McGrath, 2019 for alternative strategies, for example). My claim is simply that analytic theology deserves recognition as *a* valuable resource for Christian apologetics, just as it merits its place among the respected schools of Christian theology. If this book has helped to support either contention, or even merely aroused further interest in the discipline, then its purpose will have been well served.

Bibliography

Abraham, W., 2009, 'Systematic Theology as Analytic Theology', in Crisp, O. and Rea, M. (eds), *Analytic Theology: New Essays in the Philosophy of Theology*, Oxford: Oxford University Press, pp. 54–69.

—— 2010, 'Church,', in Taliaferro, C. and Meister, C. (eds), *The Cambridge Companion to Christian Philosophical Theology*, Cambridge: Cambridge University Press, pp. 170–82.

—— 2012, *Analytic Theology: A Biography*, Dallas, TX: Highland Loch Press.

—— 2013, 'Turning Philosophical Water into Theological Wine', *Journal of Analytic Theology*, 1, pp. 1–16.

Adams, M., 2010, *Some Later Medieval Theories of the Eucharist: Thomas Aquinas, Giles of Rome, Duns Scotus, and William Ockham*, Oxford: Oxford University Press.

Adams, M., 2014, 'What's Wrong with the Ontotheological Error?', *Journal of Analytic Theology*, 2, pp. 1–12.

Alston, W., 2000, *Illocutionary Acts and Sentence Meaning*, Ithaca, NY: Cornell University Press.

Arcadi, J. M., 2016, 'Review of Andrew Ter Ern Loke. A Kryptic Model of the Incarnation', *Journal of Analytic Theology*, 4, pp. 459–63.

—— 2018a, 'Recent developments in analytic Christology', *Philosophy Compass*, 13:4.

—— 2018b, *An Incarnational Model of the Eucharist*, Cambridge: Cambridge University Press.

—— 2021a, 'Introduction', in Arcadi, J. M. and Turner, J. T. (eds), *The T&T Clark Handbook of Analytic Theology*, London: Bloomsbury, pp. 1–5.

—— 2021b, 'On the Intelligibility of Eucharistic Doctrine(s) in Analytic Theology', in Arcadi, J. M. and Turner, J. T. (eds), *The T&T Clark Handbook of Analytic Theology*, London: Bloomsbury, pp. 463–75.

—— 2022, 'Blessing God as Pledge of Allegiance: A Speech-Act Theoretic Approach', in Crisp, O. D., Arcadi, J. M. and Wessling, J. (eds), *Analyzing Prayer: Theological and Philosophical Essays*, Oxford Studies in Analytic Theology, Oxford: Oxford University Press, pp. 149–65.

Arcadi, J. M. and Turner, J. T. (eds), 2021, *The T&T Clark Handbook of Analytic Theology*, London: Bloomsbury.

Aspenson, S., 1996, 'Swinburne on Atonement', *Religious Studies*, 32:2, pp. 187–204.

Aulen, G., 1931, *Christus Victor: An Historical Study of the Three Main Types of the Idea of the Atonement*, London: SPCK.

Baber, H. E., 2013, 'The Real Presence', *Religious Studies*, 49:1, pp. 19–33.

Baker, K., 2013, *Jesus Christ – True God and True Man: A Handbook on Christology for Non-Theologians*, South Bend, IN: Saint Augustine's Press.

BIBLIOGRAPHY

Baker-Hytch, M., 2016, 'Analytic Theology and Analytic Philosophy of Religion: What's the Difference?', *Journal of Analytic Theology*, 4, pp. 347–60.

Basinger, D., 1983, 'Why Petition an Omnipotent, Omniscient, Wholly Good God?', *Religious Studies*, 19, pp. 25–42.

Bayne, T. and Restall, G., 2009, 'A Participatory Model of the Atonement', in Nagasawa, Y. and Wielenberg, E. J. (eds), *New Waves in Philosophy of Religion*, New York: Palgrave-Macmillan. pp. 150–66.

Beall, J. C., 2019, 'Christ – A Contradiction: A Defense of Contradictory Christology', *Journal of Analytic Theology*, 7, pp. 400–33.

—— 2021, *The Contradictory Christ*, Oxford Studies in Analytic Theology, Oxford: Oxford University Press.

—— 2023, *Divine Contradiction*, Oxford Studies in Analytic Theology, Oxford: Oxford University Press.

Beilby, J. K., 2011, *Thinking About Christian Apologetics*, Downers Grove, IL: IVP Academic.

Bonhoeffer, D., 1998, *Sanctorum Communio: A Theological Study of the Sociology of the Church*, Dietrich Bonhoeffer Works: Volume 1, Krauss, R. and Lukens, N. (trans.), Green, C. J. (ed.), Philadelphia, PA: Fortress Press.

Branson, B., 2014, 'Ahistoricity in Analytic Theology', in *American Catholic Philosophical Quarterly*, 92, pp. 195–224.

Brower, J. and Rea, M., 2005, 'Material Constitution and the Trinity', *Faith and Philosophy*, 22:1, pp. 57–76.

Brummer, V., 2008, *What Are We Doing When We Pray? On Prayer and the Nature of Faith*, Farnham: Ashgate.

Choi, I., 2016, 'Is Petitionary Prayer Superfluous?', in Kvanvig, J. (ed.), *Oxford Studies in Philosophy of Religion: Volume 7*, Oxford; Oxford University Press, pp. 32–62.

Clark, A. and Chalmers, D. J., 1998, 'The Extended Mind', *Analysis*, 58, pp. 7–19.

Coakley, S., 1999, '"Persons" and the "Social" Doctrine of the Trinity: A Critique of Current Analytic Discussion', in Davis, S. T., Kendall, D. and O'Collins, G. (eds), 1999, *The Trinity*, New York: Oxford University Press, pp. 124–44.

—— 2002, 'What Does Chalcedon Solve and What Does It Not? Some Reflections on the Status and Meaning of the Chalcedonian "Definition"', in Davis, S. T., Kendall, D. and O'Collins, G. (eds), *The Incarnation*, Oxford: Oxford University Press, pp. 143–63.

—— 2009, *Analytic Theology: New Essays in the Philosophy of Theology*, in Crisp, O. and Rea, M. (eds), Oxford: Oxford University Press.

—— 2013a, *God, Sexuality, and the Self: An Essay 'On the Trinity'*, Cambridge: Cambridge University Press.

—— 2013b, 'Beyond "Belief": Liturgy and the Cognitive Apprehension of God', in Greggs, T., Muers, R. and Zahl, S. (eds), *The Vocation of Theology Today: A Festschrift for David Ford*, Portland, OR: Cascade, pp. 131–45.

Cockayne, J., 2017, 'The Imitation Game: Becoming Imitators of Christ', *Religious Studies*, 53:1, pp. 3–24.

—— 2019, 'Analytic Ecclesiology: The Social Ontology of the Church', *Journal of Analytic Theology*, 7, pp. 100–23.

—— 2021, 'Analytic Theology and Liturgy', in Arcadi, J. M. and Turner, J. T. (eds), *The T&T Clark Handbook of Analytic Theology*, London: Bloomsbury, pp. 477–88.

—— 2022, *Explorations in Analytic Ecclesiology: That They May be One*, Oxford Studies in Analytic Theology, Oxford: Oxford University Press.
Cockayne, J. and Efird, D., 2018, 'Common Worship', *Faith and Philosophy*, 33:2, pp. 33–55.
Cockayne, J., Efird, D., Haynes, G., Ludwigs, A., Molto, D., Tamburro, R. and Warman, J., 2017, 'Experiencing the Real Presence of Christ in the Eucharist', *Journal of Analytic Theology*, 5, pp. 175–96.
Cohoe, C. M., 2014, 'God, Causality, and Petitionary Prayer', *Faith and Philosophy*, 31:1, pp. 24–45.
Collins, S., 2019, *Group Duties*, Oxford: Oxford University Press.
Craig, W. L., 2000, *The Only Wise God: The Compatibility of Divine Foreknowledge and Human Freedom*, Eugene, OR: Wipf and Stock.
—— 2008, *Reasonable Faith*, 3rd edition, Wheaton, IL: Crossway.
—— 2009, 'Towards a Tenable Social Trinitarianism', in McCall, T. and Rea, M. (eds), *Philosophical and Theological Essays on the Trinity*, Oxford: Oxford University Press, pp. 89–99.
—— 2018, *The Atonement*, Elements in the Philosophy of Religion, Cambridge: Cambridge University Press.
—— 2020, *Atonement and the Death of Christ: An Exegetical, Historical, and Philosophical Exploration*, Waco, TX: Baylor University Press.
Crisp, O. D., 2007a, 'Incarnation', in Webster, J., Tanner, K. and Torrance, I. (eds), *The Oxford Handbook of Systematic Theology*, Oxford: Oxford University Press.
—— 2007b, *Divinity and Humanity: The Incarnation Reconsidered*, Cambridge: Cambridge University Press.
—— 2007c. 'Was Christ Sinless or Impeccable?' *Irish Theological Quarterly* 72:2, pp. 168–86.
—— 2009, *God Incarnate: Explorations in Christology*, London: T&T Clark.
—— 2011, 'Compositional Christology without Nestorianism', in Marmodoro, A. and Hill, J. (eds), *The Metaphysics of the Incarnation*, Oxford: Oxford University Press, pp. 45–66.
—— 2016, *Word Enfleshed: Exploring the Person and Work of Christ*, Grand Rapids, MI: Baker Academic.
—— 2019a, *Analyzing Doctrine*, Waco, TX: Baylor University Press.
—— 2019b, *Is Jesus God Incarnate?*, St Andrews: Logos Institute for Analytical and Exegetical Theology.
—— 2021, 'The Importance of Model Building in Theology', in Arcadi, J. M. and Turner, J. T. (eds), *The T&T Clark Handbook of Analytic Theology*, London: Bloomsbury, pp. 9–19.
—— 2022a, *Participation and Atonement: An Analytic and Constructive Account*, Grand Rapids, MI: Baker Academic.
—— 2022b, 'Prayer as Complaint', in Crisp, O. D., Arcadi, J. M. and Wessling, J. (eds), *Analyzing Prayer: Theological and Philosophical Essays*, Oxford Studies in Analytic Theology, Oxford: Oxford University Press, pp. 79–94.
—— 2023, 'Analytic Theology', in Allen, M. (ed.), *The New Cambridge Companion to Christian Doctrine*, Cambridge: Cambridge University Press.
Crisp, O. D. (ed.), 2009, *A Reader in Contemporary Philosophical Theology*, London: T&T Clark.

Crisp, O. D., Arcadi, J. M. and Wessling, J., 2019, *The Nature and Promise of Analytic Theology*, Leiden: Brill.
Crisp, O. D., Arcadi, J. M. and Wessling, J. (eds), 2022, *Analyzing Prayer: Theological and Philosophical Essays*, Oxford Studies in Analytic Theology, Oxford: Oxford University Press.
Crisp, O. D. and Rea, M. (eds), 2009, *Analytic Theology: New Essays in the Philosophy of Theology*, Oxford: Oxford University Press.
Crisp, T., 2009, 'On Believing that the Scriptures are Divinely Inspired', in Crisp, O. and Rea, M. (eds), *Analytic Theology: New Essays in the Philosophy of Theology*, Oxford: Oxford University Press, pp. 187–213.
Cross, R., 2002a, 'Two Models of the Trinity?', *Heythrop Journal*, 43, pp. 275–94.
—— 2002b, 'Catholic, Calvinist, and Lutheran Doctrines of Eucharistic Presence: A Brief Note towards a Rapprochement', *International Journal of Systematic Theology*, 4:3, pp. 301–18.
—— 2009a, 'The Incarnation', in Flint, T. P. and Rea, M. C. (eds), *The Oxford Handbook of Philosophical Theology*, Oxford: Oxford University Press, pp. 452–75.
—— 2009b, 'Atonement without satisfaction', in Rea, M. (ed.), *Oxford Readings in Philosophical Theology Volume 1: Trinity, Incarnation, Atonement*, Oxford: Oxford University Press, pp. 328–47.
Cuneo, T., 2014, 'Transforming the self: On the baptismal rite', *Religious Studies*, 50:3, pp. 279–96.
—— 2016, *Ritualized Faith: Essays in the Philosophy of Liturgy*, Oxford Studies in Analytic Theology, Oxford: Oxford University Press.
Davies, B., 2021, *An Introduction to the Philosophy of Religion*, 4th edition, Oxford: Oxford University Press.
Davis, S. T., 2006, *Christian Philosophical Theology*, Oxford: Oxford University Press.
—— 2009, 'Was Jesus Mad, Bad or God?', in Rea, M. (ed.), *Oxford Readings in Philosophical Theology Volume 1: Trinity, Incarnation, Atonement*, Oxford: Oxford University Press, pp. 166–85.
—— 2011, 'The Metaphysics of Kenosis', in Marmodoro, A. and Hill, J. (eds), *The Metaphysics of the Incarnation*, Oxford: Oxford University Press, pp. 114–33.
—— 2016, 'Comments on Keith Ward's *Christ and the Cosmos*', *Philosophia Christi*, 18:2, pp. 307–12.
Davis, S. T. and Yang, E., 2017, 'Social Trinitarianism Unscathed', *Journal of Analytic Theology*, 5, pp. 220–9.
Davison, A. (ed.), 2011, *Imaginative Apologetics: Theology, Philosophy and the Catholic Tradition*, London: SCM Press.
Davison, S., 2017, *Petitionary Prayer: A Philosophical Investigation*, Oxford: Oxford University Press.
—— 2021, 'Prayer', in Arcadi, J. M. and Turner, J. T. (eds), *The T&T Clark Handbook of Analytic Theology*, London: Bloomsbury, pp. 489–97.
—— 2022, *God and Prayer*, Elements of the Philosophy of Religion, Cambridge: Cambridge University Press.
DeWeese, G., 2007, 'One Person, Two Natures: Two Metaphysical Models of the Incarnation', in Sanders, F. and Issler, K. (eds), *Jesus in Trinitarian Per-

spective: *An Introductory Christology*, Nashville, TN: Broadman and Holman Academic, pp. 114–55.

Dumsday, T., 2017, 'How Modern Biological Taxonomy Sheds Light on the Incarnation', *Journal of Analytic Theology*, 5, pp. 163–74.

Dunnington, K., 2021, 'Analytic Theological Ethics', in Arcadi, J. M. and Turner, J. T. (eds), *The T&T Clark Handbook of Analytic Theology*, London: Bloomsbury, pp. 347–56.

Efird, D., 2021, 'Analytic Spirituality', in Arcadi, J. M. and Turner, J. T. (eds), *The T&T Clark Handbook of Analytic Theology*, London: Bloomsbury, pp. 439–50.

Eklund, R., 2015, *Jesus Wept: The Significance of Jesus' Laments in the New Testament*, London: Bloomsbury.

Everett, N., 2003, *The Non-Existence of God*, London: Routledge.

Fairbairn, D., 2022, 'Interpreting Conciliar Christology: An Overview in the Service of Analytic Theology', *Journal of Analytic Theology*, 10, pp. 363–81.

Fairbairn, D. and Reeves, R. M., 2019, *The Story of Creeds and Confessions: Tracing the Development of the Christian Faith*, Grand Rapids, MI: Baker Academic.

Flint, T. P., 1998, *Divine Providence: The Molinist Account*, Ithaca, NY: Cornell University Press.

—— 2011, 'Should Concretists Part with Mereological Models of the Incarnation?', in Marmodoro, A. and Hill, J. (eds), 2011, *The Metaphysics of the Incarnation*, Oxford: Oxford University Press, pp. 67–87.

Frame, J., no date, 'Analytic Theology', *The Gospel Coalition*, https://www.thegospelcoalition.org/essay/analytic-theology (accessed 21.08.2023).

Gorman, M., 2014, 'Christological Consistency and the Reduplicative Qua', *Journal of Analytic Theology*, 2, pp. 86–100.

Green, A., 2021, 'Modelling Inspiration: Perspicuity after Pentecost', in Arcadi, J. M. and Turner, J. T. (eds), *The T&T Clark Handbook of Analytic Theology*, London: Bloomsbury, pp. 21–31.

—— 2022, 'Prayer as the Road to Self-Knowledge,', in Crisp, O. D., Arcadi, J. M. and Wessling, J. (eds), *Analyzing Prayer: Theological and Philosophical Essays*, Oxford Studies in Analytic Theology, Oxford: Oxford University Press, pp. 183–201.

Griffioen, A. L., 2021, 'Nowhere Men and Divine I's: Feminist Epistemology, Perfect Being Theism, and the God's-Eye View', *Journal of Analytic Theology*, 9, pp. 1–25.

Grössl, J., 2021, 'Christ's Impeccability', in Arcadi, J. M. and Turner, J. T. (eds), *The T&T Clark Handbook of Analytic Theology*, London: Bloomsbury, pp. 215–29.

Grössl J. and von Stosch, K. (eds), 2021, *Impeccability and Temptation: Understanding Christ's Divine and Human Will*, Routledge Studies in Analytic and Systematic Theology, Abingdon: Routledge.

Harris, H., 2010, 'Prayer', in Taliaferro, C. and Meister, C. (eds), *The Cambridge Companion to Christian Philosophical Theology*, Cambridge: Cambridge University Press, pp. 216–37.

Hasker, W., 1989, *God, Time and Knowledge*, Ithaca, NY: Cornell University Press.

—— 2013, *Metaphysics and the Tri-Personal God*, Oxford Studies in Analytic Theology, Oxford: Oxford University Press.

—— 2017, 'Incarnation: The Avatar Model', in Kvanvig, J., *Oxford Studies in Philosophy of Religion: Volume 8*, Oxford: Oxford University Press, pp. 118–41.

Helm, P., 2010, *Eternal God: A Study of God without Time*, 2nd edition, Oxford: Oxford University Press.

Hereth, B., 2020, 'The Shape of Trans Afterlife Justice', in Panchuk, M. and Rea, M. (eds), *Voices from the Edge: Centring Marginalized Perspectives in Analytic Theology*, Oxford Studies in Analytic Theology, Oxford: Oxford University Press, pp. 185–205.

Hill, J., 2011, 'Introduction', in Marmodoro, A. and Hill, J. (eds), *The Metaphysics of the Incarnation*, Oxford: Oxford University Press, pp. 1–19.

—— 2018, '"His Death Belongs to Them": An Edwardsean Participatory Model of Atonement', *Religious Studies*, 54:2, pp. 175–99.

Hollingsworth, A., 2023, 'Mere Social Trinitarianism, the Eternal Relations of Origin, and Models of God', *Journal of Analytic Theology*, 11, pp. 23–40.

Holmes, S. R., 2012, *The Quest for the Trinity: The Doctrine of God in Scripture, History and Modernity*, Downers Grove, IL: InterVarsity Press.

Howard-Snyder, D., 2009a, 'Was Jesus Mad, Bad, or God? ... or Merely Mistaken?', in Rea, M. (ed.), *Oxford Readings in Philosophical Theology Volume 1: Trinity, Incarnation, Atonement*, Oxford: Oxford University Press, pp. 186–210.

—— 2009b, 'The Puzzle of Prayers of Thanksgiving and Praise', in Nagasawa, Y. and Wielenberg, E. J. (eds), *New Waves in Philosophy of Religion*, New York: Palgrave-Macmillan. pp. 125–49.

Howard-Snyder, D. and Howard-Snyder, F., 2010, 'The Puzzle of Petitionary Prayer', *European Journal for Philosophy of Religion*, 2:2, pp. 43–68.

Inman, R., 2022, 'Theology in the Second Person: Christian Dogmatics as a Mode of Prayer', in Crisp, O. D., Arcadi, J. M. and Wessling, J. (eds), *Analyzing Prayer: Theological and Philosophical Essays*, Oxford Studies in Analytic Theology, Oxford: Oxford University Press, pp. 116–35.

Jacobs, J. D., 2015, 'The Ineffable, Inconceivable, and Incomprehensible God: Fundamentality and Apophatic Theology', in Kvanvig, J. (ed.), *Oxford Studies in Philosophy of Religion: Volume 6*, Oxford: Oxford University Press, ch.7.

Jedwab, J., 2018, 'Timothy Pawl. In Defense of Conciliar Christology', *Journal of Analytic Theology*, 6, pp. 743–7.

Johnson, J., 2021, 'Eleonore Stump: Atonement', *Journal of Analytic Theology*, 9, pp. 743–8.

King, D. S., 2023, *The Church and the Problem of Divine Hiddenness*, Routledge Studies in Analytic and Systematic Theology, Abingdon: Routledge.

Labooy, G. H., 2019, 'Stepped Characterisation: A Metaphysical Defence of qua-Propositions in Christology', *International Journal for Philosophy of Religion*, 86:1, pp. 25–38.

Lebens, S., 2020, *The Principles of Judaism*, Oxford Studies in Analytic Theology, Oxford: Oxford University Press.

Leftow, B., 1999, 'Anti Social Trinitarianism', in Davis, S. T., Kendall, D. and O'Collins, G. (eds), *The Trinity*, New York: Oxford University Press, pp. 203–50.

—— 2002, 'A Timeless God Incarnate', in Davis, S. T., Kendall, D. and O'Collins, G. (eds), *The Incarnation: An Interdisciplinary Symposium on the Incarnation of the Son of God*, Oxford: Oxford University Press, pp. 273–302.

—— 2004, 'A Latin Trinity', *Faith and Philosophy*, 21:3, pp. 304–33.
—— 2011, 'Composition and Christology', *Faith and Philosophy*, 28:3, pp. 310–22.
—— 2012a, *God and Necessity*, New York: Oxford University Press.
—— 2012b, 'Time Travel and the Trinity', *Faith and Philosophy*, 29:2, pp. 313–24.
—— 2015, 'Against Materialist Christology', in Ruloff, C. P. (ed.), *Christian Philosophy of Religion: Essays in Honor of Stephen T. Davis*, Notre Dame, IN: University of Notre Dame Press.
—— 2016, 'Immutability', in Zalta, E. N. and Nodelman, U. (eds), *The Stanford Encyclopedia of Philosophy*, available at https://plato.stanford.edu/archives/sum2024/entries/immutability/, accessed 8.11.2024.
—— 2018, 'The Trinity is unconstitutional', *Religious Studies*, 54:3, pp. 359–76.
Lewis, D., 2009, 'Do we believe in Penal Substitution?', in Rea, M. (ed.), *Oxford Readings in Philosophical Theology Volume 1: Trinity, Incarnation, Atonement*, Oxford: Oxford University Press, pp. 308–13.
List, C. and Pettit, P., 2011, *Group Agency: The Possibility, Design, and Status of Corporate Agents*, Oxford: Oxford University Press.
Loke, A. T. E., 2013, 'The Incarnation and Jesus' Apparent Limitation in Knowledge', *New Blackfriars*, 94: 1053, pp. 583–602.
—— 2014, *A Kryptic Model of the Incarnation*, Abingdon: Ashgate.
—— 2022, *Evil, Sin, and Christian Theism*, Abingdon: Routledge.
MacDonald, S., 2009, 'What is Philosophical Theology?', in Timpe, K. (ed.), *Arguing about Religion*, London: Routledge, pp. 17–29.
Matz, R. J. and Thornhill, A. C. (eds), 2019, *Divine Impassibility: Four Views of God's Emotions and Suffering*, Downers Grove, IL: IVP Academic.
Mawson, T. J., 2018, *The Divine Attributes*, Elements of the Philosophy of Religion, Cambridge: Cambridge University Press.
McCall, T., 2009, 'On Understanding Scripture as the Word of God', in Crisp, O. and Rea, M. (eds), *Analytic Theology: New Essays in the Philosophy of Theology*, Oxford: Oxford University Press, pp. 171–86.
—— 2010, *Which Trinity? Whose Monotheism?: Philosophical and Systematic Theologians on the Metaphysics of Trinitarian Theology*, Grand Rapids, MI: Eerdmans.
—— 2015, *An Invitation to Analytic Christian Theology*, Downers Grove, IL: IVP Academic.
—— 2021, 'The Trinity', in Arcadi, J. M. and Turner, J. T. (eds), *The T&T Clark Handbook of Analytic Theology*, London: Bloomsbury, pp. 181–94.
McCall, T. and Rea, M., 2009, 'Introduction', in McCall, T. and Rea, M. (eds), *Philosophical and Theological Essays on the Trinity*, Oxford, Oxford University Press, pp. 1–18.
McGrath, A. E., 2016, *Mere Apologetics*, London: SPCK.
—— 2019, *Narrative Apologetics*, Grand Rapids, MI: Baker Books.
McMartin, J., 2022, 'Prayer and the Meaning of Life', in Crisp, O. D., Arcadi, J. M. and Wessling, J. (eds), *Analyzing Prayer: Theological and Philosophical Essays*, Oxford Studies in Analytic Theology, Oxford: Oxford University Press, pp. 202–19.
McNaughton, D., 1992, 'Reparation and Atonement', *Religious Studies*, 28:2, pp. 129–44.

Mihut, C. F., 2023, *Gracious Forgiveness: A Theological Retrieval*, Oxford Studies in Analytic Theology, Oxford: Oxford University Press.
Moreland, J. P. and Craig, W. L., 2003, *Philosophical Foundations for a Christian Worldview*, Downers Grove, IL: InterVarsity Press.
Morris, T. V., 1986, *The Logic of God Incarnate*, Ithaca, NY: Cornell University Press.
—— 1991, *Our Idea of God: An Introduction to Philosophical Theology*, Downers Grove, IL: InterVarsity Press.
Mullins, R. T., 2016, 'Divine Temporality, the Trinity, and the Charge of Arianism', *Journal of Analytic Theology*, 4, pp. 267–89.
Murphy, M. C., 2009, 'Not Penal Substitution but Vicarious Punishment', *Faith and Philosophy*, 26:3, pp. 253–73.
Murray, M. and Meyers, K., 1994, 'Ask and It Will Be Given to You', *Religious Studies*, 30, pp. 311–30.
Nemes, S., 2023, *Eating Christ's Flesh: A Case for Memorialism*, Eugene, OR: Cascade Books.
Nordby, S. N., 2018, 'Metaphor and the Mind of God in Nevi'im', *TheoLogica*, 2:1, pp. 51–83.
Panchuk, M., 2021, 'Gender and Justice: Human and Divine Gender in Analytic Theology', in Arcadi, J. M. and Turner, J. T. (eds), *The T&T Clark Handbook of Analytic Theology*, London: Bloomsbury, pp. 38–93.
Panchuk, M. and Rea, M. (eds), 2020, *Voices from the Edge: Centring Marginalized Perspectives in Analytic Theology*, Oxford Studies in Analytic Theology, Oxford: Oxford University Press.
Parker, R. M. and Rettler, B., 2017, 'A Possible-Worlds Solution to the Puzzle of Petitionary Prayer', *European Journal for Philosophy of Religion*, 9:1, pp. 179–86.
Pawl, T., 2016, *In Defence of Conciliar Christology*, Oxford Studies in Analytic Theology, Oxford: Oxford University Press.
—— 2019, *In Defence of Extended Conciliar Christology*, Oxford Studies in Analytic Theology, Oxford: Oxford University Press.
—— 2020, *The Incarnation*, Elements in the Philosophy of Religion, Cambridge: Cambridge University Press.
—— 2021, 'The Incarnation', in Arcadi, J. M. and Turner, J. T. (eds), *The T&T Clark Handbook of Analytic Theology*, London: Bloomsbury, pp. 197–213.
Peckham, J. C., 2020, 'The Influence Aim Problem of Petitionary Prayer: A Cosmic Conflict Approach', *Journal of Analytic Theology*, 8, pp. 412–32.
Pettit, P., 1996, *The Common Mind: An Essay on Psychology, Society, and Politics*, Oxford: Oxford University Press.
Philips, D. Z., 1981, *The Concept of Prayer*, New York, NY: Seabury.
Pickup, M., 2015, 'Real Presence in the Eucharist and Time-Travel', *Religious Studies*, 51:3, pp. 379–89.
Plantinga, A., 1999, 'On Heresy, Mind, and Truth', *Faith and Philosophy*, 16:2, pp. 182–93.
Plantinga, C., 1989, 'Social Trinity and Tritheism', in Feenstra, R. J. and Plantinga, C. Jr (eds), *Trinity, Incarnation, and Atonement: Philosophical and Theological Essays*, Notre Dame, IN: University of Notre Dame Press.
Porter, S. L., 2009, 'Swinburnian Atonement and the Doctrine of Penal Substitution', in Rea, M. (ed.), *Oxford Readings in Philosophical Theology Volume 1: Trinity, Incarnation, Atonement*, Oxford: Oxford University Press, pp. 314–27.

Pruss, A., 2009, 'The Eucharist: Real Presence and Real Absence', in Flint, T. and Rea, M. C. (eds), *The Oxford Handbook of Philosophical Theology*, Oxford: Oxford University Press, pp. 512–37.
—— 2013a, 'Omnipresence, Multilocation, the Real Presence and Time Travel,' *Journal of Analytic Theology*, 1, pp. 60–73.
—— 2013b, 'Omnirationality', *Res Philosophica*, 90:1, pp. 1–21.
Quinn, P. L., 2009, 'Abelard on Atonement: Nothing Unintelligible, Arbitrary, Illogical, or Immoral About It', in Rea, M. (ed.), *Oxford Readings in Philosophical Theology Volume 1: Trinity, Incarnation, Atonement*, Oxford: Oxford University Press, pp. 348–64.
Rea, M., 2009a, 'Introduction', in Crisp, O. and Rea, M. C. (eds), *Analytic Theology: New Essays in the Philosophy of Theology*, Oxford: Oxford University Press, pp. 1–30.
—— 2009b, 'The Trinity', in Flint, T. P. and Rea, M. C. (eds), *The Oxford Handbook of Philosophical Theology*, Oxford: Oxford University Press, pp. 403–29.
—— 2016, 'Authority and Truth', in Carson, D. A. (ed.), *The Enduring Authority of the Christian Scriptures*, Grand Rapids, MI: Eerdmans, pp. 872–98.
—— 2018, *The Hiddenness of God*, Oxford: Oxford University Press.
—— 2020, *Essays in Analytic Theology*, Oxford Studies in Analytic Theology, Oxford: Oxford University Press.
Rea, M. (ed.), 2009, *Oxford Readings in Philosophical Theology Volume 1: Trinity, Incarnation, Atonement*, Oxford: Oxford University Press.
Reichenbach, B., 1999, 'Inclusivism and the Atonement', *Faith and Philosophy*, 16:1, pp. 43–54.
Reno, R., 2006, 'Theology's Continental Captivity', *First Things*, April 2006.
—— 2009, 'Introduction', in Rea, M. (ed.), *Oxford Readings in Philosophical Theology Volume 1: Trinity, Incarnation, Atonement*, Oxford: Oxford University Press, pp. 1–18.
Rogers, K. A., 2010, 'Incarnation', in Taliaferro, C. and Meister, C. (eds), 2010, *The Cambridge Companion to Christian Philosophical Theology*, Cambridge: Cambridge University Press.
Rutledge, J. C., 2022, *Forgiveness and Atonement: Christ's Restorative Sacrifice*, Routledge Studies in Analytic and Systematic Theology, Abingdon: Routledge.
Rutledge, J. C. (ed.), 2024, *Paradox and Contradiction in Theology*, Routledge Studies in Analytic and Systematic Theology, Abingdon: Routledge.
Saemi, A. and Davison, S. A., 2020, 'Salvific Luck in Islamic Theology', *Journal of Analytic Theology*, 8, pp. 120–30.
Scott, P. S., 2024, *Identity and Coherence in Christology: One Person in Two Natures*, Routledge Studies in Analytic and Systematic Theology, Abingdon: Routledge.
Sharpe, K., 2017, 'The Incarnation, Soul-Free: Physicalism, Kind Membership, and the Incarnation', *Religious Studies*, 53:1, pp. 117–31.
Sijuwade, J. R., 2022, 'Transubstantiation: A Metaphysical Proposal', *Journal of Analytic Theology*, 10, pp. 309–31.
Smith, N. D. and Yip, A. C., 2010, 'Partnership with God: A Partial Solution to the Problem of Petitionary Prayer', *Religious Studies*, 46:3, pp. 395–410.
Sonderegger, K., 2022, 'Does God Pray?', in Crisp, O. D., Arcadi, J. M. and Wessling, J. (eds), *Analyzing Prayer: Theological and Philosophical Essays*, Oxford Studies in Analytic Theology, Oxford: Oxford University Press, pp. 136–48.

Strabbing, J. T., 2016, 'The Permissibility of the Atonement as Penal Substitution', in Kvanvig, J., *Oxford Studies in Philosophy of Religion: Volume 7*, Oxford: Oxford University Press, pp. 239–70.

Strobel, K., 2022, 'Knowing as you are Known: Prayer in the Presence of God', in Crisp, O. D., Arcadi, J. M. and Wessling, J. (eds), *Analyzing Prayer: Theological and Philosophical Essays*, Oxford Studies in Analytic Theology, Oxford: Oxford University Press, pp. 166–82.

Stump, E., 1979, 'Petitionary Prayer', *American Philosophical Quarterly*, 16:2, pp. 81–91.

—— 2009, 'The Problem of Evil: Analytic Philosophy and Narrative', in Crisp, O. and Rea, M. (eds), 2009, *Analytic Theology: New Essays in the Philosophy of Theology*, Oxford: Oxford University Press, pp. 251–264.

—— 2010, *Wandering in Darkness*, Oxford: Oxford University Press.

—— 2015, 'Atonement and Eucharist', in Crisp, O. D. and Sanders, F. (eds), *Locating Atonement: Explorations in Constructive Dogmatics*, Grand Rapids, MI: Zondervan Academic, pp. 209–25.

—— 2018, *Atonement*, Oxford Studies in Analytic Theology, Oxford: Oxford University Press.

Sutanto, N. G., 2021, 'Christian Baptism: A Reformed Account', in Arcadi, J. M. and Turner, J. T. (eds), *The T&T Clark Handbook of Analytic Theology*, London: Bloomsbury, pp. 451–61.

Swinburne, R., 1989, *Responsibility and Atonement*, Oxford: Clarendon Press.

—— 1994, *The Christian God*, Oxford: Clarendon Press.

—— 1998, *Providence and the Problem of Evil*, Oxford: Oxford University Press.

—— 2003, *The Resurrection of God Incarnate*, Oxford: Oxford University Press.

—— 2005, *Faith and Reason*, 2nd edition, Oxford: Oxford University Press.

—— 2007, *Revelation: From Metaphor to Analogy*, 2nd edition, Oxford: Oxford University Press.

—— 2008, *Was Jesus God?*, Oxford: Oxford University Press.

—— 2011, 'The Coherence of the Chalcedonian Definition of the Incarnation', in Marmodoro, A. and Hill, J. (eds), *The Metaphysics of the Incarnation*, Oxford: Oxford University Press, pp. 153–67.

—— 2013a, 'The Probability of the Resurrection of Jesus', *Philosophia Christi*, 15:2, pp. 239–52.

—— 2013b, 'Responsibility, Atonement, and Forgiveness', in Moreland, J. P., Meister, C. and Sweis, K. A., *Debating Christian Theism*, New York: Oxford University Press, pp. 361–71.

—— 2016, *The Coherence of Theism*, 2nd edition, Oxford: Oxford University Press.

—— 2018, 'The Social Theory of the Trinity', *Religious Studies*, 54:3, pp. 419–37.

Talbert, B. M., 2015, 'Knowing Other People: A Second-Person Framework', *Ratio*, 28, pp. 190–206.

Taliaferro, C., 2010, 'Religious Rites', in Taliaferro, C. and Meister, C. (eds), *The Cambridge Companion to Christian Philosophical Theology*, Cambridge: Cambridge University Press, pp. 183–200.

Thurow, J. C., 2015, 'Communal Substitutionary Atonement', *Journal of Analytic Theology*, 3, pp. 47–69.

—— 2021, 'He Died for Our Sins (in a Contextually-Sensitive Way)', *Journal of Analytic Theology*, 9, pp. 238–61.

Timpe, K., 2022, 'Toward an Account of Lamenting Well', in Crisp, O. D., Arcadi, J. M. and Wessling, J. (eds), *Analyzing Prayer: Theological and Philosophical Essays*, Oxford Studies in Analytic Theology, Oxford: Oxford University Press, pp. 95-115.

Tobin, T. W. and Moon, D., 2020, 'Sacramental Shame in Black Churches: How Racism and Respectability Politics Shape the Experiences of Black LGBTQ and Same-Gender-Loving Christians', in Panchuk, M. and Rea, M. (eds), *Voices from the Edge: Centring Marginalized Perspectives in Analytic Theology*, Oxford Studies in Analytic Theology, Oxford: Oxford University Press, pp. 141-65.

Toner, P., 2011, 'Transubstantiation, Essentialism, and Substance', *Religious Studies*, 47:2, pp. 217-31.

Tuggy, D., 2016, 'Some Objections to Ward's Trinitarian Theology', *Philosophia Christi*, 18:2, pp. 363-73.

van Inwagen, P., 1995, *God, Knowledge and Mystery: Essays in Philosophical Theology*, Ithaca, NY: Cornell University Press.

—— 2003, 'Three Persons in One Being: On Attempts to Show That the Doctrine of the Trinity is Self-Contradictory', in Stewart, M. Y. (ed.), 2003, *The Trinity: East/West Dialogue*, Dordrecht: Kluwer Academic.

Vidu, A., 2016, 'Trinitarian Inseparable Operations and the Incarnation', *Journal of Analytic Theology*, 4, pp. 106-27.

Wahlberg, M., 2014, *Revelation as Testimony: A Philosophical-Theological Study*, Grand Rapids, MI: Eerdmans.

Ward, K., 2015, *Christ and the Cosmos: A Reformulation of Trinitarian Doctrine*, Cambridge: Cambridge University Press.

Webster, J., 2007, 'Theologies of Retrieval', in Webster, J., Tanner, K. and Torrance, I. (eds), *The Oxford Handbook of Systematic Theology*, Oxford: Oxford University Press, pp. 583-99.

Weinandy, T., 2000, *Does God Suffer?*, Notre Dame, IN: University of Notre Dame Press.

Wessling, J., 2022, 'Interceding for the Lost: On the Effectiveness of Petitioning God for the Salvation of Others', in Crisp, O. D., Arcadi, J. M. and Wessling, J. (eds), *Analyzing Prayer: Theological and Philosophical Essays*, Oxford Studies in Analytic Theology, Oxford: Oxford University Press, pp. 20-37.

Williams, S. M., 2013, 'Indexicals and the Trinity: Two Non-Social Models', *Journal of Analytic Theology*, 1, pp. 74-94.

Williams, T., 2005, 'The Doctrine of Univocity Is True and Salutary', *Modern Theology*, 21, pp. 575-85.

Wolterstorff, N., 1995, *Divine Discourse: Philosophical Reflections on the Claim that God Speaks*, Cambridge: Cambridge University Press.

—— 2009, 'How Philosophical Theology Became Possible Within the Analytic Tradition of Philosophy', in Crisp, O. and Rea, M. (eds), *Analytic Theology: New Essays in the Philosophy of Theology*, Oxford: Oxford University Press, pp. 155-68.

—— 2015, *The God We Worship: An Exploration of Liturgical Theology*, Grand Rapids, MI: Eerdmans.

—— 2018, *Acting Liturgically: Philosophical Reflections on Religious Practice*, New York: Oxford University Press.

Wood, W., 2016, 'Modelling Mystery', *Scientia et Fides*, 4:1, pp. 1-21.

—— 2021, *Analytic Theology and the Academic Study of Religion*, Oxford Studies in Analytic Theology, Oxford: Oxford University Press.

Yadav, S., 2020, 'Towards an Analytic Theology of Liberation', in Panchuk, M. and Rea, M. (eds), *Voices from the Edge: Centring Marginalized Perspectives in Analytic Theology*, Oxford Studies in Analytic Theology, Oxford: Oxford University Press, pp. 47–74.

—— 2021, 'Willie Jennings on the Supersessionist Pathology of Race: A Differential Diagnosis', in Arcadi, J. M. and Turner, J. T. (eds), *The T&T Clark Handbook of Analytic Theology*, London: Bloomsbury, pp. 357–68.

Yancey, H., 2021, 'Goodness, Embodiment, and Disability: Lessons Then for Now', in Arcadi, J. M. and Turner, J. T. (eds), *The T&T Clark Handbook of Analytic Theology*, London: Bloomsbury, pp. 369–80.

Index of Names and Subjects

Abelard, Peter 86–9
Abraham, William 3, 6–7, 10, 20, 22, 109–11, 158–62
Adams, Marilyn McCord 5, 15, 24
analytic philosophy 4–10, 18–20, 65, 97, 109, 117, 121, 158, 162
analytic theology
 and church tradition 15, 18, 22–5
 and experience 32–3
 and faith seeking understanding 11–12, 22, 27
 and Scripture 6, 10, 13–15, 17–21, 27
 and reason 17, 19, 25–31
 apologetic value of vii, 12, 76, 160–5
 as a research programme 3, 13–14
 assumptions and aspirations of 10–13
 constructive 11–13, 22, 24–5
 defined vii, 4–5
 model-building in 13, 27–9, 39, 54, 82, 105, 112, 159, 163
 objections to 17–34
Anselm 11, 85–6, 91–6
Aquinas 7, 49, 84, 149
Arcadi, James 3, 7, 10–11, 14–16, 18, 28, 34, 40, 49, 57, 68, 70, 73, 109, 130–5, 145–6, 157–60
Atonement, the
 Christus Victor accounts of 86, 90–2
 conceptual analysis of 79–85
 moral influence models of 86–9
 new approaches to 103–5
 penal substitution models of 97–103
 ransom theory of 86, 90–1
 satisfaction models of 83–4, 92–6
Augustine 11, 25, 40, 57
Aulen, Gustaf 86, 90

baptism
 and church membership 111, 125, 128–30
 intelligibility puzzle of 125–7
Baker-Hytch, Max 19, 23, 164–5
Beall, J. C. 56, 71–2
Beilby, James 160–1
Bonhoeffer, Dietrich 87, 112–13
Brower, Jeffrey 24, 52–4, 57, 163

Calvin, John 97, 129–30, 134
Christology, *see also* Incarnation
 Apollinarian 60, 66–7
 abstract 64–6
 Chalcedonian 11, 22, 25, 59–61, 64, 72–6, 79, 164

concrete 64–5, 68
contradictory 71–2
kenotic 72–4
Nestorian 60, 65, 67
new avenues in 76–7
relational and transformational 68–9
two- and three-part 66–8
Church, *see also* ecclesiology
  as the body of Christ 112–15, 121–2, 128, 140, 159
  and group agency 113, 116, 122
  as interpreter of revelation 110–12
Coakley, Sarah 3, 56–7, 59–60, 117, 123–4
Cockayne, Joshua 14, 34, 86, 109, 112–15, 117–25, 128–31, 135, 137–40, 163
Craig, William Lane 6, 42, 45–8, 57, 61, 66–7, 73, 78–81, 86–7, 89–93, 96–102, 106, 151, 162–4
Crisp, Oliver 3, 5–20, 23, 28–30, 34, 39–40, 47, 49, 54–60, 64–5, 69, 76–80, 82–7, 89–93, 95, 101, 103, 106, 112, 115–16, 145, 147–8, 150, 154, 157, 160, 162
Crisp, Thomas 21
Cross, Richard 24, 57, 60, 64, 67, 71–2, 74, 85, 95–6, 133, 135
Cuneo, Terence 14, 34, 109, 117–21, 123–7, 139–40, 159

Davies, Brian 78, 150
Davis, Stephen T. 28, 42–5, 48, 51, 62–3, 73
Davison, Scott 15, 34, 145–7, 150–2, 154–5, 157, 159–60

ecclesiology, *see also* Church 14–15, 34, 38, 109–10, 112–16, 122
Efird, David 15, 124, 141–4, 159
ethics 14, 34, 38
Eucharist, the
  and church unity 137–40
  corporeal ('Real Presence') accounts of 130–5, 137, 164
  ordinary ('Memorialist') views of 130–1, 135–7
  pneumatic perspectives on 130–1, 134–5, 137

Fairbairn, Donald 60, 65
Flint, Thomas 69, 151
Frame, John 17–18

Green, Adam 21, 154

Harris, Harriet 149, 156
Hasker, William 12–13, 22–5, 30, 45–7, 50, 53, 57–8, 70, 151, 163
Helm, Paul 57, 151
Hill, Jonathan 68, 104
Holy Spirit, the 21, 34, 37–46, 48–53, 57, 61, 75, 87, 89, 104, 110, 112, 114–16, 122–9, 134, 139, 156
Howard-Snyder, Daniel 63, 145, 152–3

Incarnation, the *see also* Christology
  and Scripture 20–1
  as a hypostatic union 60, 69–70, 75, 78, 133
  evidence for 61–3
  fundamental philosophical problem of 71–6

kryptic account of 68
metaphysics of 63–70
see also Christology

King, Derek 33, 115–16, 118, 120, 123–4

Leftow, Brian 6, 26, 48–51, 53, 57, 69, 150, 163
Lewis, C.S. 33, 62
liturgy
  defined 117–24
  aptness of 119–20
  as a communal act 116, 120–3
  knowing God through 123–4
  virtues of 118–19
Loke, Andrew Ter Ern 64, 68, 147
Luther, Martin 97, 133

McCall, Thomas 3, 8–9, 18, 20–1, 23–5, 27–8, 34, 38–42, 50–2, 56, 58, 68, 73, 109
McGrath, Alister 160, 163, 165
McMartin, Jason 155–6
Moreland, James Porter 42, 45–8, 57, 61, 66, 73, 78, 163
Morris, Thomas 5, 16, 27, 31, 66–7, 72
mystery 15, 17, 27–9, 34, 53–5, 60–1, 72, 130

Nemes, Steven 136–7
Nicene creed 22, 37, 44, 55, 79, 109, 130

Panchuk, Michelle 15, 159
Pawl, Timothy 11, 22–3, 61, 66–7, 69–78
Peckham, John 150, 152–3
philosophy of religion 5, 9–10, 19, 34, 162

Plantinga, Alvin 5, 9, 64
Plantinga, Cornelius 41
prayer
  benefits of 154–7
  of adoration and praise 145–6
  of complaint and lament 147–9
  of thanksgiving 125–6, 146–7
  petitionary 149–54
Pruss, Alexander 15, 34, 132, 137, 151–2

Quinn, Peter 79, 88–9

Rea, Michael 3–4, 7–9, 15–16, 20–1, 27, 30, 32, 37–9, 42–3, 45, 48, 52–4, 57, 83, 89, 147–8, 163–4
Reno, Russell 7, 158
Resurrection, the 5, 14, 62, 74, 82, 90–1, 103–4, 139, 164
revelation 18–20, 27, 41, 55, 59, 110, 112, 116, 120
Rogers, Kathryn 60–1, 70, 73
Rutledge, Jonathan 34, 79, 104–5

sacraments vii, 104, 109, 116, 124, 127, 159
Scripture 6, 10–11, 13–15, 17, 23, 25–7, 29, 32–3, 38, 51, 55, 59, 66
spirituality 14–15, 140–5, 157, 159
Strobel, Kyle 141, 156
Stump, Eleonore 3, 5, 24, 60, 76, 79–80, 88–9, 95, 106, 117, 124, 141–2, 152, 156, 158–9
Swinburne, Richard 5–6, 16, 41, 43–5, 47–8, 57, 61–2, 66–7, 81, 84, 94, 96, 105, 110–12, 141–2, 146, 151–2, 158, 162, 164

Taliaferro, Charles 117–19
theology *see also* analytic theology
  declarative 11–13, 19, 22, 162
  historical 6, 12, 24–5
  philosophical 5–6, 9–10, 14, 41, 117, 158, 162
  scholastic 7, 163
  systematic 5–7, 24, 41, 150, 158, 162
Thurow, Joshua 81, 83–5, 90–1, 95, 102–3, 105
Timpe, Kevin 33, 148–9, 155
Trinity, the
  and divine contradiction 56
  and modalism 39, 49–51, 57
  and subordinationism 39, 57
  and tritheism 39, 42–3, 45, 47, 54
  constitutional models of 39–40, 51–4, 57, 159, 163
  Latin models of 39–40, 49–51, 53–4, 57
  logical problem of 38–9
  mysterian account of 51, 53–6
  social models of 25, 39–51, 53–4, 163

van Inwagen, Peter 52

Ward, Keith 50–1
Weinandy, Thomas 18
Wessling, Jordan 3, 11, 18, 28, 34, 40, 49, 57, 145, 153–4, 157, 160, 162
Wolterstorff, Nicholas 3, 9–10, 14, 20, 34, 109, 117–21, 123–4, 144–5, 158–9
Wood, William 3–4, 7, 11–13, 19, 22–34, 47, 75, 161–4

Yadav, Sameer 159

www.ingramcontent.com/pod-product-compliance
Lightning Source LLC
Chambersburg PA
CBHW022012290426
44109CB00015B/1148